1997-98

Michigan Vacation Guide

Cottages, Chalets, Condos, B&B's

FOURTH EDITION

Editor/Writer: Kathleen R. Tedsen

Associate Editor: Clara M. Rydel

Writer/Photographer: Beverlee J. Rydel

Business Manager: Christian Tedsen

Cover Photograph: Oak Cove Resort, Lawrence, Michigan

For information, contact:

TR Desktop Publishing
P.O. Box 180271
Utica, MI 48318-0271
(810) 228-8780

PRINTED IN THE UNITED STATES OF AMERICA

ISBN: 0-9635953-2-6

Michigan

Statehood: 1837 — 25th State of the Union

Let me take you to the land once called "Michigania" across flat planes to ever increasing slopes, hills and mountains; through virginal forests and crystal lakes, dotted by cottages resting on sugar white sand. Where falls are painted by an artist's brush and winters are blanketed in white. Here are the forests and wildlife, quaint cities and great cities, museums and shipwrecks, and so much more!

I am your dream maker ...
the great outdoors ...
the vacation land for all seasons.

HOW TO USE THIS BOOK

Welcome to the Fourth Edition of *The Michigan Vacation Guide to Cottages, Chalets, Condos, B&B's.* This simple to use publication, arranged by region and alphabetically by city, is designed to assist you with one of your first vacation priorities — WHERE TO STAY — and offers some interesting alternatives to the usual hotels/motels. We hope our Guide helps you find your perfect vacation lodging as quickly and effortlessly as possible.

Understanding Special Notes:

Editor's Note Our staff has not had the opportunity to visit every listing in this book. Many of the descriptions have been supplied by owners or chambers of commerce. When we have visited a lodging, we have made our personal comments at the bottom of the listing by using *Editor's Note.*

Editor's Choice indicates places our staff have visited which, in our opinions, meet or exceed the basic requirements of comfort, cleanliness, location and value.

REVIEWS We've significantly increased our Review Section to include more vacation lodgings, photographs and detail. All comments are solely the opinion of our staff and do not necessarily reflect the opinions of others.

Whenever possible, prices have been included. One thing you should remember, **prices frequently change or fluctuate with the seasons.** We recommend you call to verify rates when making your reservations. If the owner requires an advance deposit, verify refund policies (if any). As a renter, be sure you understand the terms of the rental agreement.

CHECK OUT OUR WEB SITE!

For The Latest Information ... Contact Our Internet Affiliate:

THE MICHIGAN TRAVELER'S COMPANION

http://www.yesmichigan.com

SEE YOU ON ... THE WEB!

REGIONAL DIVISIONS

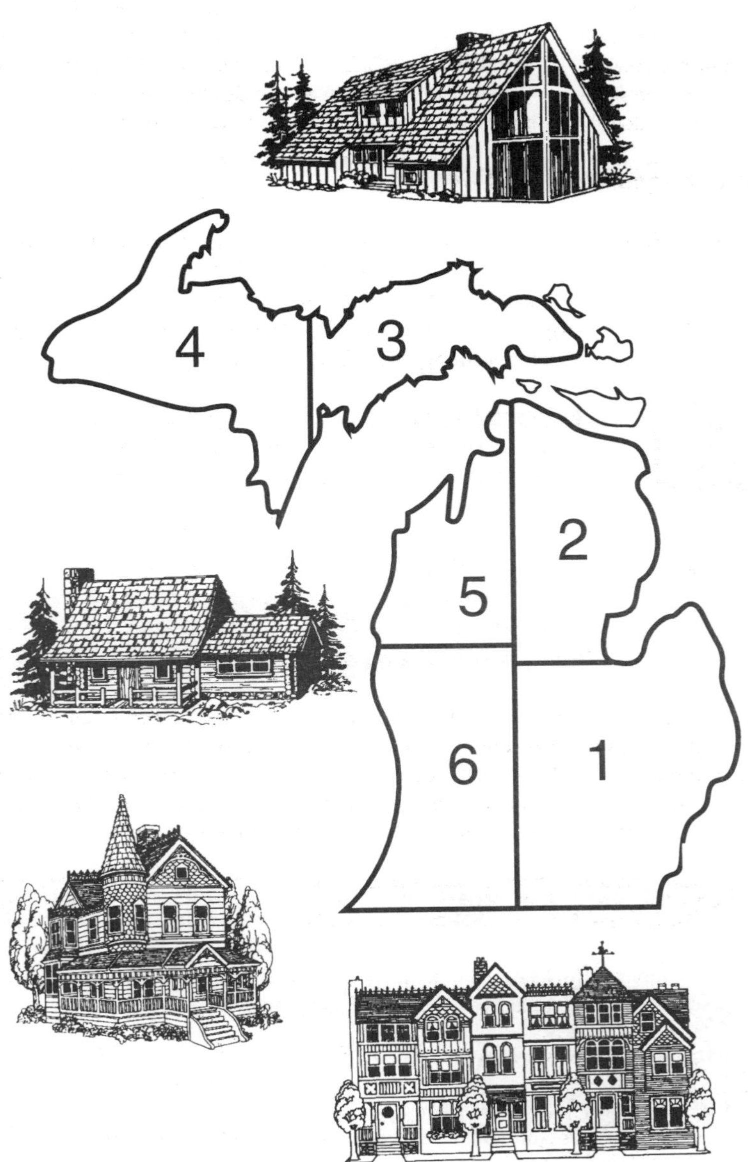

TABLE OF CONTENTS

Region 3

Region 4

Region 5

Region 6

WHICH LODGING IS RIGHT FOR YOU?

Staying at a cottage, condo or bed and breakfast is truly a unique and enjoyable experience. However, it is ***different*** than staying at a hotel or motel. We've provided some information to help you understand and appreciate the differences.

■ THE BASICS

Don't be afraid to ask the owner questions. For instance, ask about the *House Rules*. If staying at a resort, private cottage, or condo, you may want to ask what you'll need to bring and what the owner's housekeeping policies are; or other questions regarding amenities or location which are important to your comfort and enjoyment.

Always be sure you understand the terms of the rental agreement. Determine advance deposit and cancellation/refund policies prior to booking.

Clean up after yourself. Please be courteous and leave your lodging in the same condition in which it was found.

■ TERMINOLOGY

Fully Equipped Kitchens. Includes stove, refrigerator, pots, pans, dishes, eating utensils and sometimes (not always) microwaves, toasters and coffee makers.

A/C and CATV. A/C refers to air conditioning (may or may not be central air conditioning); CATV refers to color cable television.

Modern Cottage. Does not mean new. It refers to electricity and indoor plumbing (private bath, hot water, etc.). Most of today's cottages are considered modern.

On the Water. Refers to a lodging which fronts water. It does not necessarily mean the property has a swimming beach (see below) or a place to dock your boat.

Swimming Beach. A water area with gradual incline, no surprise drop offs, no strong currents. It may or may not have a smooth, sand beach.

Full Breakfast. Beverages with main course and, sometimes, dessert.

Continental Breakfast. Beverages with breads and/or pastries.

American Plan Resorts. All meals included in the price of rental.

MICHIGAN COTTAGES • CHALETS • CONDOS • B&B'S

What Are the Differences?

While it's impossible to give a single description for each type of accommodation, there are certain traits which make each distinctively different and appealing in their own way. Here's some general information in that area.

Atmosphere: Most resorts were built during the 1950's and 1960's with some dating back even further. We've found that a great many of the guests come back year after year, even generations. They like the friendly environment and diverse amenities available.

While there are cottage resorts which provide "luxury" accommodations, most are simple in nature. You may find a ceiling fan but only a few have air conditioning. Floors are covered with linoleum, wood, or simple carpeting. Furniture is sometimes a collection of older, second-hand chairs, sofas, tables, dishes, pots, pans, etc. A cozy fireplace in your cabin is not uncommon and wood is usually provided. Resorts will clean the cottage prior to your arrival, but do not expect daily maid service.

Features: There are a broad range of features provided to guests which make resorts particularly appealing to families. For example, those by the water often have a safe swimming area with a canoe or rowboat as part of the rental price. You can usually bring your own boat (not all allow high speed motors). There may be a children's play area, badminton, basketball or tennis courts. Game rooms may include pinball, video arcades, pool tables and more. Many rent motors, paddle boats or pontoon boats, with others also providing sail boats, wave runners or kayaks. Nature and snowmobile trails, fish cleaning areas and chartered fishing trips along with planned daily activities, or American Plan programs are sometimes available.

Rates/Rental Policy: Resorts often provide the most economically priced lodging, especially those not located on the water. Many begin renting as low as $400 weekly with a few exceeding $1,000. During prime season, most require weekly rentals (Saturday to Saturday). Advance deposits are generally asked with refund policies varying.

What to Bring: You may need to bring towels, bed linens, cleaning and paper products (toilet paper, trash bags, paper towels, dish soap), coffee maker, etc.

Finally, please remember, even the cleanliest cottage in the world will have an occasional spider or walking "thing" ... you're in a wooded area by the water ... it happens!

SELECTING THE LODGING THAT'S RIGHT FOR YOU

Atmosphere: Guests choosing this type of accommodation will enjoy a very private vacation. Whether overlooking the water, woods or ski slopes, this place will seem like your own private retreat.

Since this type of cottage is used by the owner, interior decor will vary greatly depending on the comforts of the owner. Some are small and simply furnished while others are spacious, contemporary and luxurious in nature.

Please note, privately owned cottages or homes may or may not have a "cleaning service" and many have special "house rules". Be sure to ask about the cleaning arrangement and the house rules. Also very important, ask who your contact is should there be any problems once you arrive (i.e. a storm takes out the electricity, plumbing, etc.).

Features: You usually won't have all of the outdoor amenities found at resorts, such as basketball/ tennis courts or video game rooms. However, interiors tend be more comfortable and owners often supply a good selection of board games or lawn games. Private cottages may have fireplaces, but you'll probably have to supply your own wood. Other extra features may include ceiling fans, air conditioning, hot tubs, stereos, TVs, VCRs and kitchens with dishwashers.

Rates/Rental Policies: Owners frequently need to be contacted during evenings or weekends when they're not working. During prime season, most choose to rent weekly (Saturday to Saturday) some will agree to a 2-day minimum stay. Prices may be a little higher than resorts with average rates from $500 to $1,200. The larger vacation homes begin around $1,200 and some, with added luxuries, may rent for over $3,000. Most require up front deposits with varying refund policies.

What to Bring: See "Cottage Resorts".

Chalets are generally an A-frame lodging frequently found at or near ski or winter sport areas. See Private Cottage for features, rental policies, etc.

Atmosphere: For those who enjoy the anonymity and comfort a hotel/motel provides but also want the added convenience of a full kitchen, living room, etc., condominiums would be a good choice. While there are a few older condos, most were built in the last 5 to 20 years. You will generally find the interior furnishings newer with matching sofa, chairs, tables and decor.

Features: Air conditioning is often available. Rooms may have Jacuzzi tubs and wet bars. Condo "resorts" frequently feature championship golf courses, heated swimming pools, tennis and health clubs. Other amenities are in-house masseuses, nature and x-country ski trails or downhill ski slopes, boat and canoe rentals, swimming, sailing and more.

Rates/Rental Policies: Units are rented by private owners or by Associations with more flexible policies (not all require week long rentals). Weekly rentals prices are similar to private cottages from $500 to $2,000+. Advance deposits are usually requested with varying refund policies.

What to Bring: See "Cottage Resorts".

Atmosphere: B&B's and Inns provide a quiet, relaxing atmosphere and are equally enjoyed by business and vacation travelers alike. While some establishments welcome well behaved children, most cater to the adult traveler. A bed and breakfast is not the place for loud parties. However, with notice, many welcome small weddings or other memorable celebration gatherings.

Proprietors take great pride in decorating and maintaining their lodgings in a style which will welcome their guests and provide a comfortable, inviting setting. As a result, courtesy and respect of property is expected.

Features: These establishments can be very diverse in features and amenities. Some are traditional homes in quiet subdivisions with one or two guest rooms and a single shared bath. Others may be contemporary, large and opulent with multiple guest rooms, private baths, designer furnishings and decorations. Still others may be old and grand featuring significant historical background with Victorian, Greek Revival or other Old World styling. They are frequently decorated with antiques and/or authentic reproductions. Several feature in-room Jacuzzis and fireplaces. Air conditioning may or may not be available.

SELECTING THE LODGING THAT'S RIGHT FOR YOU

Price/Rental Policies: Prices vary greatly with averages between $50 to $90 daily and a few luxury suites exceed $200. Most bed and breakfasts rent daily and may offer special week or weekend package rates. Advanced deposits are generally requested and refund policies vary.

What to Bring: Just your clothes and a smile.

Breakfasts: Breakfasts are part of every B&B package (those categorized as inns may not include breakfast). Breakfasts vary from continental to full. Ask the owner about serving times. Some establishments encourage guests' mingling at a common table during breakfast. Others may provide private tables or will bring breakfast directly to your room. Many owners are happy to accommodate special dietary needs but will need to be told in advance.

Just remember, if you're not sure about something ...
ASK THE OWNER.

We wish you a safe and most enjoyable Michigan vacation!

Reviews

The Munro House

Jonesville, Michigan
(517) 849-9292

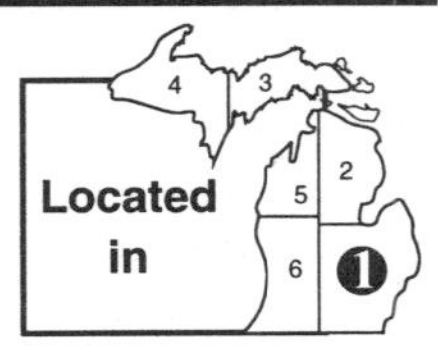

Proprietor: **Joyce Yarde**

Accommodations: **7 rooms, private baths (twin/queen beds)**

Extras: **In-room phones/CATV, fireplaces. 2 Jacuzzi rooms. No pets/ smoking. Full breakfasts**

Rates: **Daily $56 to $150**

Payment: **Check, Cash**

Open: **Year around**

Guests will be greeted with the elegance of an earlier time as they step inside the historic Munro House located in Jonesville, Michigan. Greek Revival styling with sweeping staircase, 12 foot ceilings, 10 fireplaces and numerous chandeliers effectively recreate the mood of its 1800's refinement. Over the years, considerable effort has been made to restore the house, retaining its original charm while providing the technology and comfort today's travelers require.

Munro House served as a station on Michigan's Underground Railroad

Built by George C. Munro in 1834, it remained in the Munro family for over 100 years. Originally a small cabin, it was expanded in 1843 and stands today at 6,800 sq. ft. It is considered to be the first brick home in Hillsdale. From the fur trading era through the Civil War period, this home has seen much history. It was on the original wagon train trail that passed through Michigan. It also served as a station on the Underground Railroad taking slaves to freedom along routes from Detroit to Windsor, Canada. In fact, the *secret room* still exists today and is found above the downstairs bedroom's bath area.

Joyce Yard, the outgoing and charismatic owner of The Munro House, must be commended for her sense of history and her ability to tastefully blend old with new. Each guest room is comfortably and uniquely styled from traditional to country and Shaker. All include color TV's with radios and phones. Most of these modern conveniences, however, are tactfully hidden from site in cabinets, dressers, etc. so they may be used but won't detract from the room's overall ambiance.

Located on the third floor, George's Room and Clara's Room are the newest additions at The Munro House. Each features a two-person Jacuzzi and, once again, Joyce has successfully merged old with new. George's Room serves as a tribute to Mr. Munro's friendship with the Chief of the Patawatame Indians back in the fur trading era of the 1830's. The room's styling is reminiscent of an earlier time and decorated in colors of deep red, blue and tan. The mood is definitely masculine with a portrait of the great Chief resting on the wall.

Spacious - George's Room

Clara's Room is completely different and perhaps one of the most creatively decorated rooms we've seen in our travels. The styling is that of an outdoor garden with murals of trees and flowers flowing with the curves of ceiling and walls. One and three dimensional bird houses are placed strategically on tree branches. The room is airy, bright and truly delightful. We won't tell you where Joyce has hidden the TV in this room ... you'll have to see it to believe it.

Cooking is yet another attribute of Joyce who is more than a little handy in the kitchen. Each morning guests will sit down to one of Joyce's deliciously prepared full breakfasts served in the quaint and authentically styled colonial room with windows overlooking the garden. The room's large brick open hearth fireplace makes a cozy spot for those chilly winter mornings. During the day, if your sweet tooth is calling, there's Joyce's famous "bottomless" cookie jar and in the evening guests will be treated to coffee and a freshly prepared dessert.

Clara's Room - garden setting

For those seeking daily adventures, there's plenty to do in this lovely area by the Irish Hills. Start by taking an auto tour through the scenic rolling landscapes or stop at some of the many area antique shops. For outdoor enthusiasts, there are several nearby state parks where you'll find plenty of hiking/biking trails and cross country skiing. Of course, Shipshewana, Indiana and Amish Country is just another scenic drive away.

Joyce Yard is waiting to share the history and comfort of her charming home. She welcomes both business and vacation travelers and will happily accommodate your meeting, conference, wedding or special celebration plans for groups of 10 to 130.

2452

Pleasant Lake, Michigan
(313) 426-2874

Owners: Jan Marble and Mike Stagg

Accommodations: Single Lakefront Cottage, 3 bedrooms

Extras: Fully equipped kitchen, Franklin Stove, Cable TV, VCR, wood deck, boat included, no pets

Rates: Weekly $425 to $450

Payment: Check, Cash

Open: Year around

Inviting knotty pine interior & great lake view

Jan Marble and Mike Stagg are two fun loving, active people who enjoy the unusual but also have respect and admiration for tradition. 2452 is a direct reflection of that. Over the years they have maintained, restored and renovated this 70 year old lodging to retain its original character while updating it with all the modern conveniences.

The knotty pine interior is uniquely decorated, reflecting Jan and Mike's love for nature and outdoor sports. The living area, with comfortable and overstuffed furniture, faces a wall of windows overlooking Pleasant Lake. The kitchen is fully equipped, including microwave, stove and refrigerator. Bedrooms are cozy with twin or queen size beds and simple but engaging decorations.

Their new and well made wood deck is a great way to pass some time. Several nearby oak trees providing plenty of shade. Because their property sits high above the water, stepping onto the deck almost feels as though you're sitting over the lake ... it's a great effect. Approximately 20 steps take you down to the breakwall, dock and water's edge. Here you'll find a cement patio with chairs and a little shed filled with fun water toys. Jan and Mike also provide a boat for your use. If you bring your own boat, it can be easily loaded on the other side of the lake. To ensure that all you boaters and swimmers won't miss their place, Jan and Mike have installed a regulation-size, working stoplight by the lower patio.

New deck sits high above the lake

Affordably priced with all the comforts and conveniences of home, this cozy spot makes a nice place to spend your leisure time. A short drive from Detroit and close to the Irish Hills.

Point of View

Frankenmuth, Michigan
(517) 652-9845

Owners:	**Ed and Betty Goyings**
Accommodations:	**1 Room Riverfront Cabin w/Florida Room**
Extras:	**Linens, phones, room air conditioner available, fireplace wood, bottled water, no pets**
Rates:	**Weekly $345 (based on 2 people, $25 each add'l person)**
Payment:	**Check, Cash**
Open:	**Year around**

Peeking through the covering of trees, abundant wild flowers, and greenery lies Ed and Betty Goyings' hidden gem, Point of View. The natural blend of landscaping effectively hides the cottage from the quiet, country road and the Goyings' home. Who would have thought that less than four miles from the bustling main streets of Frankenmuth, you'd find such a private spot with a definite Up North feel.

This charming little retreat was originally built after World War II, in 1945, by eight young men from the Frankenmuth/Vassar area. After it was completed, they agreed to meet there **E**very **O**ther **M**onday, and named it the E.O.M. Club. Faithfully they gathered to play cards and talk "guy talk". On alternating week-ends, they'd bring their families to enjoy picnics, make pretzels, dance to the juke box and generally just have fun. By 1986, the Vassar American Legion bought the site, adding a spacious Florida Room that overlooks the Cass River.

The Goyings took charge in 1993. They made significant renovations striving to retain the original ambiance while decorating for those who love the outdoors yet expect modern comforts.

Betty has a flair for interior design and has preserved its unique history with cheerful, homey touches. The immaculate, open styled one-room lodging has restored maple and knotty-pine floors, walls and ceilings. The original owners' presence is still felt and framed photos them and their families are displayed on several walls which evoke happy times of the past.

Comfortable and inviting 1 room cabin

Guests naturally gravitate toward the fully equipped kitchen which has been restored to its look of the 1940's with some definite 1990's features including new appliances and microwave.

Across from the kitchen, the living room includes a sofa, table and TV, with the comfortable queen-sized bed resting in the corner not far from the fireplace. Guests will enjoy the bright Florida Room. An expanse of windows looks out over the natural landscape of trees, foliage and the gently flowing Cass River— excellent for canoeing and fishing. Betty tells us it's a birdwatcher's paradise with Blue Herons and other friendly fowl and small wildlife frequently making stops. The Florida Room is furnished with wicker chairs, tables and full-size bunk bed which can sleep up to four. We tried the lower bunk bed and found it to be a little stiff for our own comfort, but others might find it more to their liking.

Fully renovated kitchen with '40's theme

Serene view from Florida Room

Amenities include linens, telephone and wood for the fireplace. A window air conditioner is available. Betty believes the drinking water may not be up to guest standards, so she provides fresh bottled water for your convenience.

Come to Point of View and enjoy a delightful blast from the past. Bring your canoe, bike or fishing rod. Listen to music, dance, play cards and enjoy the charm that was created by eight young men over 50 years ago. Join the growing membership of the E.O.M. Club.

Bed & Breakfast at The Pines

Frankenmuth, Michigan

(517) 652-9019

Owners:	**Richard & Donna Hodge**
Accommodations:	**3 Bedroom, private bath/shared bath**
Extras:	**Full breakfasts, no smoking/pets**
Rates:	**Daily $40-$50**
Payment:	**Check, Cash**
Open:	**Year around**

Looking to spend a few days in historic Frankenmuth? Why not stay with your soon-to-be new friends, Richard and Donna Hodge. Here on a quiet side street with well kept homes and lawns, a few blocks from major restaurants and shops, rests their three bedroom brick ranch home.

Located on a quiet side street in Historic Frankenmuth

The Hodges' traditional ranch home offers an excellent example of what a home-away-from-home can be. "Come as a stranger— leave as a friend" is their motto and, indeed, it holds true for guests coming to Bed & Breakfast at The Pines. Donna or Richard will be there to greet you with cheerful smiles and sincere warmth.

Well maintained with unpretentious touches, the home creates a relaxed, casual feeling — like the home of an old friend. You'll find photos of their daughter's wedding on one tabletop, Staffordshire and other pottery plates displayed along a wall and a good assortment of magazines and books begging to be read. The three bedrooms, though not large, contain double or twin beds and feature ceiling fans. Fresh flowers, heirloom bedspreads, antique dressers

add to each room's light and cheery decor. The larger bedroom offers a small, private half bath (sink and toilet) and also shares the full bath and shower with the other rooms.

If you're interested, the Hodges will be more than happy to share their extensive knowledge about the history of Frankenmuth. They're also your key source to finding interesting places to visit, restaurants or charming coffee shops. In the evenings, you may want to join them for a quiet chat in their backyard or, on those cooler nights, in front of the warming fireplace. They'll also be happy to join you in a game of cards before you turn in after your busy day.

The Hodges describe their breakfasts as Continental-plus. This allows Donna to indulge in one of her favorite past times — baking. Guests will be treated and spoiled by the tempting aromas and tastes of one of her homemade breads or rolls and, perhaps, a special egg dish which is served along with seasonal fruits and beverages. We had the opportunity of briefly speaking with one of her guests — a visiting lecturer from Colorado — who, without hesitation, eagerly volunteered that Donna's breakfasts were "absolutely wonderful". The Hodges welcome you to share their refrigerator and kitchen to store your own refreshments or lunch preparations.

Well, what more can be said? If you're looking for a friendly, homey Frankenmuth experience, come to Bed & Breakfast at the Pines ... you'll definitely "*Come as a stranger—leave as a friend.*"

Little White Cottages

Nymph and Seadog

Lexington, Michigan

(616) 669-5187

Located in Region 1

Accommodations:	**Two cottages (1-2 bedroom - waterfront/water access)**
Extras:	**Fireplaces, equipped kitchen w/microwave, Seadog with ceiling fan, screened porches, lawn furniture, firepit, board games, no pets**
Rates:	**Weekly $395-$575 (reduced off-season rates)**
Payment:	**Check, Cash, with 50% deposit**
Open:	**May-October**

Nestled in the trees, along 50 feet of Lake Huron shoreline, rests the comfortably old-fashioned Little White Cottages. Several recent improvements add to the appearance and comfort of these two traditional lodgings.

Standing closest to the water is the two bedroom Seadog. Its screened porch is a great spot to view the sloping yard, water's edge and beautiful Lake Huron sunrises. Decorated in a blend of new and old, it is highlighted by a cozy woodburning fireplace for those cooler evenings. The well maintained and fully equipped kitchen is complemented by new countertops and contains all the necessary utensils and appliances including microwave. Its full bath includes a tub with shower.

The Seadog - a cozy blend of new and old

Sitting behind the Seadog is the smaller one-bedroom Nymph. Furnished and equipped similar to its neighbor, it also includes a Franklin stove, screened porch and bathroom with shower.

1 bedroom Nymph sits behind the Seadog

All bedrooms, though small, are comfortable. Linoleum floors run throughout with freshly painted walls and ceilings adding a bright and welcoming touch.

Outside, the grounds are natural with both cottages bordered in bright flowers. The long, narrow yard leads to a scattering of chairs overlooking the water. A comfortable and inviting wooden swing rests nearest the water (...its's a real favorite of ours). You'll find it a perfect spot to sip your morning coffee while watching one of Lake Huron's beautiful sunrises.

Walking down a short inclined path to the beach is traditional Huron water with the traditional Huron stones, so bring along your aquashoes. Also at beachside you'll find the all important firepit just waiting for that traditional evening bonfire.

Everything is provided for guests at the Little White Cottages except linens, towels and fireplace wood. You'll also find plenty of board games to occupy your evenings or any free time. Also, since there is no regular cleaning service, the owners ask that you please leave your cottage clean for the next guests.

Glenview

Lexington, MI
(810) 359-7837

Located in REGION 1

Owner/Manager:	**Charles & Linda Phipps, Jr.**
Accommodations:	**Two bedroom cottage**
Extras:	**Fireplace, equipped kitchen, TV (no cable), no pets**
Rates:	**Weekly $500 (prime season)**
Payment:	**Check, Cash**
Open:	**Year around**

With its well manicured, simple exterior and tastefully decorated interior, a small delight awaits guests at Glenview. Charles and Linda Phipps have used their innovative and creative style to completely rejuvenate this older home.

Lovely interior design makes small Glenview a true delight

Tall ceilings, open styling and creative use of space makes the home appear larger than it is. Cedar walls, white wood and brick create an inviting blend of contrasts. Wood floors, area rugs and throws complemented by the comfortable and eclectic furnishings continue to add to the home's warmth and friendliness.

The living area is divided into two sections. The first resembles a verandah with wraparound windows facing the sunrise. The dark color of the corner sectional provides a rich contrast to the white wicker furniture opposite. Walking into the more formal living room, your attention is drawn to the brick fireplace dividing the dining from the living area.

Friendly, open dining alcove

The single bathroom and two bedrooms are comfortably sized, though not large. The small, fully equipped kitchen has been totally redone with white cabinets and tan Formica countertops.

Glenview rests on a very safe and quiet street. While it does not directly front water, there is access to the sandy Lake Huron beach, approximately 25-30 yards down the road. The 30 or more steps down to the water are somewhat steep, but the Phipps have completely redone the stairs making them safe, secure and easier to descend.

Stairway leads to sandy beach

Only a couple of hours from metro Detroit, this is a great little cottage for a pretty darn good price.

The Get-A-Way

Pt. Au Gres, MI
(313) 389-1793

Located in Region 2

Owners:	**Tom and Karen Wilson**
Accommodations:	**Waterfront, 3 bedroom cottage**
Extras:	**Equipped kitchen, radio, phone, color TV, VCR, book and video libraries, board games, enclosed porch, outside patio, no pets**
Rates:	**Weekly $450**
Payment:	**Check, Cash**
Open:	**Year around**

Rush hour traffic and stress getting you down ... why not getaway to The Get-A-Way?

Perched on the edge of Pt. AuGres, overlooking Saginaw Bay on a quiet cottage lane, the Get-A-Way provides a simple, comfortable escape. Approximately 800 sq. ft., this well maintained, white frame cottage offers several very nice features which make it an excellent value.

Well furnished & maintained - only 50-60 yards from Saginaw Bay

The bright and airy living and dining area is highlighted by wraparound windows and a doorwall which overlooks the lake. It's just the spot to catch a beautiful sunrise over your morning coffee. We were impressed with the new, comfortable sofas in the living room — great after an exhausting day of fun. Another nice feature is the TV and VCR which is complemented by a well stocked video library with itemized directory. Of

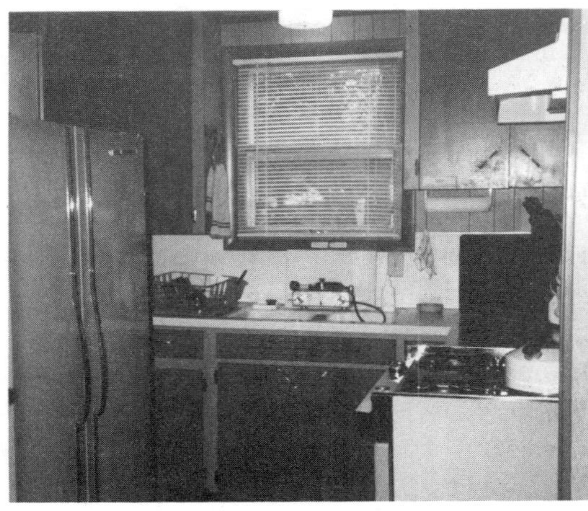

Small but efficient kitchen area

course, you'll also want to take advantage of their extensive book library, board games or outdoor bocci and croquet sets.

The small kitchen is well equipped including microwave and sported a sparkling new floor. Karen joked about the avocado colored appliances which reminded her of the 70's. However, on inspection, we found them to be in excellent condition. Karen and Tom are not particularly fond of their filtered well water and, as a result, provide guests with 6 to 8 gallons of bottled drinking water.

The Wilsons have put a great deal of pride and effort into renovating their place. The bathroom has been completely updated including new walls, shower stall/tub, sink and toilet. Their handy work is again visible in the stone wall panels in the hall and front bedroom. Speaking of bedrooms, there are three altogether. The first is highlighted by an attached, furnished and enclosed porch which overlooks the bay. The second also has a bay view and the very small third bedroom has bunkbeds and is suitable for children.

Bright and cheery interiors

The surrounding grounds are open and well groomed with several pine and shade trees dotting the property. Along side the cottage is a large, open patio furnished with a 7 ft. swing, picnic table and barbecue. Approximately 50 to 60 yards from the patio is Saginaw Bay. Its waterline is edged by a seawall with a sandy path to the water. Tom and Karen said the water is shallow and safe for swimming but there's a rocky bottom which makes it difficult to walk. For a smooth, sandy swimming beach the Wilsons recommend a nearby campground just a few minutes walking distance away (a small per person fee is charged - Tom thought it was somewhere under 50¢).

Guests at the Get-A-Way will find plenty to do in the area. One or two miles away is a marina where boats can be rented. For other things to do and see, Tom and Karen provide an excellent reference book highlighting key area attractions, restaurants, etc.

The Get-A-Way is a comfortable place to be for a private vacation offering great value and an outstanding Michigan sunrise.

Borchers Bed & Breakfast

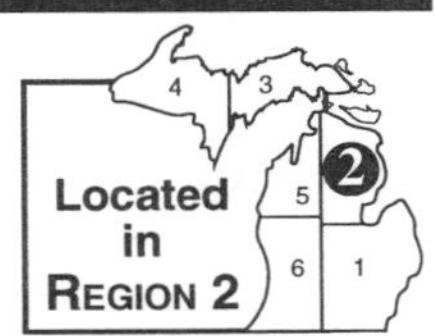

Grayling, Michigan
(517) 348-4921 • (800) 762-8756

Proprietors:	**Tink & Shirley Henry/Mark & Cheri Hunter**
Accommodations:	**Riverfront, 6 bedrooms (shared and private baths)**
Extras:	**Full breakfast, canoe/kayak rentals, planned canoe trips with pick-up and return**
Rates:	**Daily $49 to $82**
Payment:	**Major Credit Cards, Check, Cash($25 deposit per room), Corporate discounts**
Open:	**May through October (November-April open by reservation only)**

An excellent way to begin your next AuSable River adventure is in the comfort and hospitality of Borchers Bed & Breakfast.

Originally built in the early 1900's, this two-story, country-styled B&B sits along the banks of the AuSable. The two families have combined their considerable talents to renovate and maintain a lodging which provides all the atmosphere and amenities needed to enjoy your river experience.

Real down-home comfort and charm right on the banks of the AuSable River

From first-timers to the most dedicated canoeing or kayaking enthusiast, the gently flowing waters of the AuSable offer a most pleasurable experience. The proprietors of Borchers are very knowledgeable about the river and happy to help you plan the trip best suited to your needs and capabilities. They'll give you detailed maps of the area and might even be able to point out some of the best fishing spots or places to see wildlife.

Borchers' guests traditionally look forward to the morning. That's when they're treated to the aroma of freshly brewed coffee and one of Shirley's and Cheri's specially prepared full breakfasts which are delicious and hearty. If given advance notice, they will be happy to accommodate your special dietary needs.

Hearty breakfasts are served each morning in their country kitchen

After that last sip of juice or coffee, it's time to begin your day. Ready? Then meet Tink or Mark in the newly built boat house. They'll set you up with everything you'll need for your canoe, kayak or fishing adventure. If you're planning a longer journey, they'll be waiting at your final destination to bring you back.

Though Borchers is slightly off the beaten path, it's still only minutes away from several interesting shops and restaurants. They are also close to miles of hiking, mountain biking and, in winter, cross country ski trails. So, for those seeking a break from the water, you will find plenty to do to keep you busy.

Country decor highlight each room

Whatever your pleasure, after an exciting but exhausting day, it's a welcomed relief to come back to the clean comfort of Borchers. Sit back on their large porch overlooking the river. Or, if you prefer, watch a video or read a book in their sitting room. The six guest rooms continue the theme of inviting, country comfort — three have private baths and three shared. All are attractively appointed and include color TV with cable and remote control. Some rooms have window air conditioners.

Whatever season, the Henrys and Hunters welcome you to share their lovely and comfortable bed and breakfast. With open hospitality and a keen knowledge of the area, they'll help to make your next trip to the AuSable a memorable experience.

Hinchman Acres Resort

Mio, Michigan
(517) 826-3267 • (800) 438-0203

Proprietors: Sam & Natalie Giardina

Accommodations: 13 cottages (1, 2 and 3 bedrooms)

Extras: A/C, some fireplaces (wood provided), kitchens w/ microwaves, CATV, radios, phones, linens. Beach, children's play area, game room. Planned canoe trips, hiking, biking and x-country ski tails. No pets. AAA approved.

Rates: Daily $40 to $95 ; Weekly $250 to $475

Payment: Major Credit Cards, Checks, Cash. 1st night's rent deposit required for summer rentals.

Open: Year around

Built in 1932, this historic, peaceful resort rests 800' off the highway along the main stream of the AuSable River and adjacent to the Huron National Forest. Its 13 cottages are nestled among acres of natural pine and oak which provide a lovely and relaxed setting.

Peaceful grounds of Hinchman Acres

Sam and Natalie Giardina have owned and operated Hinchman since 1971. We were very impressed by the Giaradinas focus on guest comfort. As Natalie firmly states, they don't maintain and clean their lodgings simply to ensure their AAA approval ... they do it to ensure the maximum comfort of their guests.

To achieve this philosophy, their cottages continually undergo renovations. All feature fully heated and air conditioned rooms as well as cable TV, radios, phones and equipped kitchens. We were very impressed with the cleanliness and comfort of each cottage. Even the smaller one bedrooms were well maintained and comfortable with the larger cottages providing plenty of room.

The two lakes found at Hinchman add to the resort's scenic beauty. The smaller spring-fed lake serves as their private swimming beach and trout pond. The sandy beach is clean and the swimming fun and safe for all. Throwing a line into their well-stocked trout pond is almost certain to meet with success (small fee charged per trout). The second lake provides free fishing.

Decor varies significantly in each unit

Guests will find plenty to do at Hinchman no matter what season. In spring, it's a bird lovers paradise. Natalie tells us their grounds welcome diverse bird populations including the Kirtland Warbler. If you're interested, free tours are available through the U.S. Forest Service.

Besides plenty of swimming, hiking, biking and fishing in the summer, guests can also rent a family size canoe for a trip on the AuSable. In the evenings there are bonfires, and kids of all ages will enjoy the game room or outdoor play area. Horseback riding, paddle boat trips on the AuSable and golf courses are only a few miles away.

The scenic, natural grounds of Hinchman Acres are an excellent spot for your fall color retreat. Enjoy a full day of visiting area antique shops or walking through the breathtaking fall colors before you kick back in your cozy cottage to warm by its fireplace. Let's not forget winter! When the snow flies, Hinchman again comes alive. With over 25 kilometers of groomed and double tracked cross country ski trails in the Huron National Forest and along the beautiful AuSable River you're sure to keep your days full. Hinchman provides complete rental equipment, warming hut and free instructions.

Any time of year, Hinchman Acres provides the comfort and cleanliness vacationers seek in a setting that's sure to please.

NettieBay Lodge

Hawks, MI
(517) 734-4688

Owners:	**Mark & Jackie Schuler**
Accommodations:	**Waterfront Cottages, Duplex and Lodge**
Extras:	**Equipped kitchens, some fireplaces, boats, children's play area, nature trails, no pets**
Guided Programs:	**Bird Watching, Log Building, Stone Masonry, The Outdoor Woman. (meals included with packages only)**
Rates:	**$339 to $498**
Payment:	**Check, Cash**
Open:	**Year around**

A Michigan adventure awaits guests at NettieBay Lodge — whether you're a true naturalist or simply seeking something different, one of their many guided, outdoor programs could be an excellent choice. Of course, if you're a traditional family vacationer wanting to have fun in the woods or by the water, NettieBay has the setting.

Scenic Nettie Bay

For those interested in one of their special activities, Mark and Jackie along with their expert trainers and guides will keep you entertained and informed during your stay. Their programs are very diverse and have been highlighted in several magazines including *Michigan Out-of-Doors.* They've also received the Michigan Audubon Society Small Business Award for their birding efforts.

Our adventure began during their Spring Migration Birding Weekend (the second weekend in May). The mood was set the minute we entered the grounds, with its 2,000 acres of undeveloped woodlands, marshes and meadows. Strategically placed bird feeders were attracting a variety of birds one does not often see in the city, and loons had already nested on the nearby island.

"Sun's rising in the swamp" is the call summoning birders to begin the adventure

The program started with a Friday night get-together where the group met to review the weekend itinerary. We soon discovered our fellow birders were very knowledgeable... which was great for us since we have a hard time distinguishing Sparrows from Blue Jays.

Exploration takes you through the serenity of nature

Early the next morning (about 5:15 a.m.) we heard Mark's knock and his traditional call, "Sun's rising in the swamp", which told us it was time to begin. By 5:30 everyone, though groggy-eyed, was eager and congregated in the lodge with binoculars in hand. After coffee and morning pastries, we were off.

Even as inexperienced birding newbies, it didn't take us long to get wrapped up in the camaraderie of our group, the quiet beauty of the woodlands, the magical song of birds, and the excitement of discovery. With Mark's knowledge of the area and birding, along with our experienced group, more than 50 varieties of birds were spotted in one day which included eagles, osprey, warblers and a variety of finches and raptors. My partner and I personally spotted countless LBBs (Little Black Birds) which is a term frequently used by inexperienced birders, like us, to describe some type of flying object smaller than an eagle. Our travels also brought us to a number of deer, muskrat and beavers. Finally, after the end of an exciting and exhausting day, it was nice to come back to relax in the warmth of our room which was simple but very clean and comfortable, with an excellent view of the Bay.

Simple but comfortable and clean rooms

Most exploration is by van or boat with stop offs that take you through farmlands, wetlands and several remote locations (come prepared with appropriate clothing and foot wear). Great physical dexterity is not required to enjoy your trip. There are rest periods and stops for brunch and dinner where guests are treated to Jackie's specially prepared meals (meals included with package programs only).

We left NettieBay with great memories of a fun and informative adventure. Whether you're a traditionalist or a naturalist, make NettieBay your next adventure.

Sid's Resort

Greenbush MI
(517) 739-7638 • (810) 781-3845

Proprietors:	**Carol Sizydik**
Accommodations:	**Waterfront resort with 11, 1-3 bedroom cottages**
Extras:	**Well decorated cottage interiors, private baths, equipped kitchens, CATV. Gameroom, playground, water bicycles, paddle boards, kayaks, wave runner rentals. Bring beach and bath towels. No pets.**
Rates:	**$450-$1,100 Weekly (July/Aug.); 15% Discounts offered during off-season (May, June, Sept. Oct.)**
Payment:	**Check, Cash or Money Order ($50.00 non-refundable deposit required)**
Open:	**May through October**

A smooth stretch of inviting sandy beach, freshly painted cottages among a scattering of trees and bright annuals set the stage for an outstanding vacation experience. Only seven miles north of Oscoda along the shores of Lake Huron, Sid's stands as a premiere family resort on Michigan's sunrise side.

Exceptional accommodations and beach

Back in 1993-94 the friendly and busy owner of Sid's, Carol Sizydik, decided it was time to *freshen up* the resort. She and her family rolled up their sleeves and got to work. When the dust settled, a new Sid's emerged with a beautiful, shiny facelift. Old walls had been removed or refurbished. Ceilings were opened to reveal their high-peaked log beams. Interiors were thoughtfully re-designed and re-furnished with custom draperies, dishes, furniture, even leaded crystal light fixtures. Grounds were landscaped with care given to retain the natural beauty. All this, Carol said, to ensure her lodgings

Well furnished and decorated interiors

maintained a quality and comfort which would set her resort apart from others. Carol has accomplished her goal.

The cottages we visited were indeed appealing and maintained a quality not often found in traditional cottage resorts. Kitchens were sparkling with well-matched assortments of dishes, glasses and utensils. Interiors were well thought out with loft sleeping rooms in the larger cottages creating an open, spacious feel. Even the small, one bedroom cottage was comfortable and inviting.

Of course let's not forget the wonderful sandy beach. Here's the spot where families or couples will find hours of enjoyment burying each other in the sand, building gigantic sand castles, or simply laying back in the sun. The water has a gradual sandy incline which makes it safe and fun for all ages. For those seeking more water *action*, rent a wave runners, family-sized jet boat, kayaks (including the children-sized Penguin), water bicycles, or paddle boards. The well landscaped grounds also feature a playground. badminton, basketball, volleyball and shuffleboard area. Everyone will enjoy the game room with pinball machines, pool table and juke box.

It seems inevitable that guests at Sid's will leave spoiled and happy ... and that's just what Carol wants. Make your reservations early.

Best Western
Thunder Bay Resort

Hillman, Michigan
(800) 729-9375

Located in Region 2

Owners:	**Jack & Jan Matthias**
Accommodations:	**30 Villas & Suites (132 beds)**
Extras:	**Golf course, restaurants, lounge, gift shop, tennis court, hot tub, sport equipment rentals, meeting and conference facilities. Condos with kitchens, CATV, phones, balconies, some whirlpool tubs.**
Package Programs:	**Customized golf packages, "October" Fest Hayrides & Elk Viewing Sleigh Rides w/Gourmet Dinner, Cross-Country Skiing, Snowmobiling**
Rates:	**Varying rates starting at $41 (2 day/1 night, per person, based on quad occupancy)**
Payment:	**Major Credit Cards, Checks, Cash**
Open:	**Year Around**

There's no question that Thunder Bay stands as a premiere golf resort on Michigan's Sunrise Side giving you one of the best package values in the state. Its challenging, well groomed 18 hole course and several unique seasonal packages make it an appealing place to stay throughout the year.

Uniquely challenging golf course

During spring, summer and fall, you can play unlimited golf (with cart) at Thunder Bay, or select a customized package to include Elk Ridge, Bay Valley, White Pine National, and several other area courses. Thunder Bay's fairways and greens present unique challenges that have been etched into the natural woodlands. Their Par 73 (women's 75) course features a fairly tight layout that includes several doglegs and specially contoured greens that require precise accuracy. Though it is not a long course (6,466 yards), it does require skill with most Par 5's requiring more than 2 shots to hit the green. According to Jack, their toughest hole is the Par 5, No. 9.

Thunder Bay is more than just great golfing, however. In the fall, join in their October Fest Weekends held late September through October. The highlight of these weekends is the horse-drawn hayrides through the woods. Bundle up with someone special, enjoy the crisp air and keep your eyes open. It's almost inevitable that you'll see deer and elk roaming the trail. To add to this experience, your ride will take you to a special rustic log cabin deep in the woods where you'll be treated to a five-course gourmet meal prepared on a wood cook stove. When the snow falls the hayrides turn into sleigh rides and the fun continues. Their fall and winter Elk Viewing/Gourmet Dinner Packages have proved to be very successful. Call early for reservations.

Elk viewing sleigh rides combined with a gourmet meal package are very popular

In winter, Thunder Bay is a good central point to explore Elk Country and hundreds of miles of state groomed trails. To accommodate guests, the resort offers snowmobile and cross country ski equipment rentals.

The lodgings are an added bonus to the many amenities at Thunder Bay. The newly built suites are spacious and contemporary with separate living/sleeping areas. Kitchens are fully equipped. Some first floor rooms feature whirlpool tubs. Since sound travels easily in these suites, guests are asked to be courteous and keep noise down after 10 p.m.

Contemporary & comfortable lodging

For golfing and year around fun, Thunder Bay provides the setting and activities which will keep you entertained and your experience memorable.

River Cove Condominiums

Sault Ste. Marie, MI
(906) 632-7075

Located in Region 3

Proprietor:	**Al Tipton**
Accommodations:	**Three, two-bedroom waterfront condominiums**
Extras:	**Ceiling fans, equipped kitchens w/dishwasher, microwave, queen beds, linens , CA TV w/remote, VCR, decks, handicap accessible; parking garage; no swimming. No pets.**
Rates:	**Daily $99 (2 people) to $149 (4 people), 2 night min.** **Weekly $600-$800 (call for special off-season rates)**
Payment:	**Cash, money orders (preferred), credit cards accepted**
Open:	**Year around**

A wonderful surprise awaits guests at Al Tipton's River Cove Condominiums in Sault Ste. Marie. From the fully equipped kitchen to the comfortable and cheerfully appointed rooms, you'll be greeted by a welcomed freshness that invites you to unwind at the end of your journey.

Nautical themed, contemporary decor

Guests will find all the lodgings fully equipped, so just bring your luggage and food (should you choose to cook). The three available condo units (two on the second floor, one on the first floor) have well designed, compact interiors. The first floor unit is handicap accessible with no steps required for exit or entry. Each features a full kitchen including dishwasher, microwave, coffeemaker, stove and refrigerator as well as a complete assortment of utensils, pots and pans. There's a combined dining and living room, bathroom with tub shower and two bedrooms each with queen size beds. Ceiling fans in all rooms help to keep the interiors cool even during those rare, hot summer days in the Upper Peninsula.

Comfortable queen beds

All rooms are decorated in a contemporary nautical theme. This definitely sets the stage for the view seen from windows and doorwall. Here, across groomed lawns, you'll have a clear path to the river where the great freighters pass. Of course, you may prefer to watch from your private deck. If you do, be sure to bring your binoculars to check out the ospreys nesting on Sugar Island just across the river. Don't be afraid of scaring off the ducks meandering along the water's edge. They're happy to see you, especially if you're carrying one of Al's corn and seed buckets (found on each deck). Swimming is not permitted, but there is a dock available for your boat with a marina only one-half mile down the road.

When you arrive, we suggest you check out the black binder on the kitchen counter. In it you'll find the simple "house rules" along with descriptions and locations of area restaurants, maps and several recommended scenic tours. If you're feeling lucky, the Kewadin Casino is only two miles away. Also just down the road are the Soo Locks and boat tours. An hour's drive will take you to Taquamenon Falls, Whitefish Point, or St. Ignace where you can catch a boat to Mackinac Island.

All units offer excellent river views

The Tiptons welcome all to come and enjoy their scenic and relaxing accommodations. They do not, however, recommend you bring young children. There is no children's play area and the cold, deep river has surprisingly strong undercurrents.

Twin Cedars Resort

Trout Lake, Michigan
(906) 569-3209

Located in Region 3

Proprietors: **Harold & Judy Klave**

Accommodations: **5 cottages (1-2 bedroom) and 2 motel rooms**

Extras: **Equipped kitchens, some ceiling fans. Motel rooms with A/C, in-room coffeemaker, microwave. TV (no cable), boat, bait/tackle shop and fish cleaning area. Pets O.K. in bird season.**

Rates: **Competitive to the area**

Payment: **Check, cash**

Open: **May through November**

Located off Highway 123 in a private wooded setting, along the quiet shores of Frenchman's Lake, you'll find the traditional and homey Twin Cedars Resort.

Aerial view of Twin Cedars

Three of the five resort cottages face the water. Open, beamed ceilings with ceiling fans in two of the lodgings provide improved ventilation and can be a bonus on hot summer days.

The lodgings we visited were very clean with new bathroom tile and hot water heaters seen in several units. Kitchens have all the basics which include microwave, toaster and electric perk coffee makers. Each also includes a TV (cable not available). Sofas and chairs showed some wear but were serviceable. An interesting touch is the chain saw wood tables and bedroom furniture — a reminder of the resort's original German owner who was an avid wood craftsman. You'll also find many of the cottage walls decorated with paintings and photographs of area wildlife and nature scenes. These, Judy said, are gifts from former guests.

Clean and simply furnished cottages

For those preferring the comfort of a motel, the Klaves have built two motel units which sit back from the cottages. Built in the mid-1970's, the two rooms offer A/C, TV with remote control, microwaves and coffee makers. These units may be rented daily or weekly. These rooms were nicely laid out and certainly compared with some of the nicer motel units we've seen. Each motel room has a small, private deck with furniture.

At water's edge there's a central wooden deck with tables. The scene here is peaceful and provides a good view of the surrounding area. While there is no sandy beach, the water by the seawall is shallow enough for swimming.

Frenchmen's Lake offers good fishing

Harold tells us the fishing in Frenchman's Lake is quite good with frequent catches including pike, perch, walleye, bass as well as a variety of pan fish. The lake itself covers more than 220 acres with many cove areas and, in addition to fishing, is also fun to explore in your boat. To accommodate your fishing trip, the resort offers a bait and tackle shop along with a fish cleaning area.

We enjoyed our brief stay and wish we could have lingered. If you're looking for a simple, homey vacation by the water, enjoy fishing and boating, Harold and Judy are waiting to meet you. Open mid-May through the end of November.

Whitefish Lodge

Deerton (Marquette), Michigan
(906) 343-6762

Proprietors:	**Karen Hart and Steve Pawielski**
Accommodations:	**2, 2 bedroom units; 1, 3 bedroom lodge**
Extras:	**Cooking facilities with full-size refrigerators, ovens and coffeemakers. VCR, stereo, microwave in larger unit. Gas available on premises**
Rates:	**Weekly $350-$675 (Daily rates available)**
Payment:	**Visa/Master Card, Check, Cash (2 night min.)**
Open:	**Year around**

If you're looking for a remote, back road vacation experience in the Upper Peninsula but don't want to leave all your modern comforts behind, checkout the Whitefish Lodge. It's located off Highway 38 down several miles of dirt back roads.

The young, energetic proprietors, Karen Hart and Steve Pawielski, opened the lodge in 1993. Karen, originally from Atlanta, and Steve, born and raised in the Munising area, have made Whitefish a welcoming oasis in the middle of the wilderness.

An oasis in the wilderness

Set between the heavily wooded borders of the Laughing Whitefish Preserve and a scenic, rippling section of the Laughing Whitefish River, its nightsong is the sound of nature. Don't be fooled by its remoteness. It's only five minutes from Lake Superior's sparkling, cool beaches; 15 minutes from Munising; and 30 minutes from Marquette.

The two-story lodge has a freshly stained wood exterior and a large multi-tiered deck open to guests. On the first floor, two smaller units have bedrooms with queen-size beds. Their small kitchens provide a good gathering spot for families or friends and feature new oak-cabinets, and appliances which include full refrigerators, oven, range and automatic coffee maker. While not large, these rooms do provide enough space to comfortably sleep four adults. The new bathrooms have stall showers and are stock with plenty of soft towels.

The bubbling Whitefish River runs nearby

The upper level is devoted to a spacious lodge unit called the Sugar Maple. It's great for large families or small groups. Your party will love the combined great room/kitchen, stocked with all the basics. There's a stereo, TV (no cable) and VCR—so bring along your VHS tapes. Down the hall are three bedrooms, each with a small private bath.

Open kitchen in the spacious, upper level lodge

If you're wondering what to do while in the area, the owners are happy to inform you about special events or activities. Guided scuba diving or wilderness adventure tours can be found nearby. Or, just outside your door, enjoy miles of hiking, canoeing, snowmobiling and cross-country ski trails. Whitefish also provides mountain bikes for their guests.

If you're seeking tamer adventures, there are plenty of wilderness driving tours or nature walks that will take you to the heart of picturesque waterfalls or nearby overlooks. You may just want to spend time relaxing and contemplating nature on one of Lake Superior's many nearby beaches.

Getting to the lodge in summer months is easy enough. However, in the winter months, four-wheel drive vehicles will come in very handy. And, speaking of winter, that season is a busy time at Whitefish. If you're planning a winter excursion, we suggest you book as far in advance as possible.

Karen and Steve have found a special place in nature and they look forward to sharing what it has to offer with all of their guests. Come to the Whitefish Lodge and enjoy a *comfortable* wilderness vacation.

Thunder Bay Inn

Big Bay, MI 49808
(906) 345-9376 • (800) 732-0714

Proprietors/Owners: **Darryl and Eileen Small**
Accommodations: **14 guest rooms, 3 suites (private/shared baths)**
Extras: **Restaurant/ pub, corporate meeting facilities**
Rates: **$49-$85 Daily**
Payment: **Major Credit Cards, Check, Cash**
Open: **Year Around**

The Thunder Bay Inn is rich in Upper Peninsula legend and lore, not to mention famous people. Built by early lumber barons in 1911, the site served as a warehouse, general store, office and barber shop for community-based lumber companies.

Henry Ford's former retreat served as the setting for the movie, "Anatomy of a Murder"

In 1940, along came automaker Henry Ford who was searching for an executive vacation retreat. Realizing it was the perfect getaway spot, Ford bought the site almost instantly and renovated it extensively. For years, it was called the Ford Hotel and played host site to busy executives and their families.

In 1959, Hollywood discovered the hotel and brought it instant fame as the setting for "Anatomy of a Murder," an Alfred Hitchcock classic starring James Steward and Lee Remick. The book and movie are based on a true story of murder and intrigue in Big Bay in 1951. The inn's present-day pub was built just to film the movie. But weary travelers don't have to worry—the actual murder occurred down the road at the Lumberjack Inn.

The pub's back wall still displays newspaper clippings of the murder and trial and photos taken during the movie filming.

Current owners Darryl and Eileen Small bought the hotel in 1986, giving it the present name. The Thunder Bay Inn is actually the fictional name of the hotel in the "Anatomy" novel and movie. In restoring the hotel, the Smalls have taken great care to have the decor reflect its history and preserve its natural beauty.

Adding to its charm, the hotel overlooks the original saw mill which produced wooden panels for early Ford station wagons. Peeking from behind a cluster of trees, sky-blue Lake Independence is visible. Guests can't help but appreciate the unique touches found in the 14 guest rooms and suites. The rooms and bathrooms reflect the earlier Ford renovation period. Guest rooms share two general bath areas, but suites have private baths.

Ford's Room maintains historical theme

Recently the Smalls have been involved with finishing the Inn's upper level and expanding meeting and conference facilities. They plan to continue expanding these services for corporate events and gatherings.

Make it a point to stop at the Inn on your next U.P. vacation. Reserve ahead if possible. It's close to popular Marquette with numerous trails, waterfalls and guided wilderness tours nearby. Outdoor recreational equipment is available to rent at the Inn year round.

Château Chantel

Traverse City, Michigan
(616) 223-4110

Located in Region 5

Proprietors:	**Robert and Nadine Begin**
Accommodations:	**1 room, 2 suites, private baths**
Extras:	**Full breakfasts, handicap accessible rooms, conference/event planning**
Rate:	**$95-$125 daily**
Payment:	**Major credit cards, checks, money orders**
Open:	**Year around**

Forget Paris, we say. An Old World chateau setting can be yours right in northern Michigan, at far less cost than a trip to Europe. Overlooking the Old Mission Peninsula on Traverse City's east bay, this grand estate offers visitors a spectacular view of the area — from Grand Traverse Bay to Power Island.

Open the massive oak doors to the chateau's entrance and you're transported to another time and place. Voila! Here's a stately French country inn in northern Michigan. Most impressive is its spacious Great Room that's both elegant and comfortable. It boasts a high ceiling, huge granite fireplace, oak bar and charming dining area. The surrounding windows allow a panoramic view of the Old Mission Peninsula.

A taste of France in the Old Mission Peninsula - Château Chantel

Another windowed alcove is reserved for a white concert piano, whose keyboards get a workout by performing artists on Tuesdays and Thursdays. In the warm months, guests can relax in the outdoor patio or Great Room, sip wine and nibble cheese, crackers, fresh fruit or other goodies while listening to the cool sounds of "Jazz at Sunset". There is a small charge for this event which is also open to the public.

The Chateau's three guest rooms offer splendid views of the Peninsula. All are attractively appointed with queen-size beds, air conditioning, private bath, TV and phones. The two first-floor suites have separate sitting areas and are handicap accessible and equipped. Rooms are decorated in delicate shades of dusty blue, rose or lavender and gray, making them a perfect relaxing and romantic setting. The upstairs Pansee Room (pronounced pansy) features a queen-size canopy bed. Nadine has added her own homey touches to this cheerful and bright room — such as a creatively stitched bedspread, pillow covers and wall hangings.

Enjoy panoramic sunsets while listening to jazz on Tuesdays & Thursdays

With a masters degree in home economics, Nadine is well suited for her role as hostess and head chef. Breakfasts begin with fresh fruit, juice and an entree — Eggs Mornay, Angle Puffs, or Belgium Waffles are popular. You'll finish up with homemade desserts such as spiced muffins, rolls or coffee cakes.

Bob takes great pride in his wine offerings. He lived in France, formerly working as a wholesaler of German and French wines. He now oversees the vineyards and the wine-making operations at Chateau Chantel. The Chateau's Pinot Noir, Merlot wines and their champagne have won many awards.

Delightful Pansee Room

The Begins appreciate their guests' need for privacy which makes the chateau a perfect choice for those special getaways. Also, should you be planning a special event or conference, the Chateau also offers full planning services to make the event memorable and successful.

Best of all, the Chateau is open year round and serves as the gateway to all the good times the Traverse City region promises. We suggest booking ahead to assure availability.

Judy's Place

Interlochen, Michigan
(616) 275-6561 or (810) 626-2464

Proprietor/Owner:	**Judy Jacobson**
Accommodations:	**4 bedroom, 3 bath waterfront log home (sleeps 8-10 people)**
Extras:	**Equipped kitchen, dishwasher, microwave, washer/dryer, phones, CATV, VCR, A/C, stereo, ceiling fans, fireplace, hot tub, linens, BBQ, well behaved pets OK, handicap accessible, prefer non-smokers**
Rate:	**Weekly $1200; Daily $200**
Payment:	**Check, Cash**
Open:	**Year around**

If you're looking for the luxury of a fine hotel but want the privacy of a lakefront cottage in the woods, look no further. Judy's Place will pamper your every need, provide the solitude you seek, and put you close to all area activities.

It was built about five years ago by Judy Jacobson, one of the most exuberant, friendly and warm people you could ever want to meet. She likes comfort, quality, activity and good friends. She also has impeccable taste. The cottage is a reflection of Judy.

A perfect setting by the water

A few miles off the main road to Interlochen on a densely wooded, unpaved side street of large residential and vacation homes, you'll find Judy's Place. The light pine log cottage is impressive against the dark colors of tall pines and trees, and its one *plus* acres of land will surround you in solitude and nature.

As you enter the home from its large front deck (equipped with handicap ramp), you'll be welcomed by the bright and airy great room punctuated by high-peaked ceiling, suspended ceiling fan, and large stone fireplace. The two overstuffed sofas and chairs are the type you could sit in for days without ever wanting to leave. Naturally we can't forget the TV, VCR and stereo equipment which sits just to the right of the fireplace.

Comfortable with inviting decor

The entire home is carpeted in rich Berber and the decor perfectly blends in a continued theme of quality, comfort and friendly warmth. You'll want to take note of Judy's interesting wall hangings which reflect Michigan's history and natural wonders.

On either side of the great room and directly back, you'll find the four bedrooms. Each offers either king, queen or twin beds and ceiling fans. The two master bedrooms have a private bath — the two smaller rooms share a bath. It goes without saying the beds are very comfortable and made for sleeping in late.

The kitchen is small, efficient and fully equipped. In the adjoining dining area, a large oak table faces the windows and doorwall overlooking the deck and wooded grounds. An outside path takes you to water's edge where you'll find a firepit ready for roasting marshmallows as the sunsets. Later, as the evening cools, what better way for friends or family to relax than in the invigorating bubbles of the spacious and private hot tub located right off the back deck.

For those who have been dreaming of a beautiful log cottage by the lake, it's time to stop dreaming, you've found it — Judy's Place.

L'DaRu Lakeside Resort, Inc.

Traverse City (Spider Lake), Michigan

(616) 946-8999

Proprietors:	**Jill and Danny Rye**
Accommodations:	**17 cottages, varying in size**
Extras:	**Waterfront resort, equipped kitchens, CATV, linens (bring beach towels), on-site recreational activities, no pets**
Rates:	**Weekly $280-$675 (Sept.- May); $445-$800 (June-Aug.)**
Payment:	**Major Credit Cards, Check, Cash**
Open:	**Year around**

A little piece of heaven can be found at scenic L'DaRu Lakeside Resort located on beautiful Spider Lake.

If you arrive like we did—hot, exhausted and stressed from long work hours and too much freeway traffic—you'll appreciate the resort's calming, naturally wooded grounds. Not to mention a shaded overlook to 450 ft. of smooth, sandy beach. Guests must feel the same sense of release and relaxation since more than 80% of them come back year after year. Some families have been returning for over 30 years.

Scenic L'DaRu - built by notorious mobster, Al Capone

Present owners Jill and Danny Rye have been there for more than 10 years. They've updated and maintained the lodgings to assure today's families are comfortable. Danny, our host, told us that all cottages are kept fully updated — even mattresses are replaced every five years.

Set on gently sloping grounds, L'DaRu contains its own bit of historical excitement. The lodge was built in 1923 by renown mobster Al Capone for his favorite bookkeeper. Legend has it, Capone so loved the place, he and his cronies made it a favorite hideaway haunt. Three more lodgings were added in the Prohibition era, and the remaining lodges were completed in the 1950's.

The resort's name, L'DaRu, came from one of its first "legit" owners who combined the letter of their wives' and daughter's names, Eleanor, Diane and Ruth—hence, L'DaRu.

Well maintained cottages on 450 ft. of sandy Spider Lake beach

Cottages vary in size with the largest being 1,400 sq. ft. Each has a private bath, fully equipped kitchen, dining table and living area with color cable TV. Most offer a lake view and one includes a gas log fireplace.

Guests can enjoy many traditional family activities, from horseshoes to volleyball and badminton. There's even a combined tennis/basketball court and children's playground. If that's not enough, the game room has ping pong table, video and pinball games. A small library and sauna are also available to guests.

L'DaRu is also the place for all you fishing enthusiasts who will find Spider Lake stocked with large mouth bass, pan fish and an occasional muskie or pike. Rowboats are available to guests and outboard motors, canoes and paddle boats may be rented. There's also a beachside firepit perfect for roasting marshmallows or hot dogs at the end of the day.

During the winter, there are plenty of fully groomed snowmobile and cross-country ski trails only a few miles away.

We suspect that after one visit, L'DaRu will become one of your favorite year around hideaways—just as it was for the famed and infamous more than 60 years ago.

Linden Lea on Long Lake Bed and Breakfast

Traverse City (Long Lake), Michigan
(616) 943-9182

Proprietors:	**Jim and Vicky McDonnell**
Accommodations:	**Two bedrooms, private baths**
Extras:	**A/C, ceiling fans, one room with access to two-person Jacuzzi, full breakfast**
Rates:	**$80-$95**
Payment:	**Check, Cash**
Open:	**Year around**

Secluded behind a cluster of trees overlooking beautiful Long Lake, you'll find Jim and Vicky McDonnell's special retreat, Linden Lea. Only minutes from Interlochen and several well-known restaurants, Linden Lea provides all the ingredients for a relaxing vacation — caring and gracious owners, and a lovely home in a serene setting.

View of home from Long Lake

Linden Lea was originally built as a small summer cottage by three Civil War veterans at the turn-of-the-century. It was eventually vacated and fell into disrepair. As Vicky tell us, the cottage was in deplorable condition when they first visited in 1979. However, with one look at the perfect setting and beautiful view, Jim and Vicky knew it had to be theirs. Today, after several major expansions and renovations, it's hard to imagine it was ever a small cottage. Its multi-story exterior is contemporary country with gray stained wood and multi-tiered wood decks. The private and naturally landscaped backyard leads to a small sandy beach which offers good swimming and a great lake view. A rowboat or paddle boat is available for guests' use or they can bring their own boat for mooring at the 60 ft. dock.

The inviting interior of Linden Lea is casually sophisticated with a comfortable blend of modern and antique decor. The combined dining and living area is graced with a wall of windows overlooking Long Lake. A carved cherrywood fireplace, dating from the late 1800's, and an overstuffed couch and chair add to the room's warmth and comfort. To the back, there's an antique player piano dating to 1871 and a large dining table where breakfast is served.

Our arrival at Linden Lea occurred during one of those unbearably hot summer days. It was a welcomed relief to be cheerfully greeted by the McDonnell family. We were immediately offered cool drinks and some of Vicky's delicious homemade muffins which we gratefully accepted as Jim led the way to our upstairs room. Though not large, we found the room to be charmingly decorated with cozy quilted bedcover draping a very comfortable queen size bed. An antique dresser rested against one corner and the bright window seat provided another lovely view of the lake. A short hallway led to a private bath with plenty of fluffy towels. We understand the second room was similar to ours with the addition of a two-person Jacuzzi tub in a private bath across the hall.

Well presented interiors effectively blend modern with antique decor

When dinner time came, we called for Vicky's assistance. She was there and more than willing to describe and offer suggestions regarding some of the many fine local restaurants. In fact, both Vicky and Jim are very knowledgeable on just about everything in the area — restaurants, places to visit, and sites to see.

The next morning we awoke to the greeting sound of birds, the gentle rustle of leaves outside our window and the inviting scent of freshly baked bread and brewing coffee. We came downstairs ready to experience what Vicky calls her "monstrous" breakfast. Over the years, Vicky has developed a vast collection of breakfast recipes. By adding her own creative touch, she has

Cheerful rooms offer window seats with scenic view of Long Lake

come up with selections that are sure to delight. Our memorable and, indeed, monstrous breakfast began with coffee, tea and juice with an abundant fresh fruit salad, baked bread, muffins, jellies and jams. The main course was a bountiful quiche packed with potatoes, bacon, cheese and other "secret" ingredients which made it a truly tasty treat. Of course, if you have special dietary requirements, Vicky will be happy to prepare a breakfast to suit your needs.

Linden Lea is a lovely name and a lovely bed and breakfast. One visit here will bring you back time and time again.

Northaire Resort

Clam Lake, Michigan
(616) 347-1250

Located in Region 5

Proprietor/Manager: **Mike & Helen Lambert**
Accommodations: **Waterfront resort, six cottages**
Extras: **Equipped kitchens, docks, boats, no pets**
Rates: **$455 to $595 Weekly**
Payment: **Check, Cash**
Open: **Year around**

Remember the first time you went up north with mom and dad and stayed at that first cottage. The experience is one you've never forgotten. Northaire will take you back to those nostalgic days of the 1950's and 60's with its simple and unchanged style.

Mike and Helen Lambert took a major step a few years back when they left their careers in our country's most active political hub, Washington, D.C. Deciding to leave the crazy pace of big city living behind, they purchased Northaire and have never looked back.

Initially they had thought to make major changes to the old resort, but the many long-time return guests encouraged them to leave things alone ... to keep things simple and their memories intact. As a result, much of the resort's initial furniture and styling remains relatively unchanged. Most units have the original tile or linoleum floors, Formica counter tops, and traditional 50's vinyl furnishings. The cottages we visited were clean with appliances and furnishings ranging in age.

Despite their guests' resistance, the Lamberts were in the process of making some renovations to the lodgings. We were particularly pleased with one cottage highlighted by a tall cathedral ceiling and new, light paneling. We look forward to seeing more of these renovations as things progress.

Clean interiors - decor reminiscent of the 1950's & 60's

Guests to Northaire will appreciate the large, natural grounds which front 300 ft. of Clam Lake. Trees are abundant with the most beautiful being an old weeper which overhangs water's edge. An other nice feature was that all of the cottages offered a view of the lake and were scattered on the grounds which set each apart from the other.

For you fishing enthusiasts, the Lamberts tell us Clam Lake is an excellent spot for catching pike, trout and a variety of other lake fish.

If you'd like to stay at a resort where you don't have to worry about putting your feet up, where childhood memories can begin , the simple and traditional Northaire Resort just might be your place.

Wyndenrock on the Bay & Le Petite Maison Sur L'eau

Northport (West Bay), Michigan (616) 386-5462

Proprietor:	**Theda Connell**
Accommodations:	**Two waterfront cottages**
Extras:	**Equipped kitchens, TV's, linens, no pets/ smoking, swimming not recommended**
Rates:	**$525 - $975 (Lower rates during off-season)**
Payment:	**Check, Cash - 50% Deposit**
Open:	**Year-round**

Wyndenrock on the Bay is named for the large rocks which break the rolling waves to a gentle flow along the 166 ft. of its shoreline. Theda Connell speaks with loving pride of her three bedroom (two bedrooms plus sleeping port), 1920's summer home located in the lovely Northport area. She admires its nostalgic charm and, when completing updates or renovations, takes great effort to retain the flavor of the era in which it was built.

View of Wyndenrock from the shoreline

As you enter the open first floor Great Room of this two story lodging, you'll be wrapped in the warmth of its original log styling with high peaked ceiling and dark wood walls. An Indian blanket overhangs the second story railing and a large floor-to-ceiling stone fireplace graces the center wall of the main room. To add to its nostalgia, an old model schooner is perched on top of the fireplace's mantel with antique snow shoes decorating either side. The Turn-Of-The-Century upright piano sitting in the corner still keeps a pretty good tune. Also, within the great room, you'll find a cozy alcove and a second sitting room to the right. The newly restored wood floors shine and the French Doors at the back lead to a screened porch with a view of Grand Traverse Bay.

The kitchen, with older cabinets and countertops, is immaculate and fully equipped including newer stove and refrigerator. Also, on the first floor, you'll find the single bathroom with shower stall, toilet and small sink. It should be noted that the bathroom is very small, almost closet size, and may pose a problem for those who like room in their morning preparations.

To the right of the cottage's entrance is a wooden staircase which leads to the upstairs bedrooms and loft area. The first bedroom has built-in, single level bunk beds which are tucked under a jetting wall with small, in-wall lights. I tried one bed and found it very comfortable. This room is cozy and "secret". Children might find it a perfect hideaway... even though Theda tells us adults often use it. This bedroom leads to the second, which is set in a bay window room. Though also small, the room fits a queen size bed and is inviting with its view of the Bay through the surrounding tall trees. Several of the windows here can be opened to allow the cooling breezes to flow through. The third sleeping area is down the hall. Theda refers to this as a "sleeping port" because it is not a room as much as an alcove area. It is a new addition to the cottage and very inviting.

Charming sitting room

Of course, Theda tells us, the styling of Wyndenrock may not be for everyone. She mentioned that as soon as she hears people ask "How many bathrooms does it have?" she automatically knows the place isn't right for them. Wyndenrock doesn't offer all the newer conveniences — there may not be as many electrical wall outlets as you'd like or the bathroom may be too small. But for people seeking a genuine nostalgic cottage, then your stay at Wyndenrock on the Bay will be a wonderful and memorable experience. The waterline here is rocky and does not provide the best swimming.

The second vacation cottage, *Le Petite Maison Sur L'eau* (Little House on the Water) is located a short distance from Wyndenrock. As its name represents, it is a small but charming cottage. The large picture window overlooks a deep lot leading to water's edge. As in Theda's other property, it is nicely decorated, very clean and comfortable. The newly tiled bathroom contains tub/shower, sink and toilet. The kitchen is also fully stocked and equipped. Its single bedroom holds two twin beds which, when placed together, can be turned into a queen size bed. The sofa sleeper in the living room opens to a double bed. Here is a nice spot for honeymooners, a small family or anyone else who wants a little seclusion. The small sandy beach here provides better swimming with fewer rocks.

Cozy interior of Le Petite

Charlevoix South Arm Properties

Charlevoix, MI
(616) 536-7343

Owner/Manager	**Marie Yettaw**
Accommodations:	**Various waterfront/non-waterfront, economical cottages, private homes, condos, cedar log cabin**
Extras:	**Various, no pets**
Rates:	**$430 to $1580 weekly**
Payment:	**Check, cash**
Open:	**Year around**

Whether it's on a lake or in a quite country setting, economical cottages, spacious private home, contemporary condos, or charming cedar log cabin — Marie Yettaw's properties will provide a setting and a price right for you.

The first and most economical of the properties are the Lake Charlevoix Cottages. These four small, well maintained lodgings are simply furnished with equipped kitchens, furnished living rooms and two bedrooms. They sit side-by-side across the street from their private pebbled beach and dock area. They provide a good, basic accommodation for your stay in the lovely Charlevoix area.

For those seeking more contemporary comfort, Smuggler's Cove Condominiums would be your choice. Located on the lake's southarm, each of these one to two bedroom units offer great views from patios or decks. CATV, ceiling fans and fully equipped kitchens are provided in all with some offering air conditioning. There's plenty of docking available for your boat. The water is good for swimming with a pebble and sand mix bottom.

Contemporary comfort at Smuggler's Cove

If you want the privacy of a lakefront home, then the 2,000 sq. ft., ranch styled Charlevoix Lakefront House provides an excellent choice. This 1960's home has undergone several expansions and now features three bedrooms (sleeps 12), two baths, and a spacious, well-stocked kitchen with dishwasher and microwave. There is no air conditioning, but the cool lake breezes keep the home comfortable. The main living room is highlighted by a surrounding expanse of windows which leads to a large deck overlooking the lake. There's also a warming fireplace for those cooler nights and a 20" CATV with remote (19" TV's with remote can also be found in all bedrooms).

Spacious Charlevoix Lakefront Home

Because of its quiet and scenic location, we took a particular liking to The Log House. This classic, 900 sq. ft. red cedar log cabin is in a very picturesque, quiet country setting along the Jordan River. Unfortunately, we were unable to view the interior but Marie assures us it's "clean as a pin" with finished log interior, country blend furnishings, carpeting and hardwood floors throughout. There's two bedrooms, two baths and a fully equipped kitchen. The main living area features a fireplace and relaxing view of the grounds and Jordan River. This is a truly lovely setting and a very nice family or couples retreat.

Peaceful retreat - the Log Home

Briar-Cliffe

Saugatuck, MI
(616) 857-7041

Located in Region 6

Proprietors:	**Shirley & David Witt**
Accommodations:	**1 Luxury Suite, private bath**
Extras:	**Scenic grounds with beach access. Fireplace, two person Jacuzzi, CATV, VCR, small refrigerator, microwave and coffeemaker. No smoking/no pets. Handicap accessible.**
Rates:	**Daily $125**
Payment:	**Check, Cash**
Open:	**Year around**

David and Shirley Witt are not first timers when it comes to providing quality guest accommodations. As former owners/operators of popular bed and breakfasts, they have established a reputation in the Midwest as outstanding hosts with an eye for style and comfort. Back in 1995, they decided it was time to try something different. Not a bed and breakfast this time, but a luxury suite designed for those seeking a private and very special break from the stress and pressures of today's life-styles.

Unpretentious, quiet setting of Briar-Cliffe

Their search for the perfect location took them to a picturesque, quiet back road and a place they now call Briar-Cliffe. This lovely, unpretentious home sits back from a scenic bluff overlooking Lake Michigan. Its backyard is the gateway to five acres of natural woods with walking trails and plenty of privacy. It's apparent the Witts have found a most peaceful setting and one that should achieve their goal.

The creativity, quality and style guests have come to associate with the Witts has now been extended into their guest suite. Antiques, rich colors, inviting patterns, textures and furnishings set an intimate and relaxing mood. The sitting room is highlighted by a fireplace and large picture window offering a view of well manicured lawns and the bluff overlooking Lake Michigan. Down a short hall is the bedroom with luxurious, queen-size canopied bed. To the side, a private bath with two-person whirlpool tub. To ensure your comfort, there isa small refrigerator, microwave, coffee maker as well as CATV with VCR.

Antiques and classic styling highlight the luxury suite at Briar-Cliffe

Outside, just past the quiet road, you'll come to the bluff. Here the view of Lake Michigan and its stretch of white, sandy beach is breathtaking. Dave and Shirley have recently built a stairway which will safely take you down to enjoy the sun, sand and clear waters.

Continuing their tradition, the Witts have again combined an excellent location with a guest suite offering quality, grace and style. A lovely place to spend some special time. Briar-Cliffe is just minutes away from downtown Saugatuck with Grand Rapids and Holland only a short drive away.

The Lamplighter Bed & Breakfast

Located in Region 6

Ludington, Michigan
(616) 843-9792 • (800) 301-9792

Proprietors:	**Judy and Heinz Bertram**
Accommodations:	**4 bedrooms, private baths**
Extras:	**Full gourmet breakfasts. A/C, CATV, phones. Fireplace and Jacuzzi rooms available. Murder Mystery weekend packages. No smoking. Proprietors fluent in German. Corporate rates.**
Rates:	**Daily $75 to $135 (special rates for Murder Mystery weekends)**
Payment:	**Major Credit Cards, Check, Cash**
Open:	**Year around**

The lovely gazebo, wood deck and brick terrace beckon visitors to stay at this beautifully restored turn-of-the-century home in scenic Ludington. Originally constructed in 1895 during the Great Lumber Baron days, the home was built by a surgeon as his home and office. Speaking tubes are still visible in the walls which were used by the doctor to communicate with patients and family members. Since then it has served as a rooming house and home to various small businesses. In 1991 it was first converted to a bed and breakfast with the Bertrams taking ownership in 1993.

Attentive owners in an historic B&B with a distinctive European flavor

The graceful interior styling of The Lamplighter reflect the influence of Heinz's German heritage and Judy's own memorable years in Germany. Fully restored wood floors, lead crystal chandeliers, lace table linens and curtains create a European ambiance which give The Lamplighter a distinctive appeal. Rooms are decorated in rich colors of brown, light rose, cream, deep blue and green. The Bertram's special collections of antiques, original paintings and lithographs from American and European artists add to the interior warmth.

The four comfortable, well appointed guest rooms are upstairs and feature queen size beds, private baths, cable TV and telephones. Their newest room blends new with old and is accented by a two-person whirlpool tub...ideal for honeymooners or that special getaway.

Comfortable and inviting rooms

In the morning, before you begin your exploration of beaches, parks or shops (all only minutes away) you'll be treated to one of Judy's special *gourmet* breakfasts which include fresh fruit, juice, coffee, baked goods along with a main course. Some of her specialties include German Apple Puff Pancakes, delicious baked omelets, and decadent mocha-chocolate apple muffins. Whatever the choice, it's sure to be memorable. After breakfast or later in the day, if you're interested, Judy or Heinz will be happy to assist you in locating area restaurants or direct you to nearby beaches, parks or special events.

In November, January, February and March secret shrouds The Lamplighter. During these months the Bertrams take part in the Ludington Association's Murder Mystery events which are a combined effort of several area bed and breakfasts. Of course the weekend begins when, during a gathering of guests, a dastardly murder occurs. Suddenly everyone is converted into crack detectives. Noteworthy activities, clues and investigations take you to several locations where actors assume roles of the innocent and the guilty. It's up to you, the *investigator*, to solve the murder before the weekend is out. Meals are included during Mystery Weekends. Judy encourages all to come and enjoy these fun and challenging events which, Judy says, she enjoys as much as the guests.

Whatever time of the year, there's always plenty to do in Ludington. The next time you stop in the area, whether business or pleasure, why not make the European charm of The Lamplighter Bed and Breakfast your next choice. The Bertrams will welcome you as will their cuddly cocker spaniel *guard dog,* Freddie.

North Shore Inn

Holland, Michigan
(616) 394-9050

Located in Region 6

Proprietor/Owner:	**Beverly Van Genderen**
Accommodations:	**3 bedroom, private and shared baths**
Extras:	**Full breakfast, waterfront, AC**
Rates:	**$90 to $110 Daily**
Payment:	**Check, Cash**
Open:	**Year around**

Down a quiet lane of large homes on Lake Macatawa, you'll see the sign for North Shore Inn. Hidden behind the protective growth of wild shrubbery and trees, the home remains a secret until you turn into the drive. Suddenly the wild terrain is transformed into perfectly manicured lawns with natural gardens of annuals and perennials fronting and surrounding the impressive two-story home.

Impressive home on Lake Macatawa

A peaceful arbor and sitting area are located in the front yard. Shaded by and scented with pines and an array of bright flowers, it is an excellent spot for reflection. The grounds and natural gardens continue their path around the home and into the backyard. This will lead you to a dreamy view of tall Austrian pines and beautifully groomed lawns sloping to the blue waters of Lake Macatawa. To enhance the vision, another natural garden sits to the right with a small walking path taking you to a sitting area and pond complete with jumbo-sized goldfish.

The expansive home is beautifully furnished with the living room accented by a small concert piano and fireplace. Off to the left is the formal dining area. The three upstairs bedrooms have king, queen, double or twin beds and though not large are comfortably furnished with antiques and bright quilts. One features a spacious private bath and two other rooms share a bath.

Lovely gardens and well groomed lawns create a picturesque setting

With nice weather, breakfast is normally served on the enclosed verandah that stretches along the back of the house and provides an excellent view of the lake. The airiness and lovely view from this room sets the perfect mood for enjoying one of Beverly's well prepared and beautifully presented breakfasts which effectively blend a touch of Holland with traditional American cuisine.

Our white linen-covered table was set with a colorful centerpiece of fresh annuals and individual flowers (such as pansies and marigolds) accenting our napkins and dishes. Bev assured us that all the flowers decorating our dishes were fully edible (we tried a couple ... they were remarkably good).

Cheerfully decorated guest rooms

Our breakfast began with a choice of fresh fruit cup or special, homemade rhubarb sauce. The main course consisted of specially seasoned scrambled eggs and pigs-in-a-blanket using sausage from Holland which has a milder flavor than traditional American sausage. The light and crispy toast was also a Dutch favorite. Naturally, breakfast wouldn't be complete without Bev's homemade strudel which, by the way, was absolutely delicious.

If you're planning a visit to historic and picturesque Holland, the North Shore Inn is sure to add to your memorable experience.

The Sand Castles

Hagar Shores, MI
(616) 849-0240 • (800) 972-0080

Located in Region 6

Proprietor	**Sharon Turnbow**
Accommodations:	**10 cottages ranging in size**
Extras:	**Kitchenette or full kitchens, microwaves, linens (no towels), ceiling fans, some with C/A or fireplace, cable hook-up (bring your TV), beach access one-mile**
Rates:	**Weekly $250 - $600 (approx.)**
Payment:	**Check, Cash**
Open:	**Year around**

Accommodations range in size

Located near the center of town, the Sand Castles offers small to large cottages on a well maintained lot. The fun-loving owner, Sharon, spends a great deal of time with their upkeep and it shows. Interiors/exteriors are clean as a button and in very good condition with several new renovations including floor coverings, cheerful bedspreads, draperies and more. Attractive pictures and other wall hangings add to an air of homey comfort. All units have fully equipped kitchen or kitchenettes with stove, refrigerator, microwave and the basics. The living areas have comfortable

sofas and chairs. Most eating areas were furnished with matching tables and chairs. We were pleased to note that bedrooms were bright and appealing with firm twin, full or queen mattresses and plenty of closet space. Large decks with patio furniture were a nice feature on two of the larger cottages.

Interior of larger cottage

Though not on the water, the cottages are on a lot with plenty of trees for shade and space for yard games. There are also picnic tables on the premises. If you'd like to spend some time by the water, cottage renters have access to the private city park with an excellent sandy beach about a mile down the road. Since the park only permits Coloma residents (and, of course, Sharon's renters), you'll never find it crowded like public beaches.

Access to the private city beach only 1 mile

The Sand Castles' cottages are a good value for their size and comfort. They're also close to many shops, restaurants, and just minutes from Kalamazoo, Portage and the Indiana border.

REGION 1

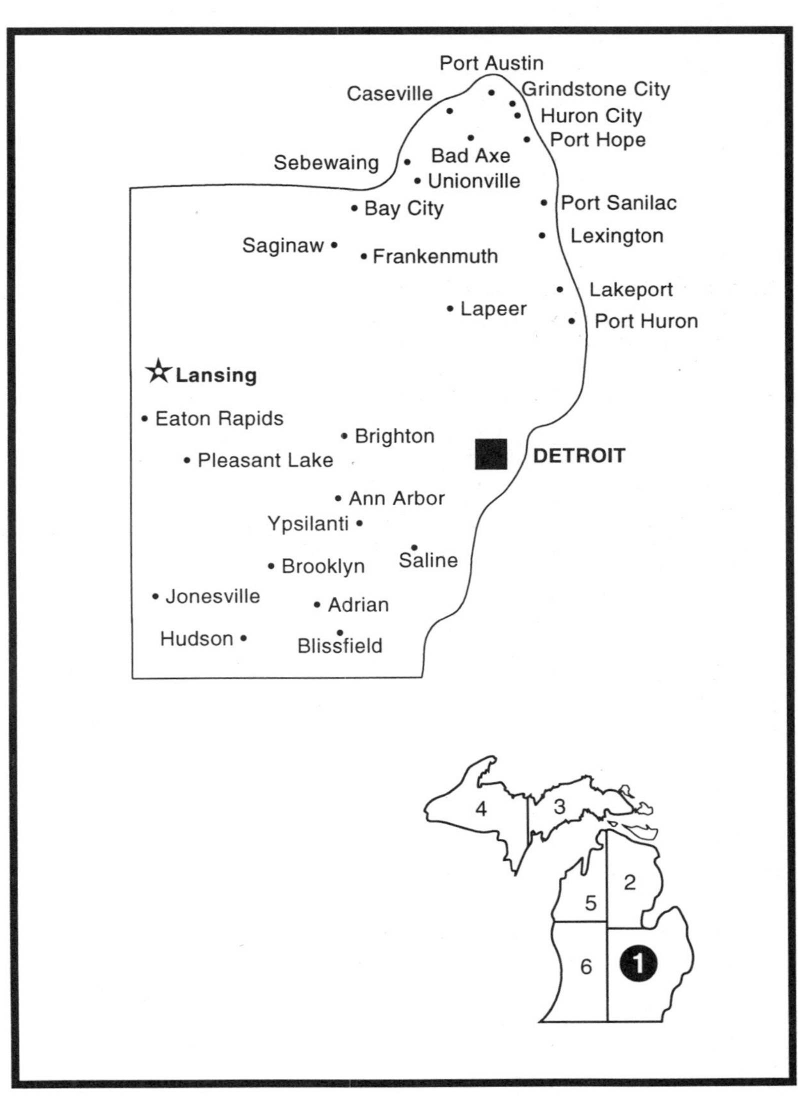
Port Austin
Caseville
Grindstone City
Huron City
Port Hope
Bad Axe
Sebewaing
Unionville
Bay City
Port Sanilac
Lexington
Saginaw
Frankenmuth
Lakeport
Lapeer
Port Huron
Lansing
Eaton Rapids
Brighton
DETROIT
Pleasant Lake
Ann Arbor
Ypsilanti
Saline
Brooklyn
Jonesville
Adrian
Hudson
Blissfield
4
3
2
5
6
1

REGION 1

The southeast side of Michigan, the Heartland, is the only area in the state without links to the Great Lakes. Here, too, the territory is agricultural with faded red barns and rolling fields of oats. As you travel along, you will see gentle hills and vails of lush green as far as your eye can see. Crystal lakes, rippling streams, waterfalls, hot air balloon races, air shows and many tours of historic homes, art fairs, unusual shops and stagecoach towns of long ago. Vibrant cities that never seem to sleep. Its treasure lies in the scenic beauty of its woods, lakes and streams made even more beautiful by the fine people and relaxed atmosphere of the area.

Shaped by the Saginaw Bay to the west and Lake Huron to the east, the "Thumb" is a world apart from the urban communities that are less than two hours away. Here the interstate highways turn to country roads and suburbs turn into distinct villages, the hectic life of the city turns into rural country charm. There are 90 miles of lake shorelines to view, small museums, beaches, country markets, antique shops, roadside parks, and picturesque bluffs, lighthouses, and an easy way of life to soothe the soul and rest the weary urban mind.

Welcome to "the gateway close to home".

ADRIAN • IRISH HILLS AREA

COVERS: BLISSFIELD • BROOKLYN • HUDSON • JONESVILLE

Adrian, a unique blend of modern and historic! Visit the Croswell Opera House, the oldest continuously operating theater of its kind in Michigan! It features live theater productions as well as special art exhibits. Michigan Futurity is the place to be for horse racing excitement.

Surround yourself by the beauty of the **Irish Hills**! Picnic by one of the area's 50 spring-fed lakes, ride amongst its beautiful rolling hills, and take a trip to historic Walker Tavern in Cambridge State Historic Park. Enjoy a nature walk through the 670-acre Hidden Lake Gardens at Michigan State University. Of course, there's always the fun of Mystery Hill. Ready for more? Then step back in time to the 1800's and enjoy the pioneering spirit that lives on at Stagecoach Stop U.S.A. Sit back with a sarsaparilla in the Saloon, pan for gold, or take a train ride ... but be careful ... we hear there's masked bandits in the area!

Join the excitement of Indy and stock car races each summer (June-August) at the Michigan International Speedway in the Irish Hills. While enjoying the beautiful fall colors, don't forget to stop in **Brooklyn** and join the fun at Oktoberfest or their arts and crafts festival. Anyone for cross-country skiing or snowmobiling? Cambridge State Historic Park is waiting. No matter what time of year, the Irish Hills are always waiting.

ADRIAN

BRIAROAKS INN (800) 308-7279 • (517) 263-1659
CONNIE & DALLAS MARVIN BED & BREAKFAST

Set among century old oak trees, overlooking Beaver Creek, this charming, completely renovated Williamsburg style inn awaits its guests. Features private baths, A/C, TV and phones. Their special guest rooms feature canopy bed, whirlpool for two and fireplace AAA approved. 3 rooms/private baths.

Daily $75-$145

BLISSFIELD

HIRAM D. ELLIS INN (517) 486-3155
BED & BREAKFAST

All rooms in this 1880's, 2-story brick Victorian inn offer phones, CATV, private baths, and complementary use of bicycles. Come, relax and enjoy the many antiques and specialty shops in the area. Continental breakfast served each morning. 4 rooms. Business discounts available.

Weekly $425 Daily $75-$95 (Corporate/Business $50)

BROOKLYN (IN THE IRISH HILLS)

CHICAGO STREET INN **(800) 252-5674 • (517) 592-3888**
KAREN & BILL KERR **BED & BREAKFAST**

Antique furnishings, original electric chandeliers, European stained glass windows, and a wicker filled veranda decorate this 1800's Queen Anne Victorian home. Wonderful full breakfasts featuring homemade baked goods are unexpected treats! Minutes from numerous lakes, golfing, hiking, antiquing. 4 suites with Jacuzzis, 3 also include fireplaces. 7 rooms w/private baths, A/C.

Daily $80-$165

DEWEY LAKE MANOR **(517) 467-7122**
THE PHILLIPS FAMILY **BED & BREAKFAST**

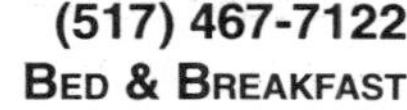

Sitting atop a knoll overlooking Dewey Lake on 18 scenic acres, a "country retreat" awaits Manor guests! Picnic by the lake — enjoy evening bonfires. Hearty breakfast buffet served on the glass enclosed porch (weather permitting). At night, snack on popcorn or sip a cup of cider...there are always cookies! 5 rooms w/private baths, A/C.

Daily $55-$75

KAREN KERR **(517) 592-3888**
COTTAGE

Located on Clark Lake this single lakefront cottage sleeps 4 to 6 people. Fully furnished with equipped kitchen, offers TV and A/C. No pets.

Call for Rates

DUANE LOCKE **(313) 971-7558**
COTTAGE

Lakefront cottage on Wamplers Lake, in the Irish Hills, sleeps up to 6. Features large enclosed porch, excellent swimming and fishing boat. No pets.

Weekly $500

JANET WITT **(419) 878-7201**
COTTAGES

On Clock Lake, 2 fully furnished cottages, 1 lakefront/1 with lake access. Clean and comfortable home-away-from home. Both have equipped kitchens, microwave, CATV, VCR, picnic table, grill, campfire ring and boat. The cottage with direct lake frontage has a screened porch and pier.

Weekly $700 (lafefront); $500 (lake access)

HUDSON

Sutton's-Weed Farm B&B **(517) 547-6302 • (800)-826-FARM**

Bed & Breakfast

You'll step back in time when you're a guest at this 7 gable Victorian farmhouse (built 1874) decorated with five generations of antiques. Stroll along the 170 acres of wooded trails and watch for deer and wildlife. Breakfast to your taste—reservations, please. No, smoking. No pets. 4 rooms.

Daily $55-$70

JONESVILLE

The Munro House **(517) 849-9292**

Joyce Yarde

Bed & Breakfast

EDITOR'S ★ CHOICE!

This 1840 Greek Revival home was a station on the underground railroad. Enjoy an old fashioned stroll in our small town, or snuggle in front of a fireplace in your room. Coffee and dessert in the evening and a full breakfast in the morning. Golf, x-country skiing, theater and antiquing. 7 rooms with private baths, phones, TV, includes 2 rooms with Jacuzzi.

Daily $56-$150

Editor's Note: The history associated with this lovely B&B and its charismatic owner combine to make the Munro House an excellent choice. See our review.

ANN ARBOR • BRIGHTON • SALINE • YPSILANTI

Ann Arbor, home of the University of Michigan. This cosmopolitan area offers year around activities for its visitors — from arts and crafts to live theater and entertainment. While here, be sure to stroll the many unique shops, visit the University of Michigan planetariums, canoe, swim or hike in Gallup Park. In late July, arts and craft enthusiasts never miss the Ann Arbor Art Fair featuring noted artisans from across the country. Only 10 miles from Ann Arbor rests **Saline.** Noted for its historic homes and antique shops, the area hosts nationally recognized antique shows from April through November. **Ypsilanti**, home of Eastern Michigan University, is also a city of diverse activities. Among its many points of interest include Wiard's Orchard which offers fresh cider, tours and hayrides. Enjoy the festivities for a yearly Heritage Festival (celebrated each August) commemorating its early French settlers.

Surrounded by lakes, the **Brighton** area offers excellent golf courses, parks, downhill and cross country skiing. In the summer, Independence, Folk Art and Farmer's Market festivals abound at Mill Pond located in the heart of the city.

ANN ARBOR

THE URBAN RETREAT BED & BREAKFAST — **(313) 971-8110**

BED & BREAKFAST

Contemporary ranch-styled home, antique furnished, set in a quiet neighborhoo, it is only minutes away from downtown and UM/EMU. Walking and jogging trails. A National Wildlife Federation "Backyard Wildlife Habitat". Full gourmet breakfasts. A/C. 2 rooms.

Daily $44-$65

BRIGHTON

BRIGHTON HOMES — **(810) 227-3225**

VACATION HOME

Built in 1990, this home sleeps 8 and is completely furnished. Located in a secluded area. The balcony overlooks the water only 10 ft. away. Features fully equipped kitchen, microwave, freezer, dishwasher, washer and dryer, use of rowboat and dock.

Weekly (summer) $600 (winter) $450

Island Lake Resort — **(810) 229-6723**
Charlotte Baprawski — **Cottages**

With frontage on both Briggs and Island Lakes, this year around resort offers 1-3 bedroom housekeeping cottages and duplex units. Completely furnished and equipped (bring bed linens and towels). Use of boat is included. Excellent fishing. Beautiful sandy beach, playground, picnic tables and more. 50% deposit required.

Weekly $200-$450

SALINE

The Homestead Bed & Breakfast — **(313) 429-9625**
Shirley Grossman — **Bed & Breakfast**

1851 circa brick farmhouse filled with period antiques, features comfort in Victorian elegance. Cross-country ski, stroll or relax on 50 acres of farmland. Only 10 minutes from Ann Arbor. A/C. Corporate rates. 5 rooms.

Daily $35-$75

YPSILANTI

Parish House Inn — **(800) 480-4866 • (313) 480-4800**
Chris Mason — **Bed & Breakfast**

1893 "Queen Anne" styled home first constructed as a parsonage. Extensively renovated in 1993. Victorian styled with period antiques. Fireplace, Jacuzzi, CATV, central A/C, and telephones. Hearty breakfast. Enjoy near-by golfing, antiqueing, biking and restaurants. No smoking. 9 rooms w/private baths.

Daily $85-$115 (Corporate Rate $60-$65)

LANSING

Covers: Eaton Rapids • Pleasant Lake

Lansing, home of our State Capital since 1847. Visiting the Capitol building is an absolute "must do" for travelers in the area. Guides conduct free tours daily! Also take some time to visit the Michigan Historical Museum and explore the state's dynamic and exciting past. Relax on a riverboat cruise on the Grand River. There's also plenty of excellent golfing, shops, galleries, live theater and restaurants. The Boars Head Theater (Michigan's only resident theater) and Woldumar Nature Center are additional attractions.

If you're looking for an intimate and distinctive dining experience, you'll want to try Dusty's English Inn in Eaton Rapids — only a short drive

LANSING (EATON RAPIDS/PLEASANT LAKE)

(continued...)

from Lansing. For simpler yet well prepared homemade meals, you'll enjoy *Ellie's Country Kitchen* on East Grand River in Williamston for breakfast, lunch and dinner. Just down the street, is the *Red Cedar Grill* with its casually upscale atmosphere.

LANSING & EATON RAPIDS

Dusty's English Inn — **(517) 663-2500 • (800) 858-0598**
Bed & Breakfast

Resting along the Grand River, amidst lovely gardens and woodland trails, this elegant English Tudor-style home is decorated throughout with antiques and reproductions. Its intimate restaurant offers fine dining and cocktails in the European tradition. Full English breakfast is served each morning.

Daily $85-$155 (dbl.)

Maplewood Bed & Breakfast — **(517) 372-7775**
Pat Bunce — **Bed & Breakfast**

3 acres of natural, scenic beauty greet visitors to this 1890 built B&B. Close to MSU and the State Capitol, Maplewood is located on the corner of Wood Road and State Road. Full breakfasts included. Major credit cards accepted. 3 rooms.

Daily $55-$65

Wheatfield House Bed & Breakfast — **(517) 655-4327**
Bed & Breakfast

A massive house designed for relaxation and enjoyment. Wheatfield House features hot tub and tanning booth, acres of woods for hiking, decks and balconies overlooking Deer Creek and the adjacent woods. Rooms range from modest to luxurious. Nearby Williamston hosts an impressive collection of antique dealers, restaurants and specialty shops.

Daily $55-$110

PLEASANT LAKE

"2452" **(313) 426-2874**
JAN MARBLE/MIKE STAGG **COTTAGE**

Vacation cottage on all sports lake with sandy bottom. 3 bedrooms, sleeps 5-7, one bath, fully carpeted, with large fully equipped kitchen. Walk to fine dining, playground and 18 hole golf course (x-country skiing in winter). Enjoy fabulous sunsets, grassy sunbathing area, private dock, TV with VCR. Grill provided, linens extra. Open year around.

Weekly $425-$450 (call for weekend, monthly and off-season rates)

Editor's Note: Well maintained cottage on narrow lot. The new wood deck offers a great view of lake. Good value. See our review.

PORT HURON • LAKEPORT • LAPEER

Port Huron, where Lake Huron's waters become the St. Clair River. This port town is the home of the Blue Water Bridge, arts and craft fairs, waterfront dining and wonderful views from the shoreline. While in the area, visit Fort Gratiot Lighthouse and the Knowlton Ice Museum. In July, enjoy the excitement of the Blue Water Festival and the 3-day Port Huron to Mackinac Island Yacht Races.

Approximately 35 miles west of Port Huron, is the scenic countryside of **Lapeer**. Surrounded by orchards, the area is known for its blueberry farms. The many lakes and streams in this region offer good fishing. In the winter, enjoy one of Lapeer's groomed x-country ski trails.

LAKEPORT

HURON LAKE HOME **(810) 364-4820**
PAUL NAZ **HOME**

Located north of Lakeport State Park, this 3 bedroom (sleeps 8) brick bi-level house is approximately 1500 sq. ft. and offers a large yard and nice beach. Very convenient location, 50' x 700' lot, the home is completely furnished with fully equipped kitchen. Linens included (bring your own towels). Deck overlooks Lake Huron. Excellent swimming.

Weekly $650 (July/Aug.) $400 (June/Sept.)

LAPEER

HART HOUSE **(810) 667-9106**
ELLIE HAYES **BED & BREAKFAST**

Listed on the National Historic Register, this Queen Anne B&B was home of the first Mayor, Rodney G. Hart. Full breakfasts served each morning. Private baths. 4 rooms. No smoking.

Daily $30-$35

PORT HURON

THE VICTORIAN INN **(810) 984-1437**
BED & BREAKFAST

Queen Anne styled inn, authentically restored, offers guests a timeless ambiance. Each room uniquely decorated. Enjoy the Inn's classically creative cuisine and gracious service. One hour from Detroit. 4 rooms, private/shared baths.

Daily $65-$75

LEXINGTON • PORT AUSTIN • CASEVILLE • BAD AXE

Covers: Grindstone City • Huron City • Port Hope • Port Sanilac Sebewaing • Unionville

Known for its historic homes, **Lexington** has excellent boating, fishing and swimming. Visit the general store (dating from the 1870's) and indulge in the tasty nostalgia of their "penny candy" counter. Walk to the marina and visit the old lighthouse which was built in 1886.

Further north is **Port Hope**, home of the Bottom Land Preserve. The Lighthouse County Park, just outside town, is an ideal spot for scuba diving enthusiasts to view the under water wrecks of 19th Century vessels.

Take the turn off to **Huron City,** and stroll among the historic recreations of a 19th Century village. Visit **Grindstone City** and see if you can spot some of the original grinding wheels made from sandstone. We understand the general store in Grindstone serves ice cream cones big enough to satisfy the hottest and hungriest of visitors.

Celebrate both outstanding sunrises and sunsets at the tip of the thumb in **Port Austin**. Stop at Finan's Drug Store's nostalgic soda fountain in the area's restored business district. Discover the rolling sand dunes hidden behind the trees at Port Crescent State Park. Relax on its excellent 3-mile beach. This is also a bird watcher's haven with abundant numbers of hawk, oriole, osprey and bluebird populations.

LEXINGTON • PORT AUSTIN • CASEVILLE • BAD AXE

(continued...)

Moving around the thumb is **Caseville**. Drive along its half-mile stretch of Saginaw Bay Beach. Here's a great area for perch fishing, boating, swimming and just plain relaxing.

For a unique dining experience in Port Austin, try *The Bank* on Blake Street ... a little pricey, but worth it. This historic former bank is now an excellent restaurant, noted for its sourdough bread with herb butter and freshly prepared meals. Another excellent dining treat is offered at the *Garfield Inn* on Lake Street that serves as both a B&B and elegant restaurant. For more casual, relaxed dining you'll want to stop at the *Port Hope Hotel Restaurant* (in Port Hope) where we understand they prepare some hearty and very tasty hamburgers and other basics at affordable prices.

BAD AXE

GRAYSTONE MANOR **(517) 269-9466**
BOB & JO VANSCHEPEN **BED & BREAKFAST**

In town on 2.5 acres. 6 traditionally furnished rooms with private baths, A/C and CATV. Fireside suite with queen half-poster bed. Perfect for weddings, special occasions. Princess room with king-size bed and whirlpool tub. Open Year around. Children 12 yrs. and up welcomed. MC /Visa. Business rates.

Daily $65-$85

CASEVILLE

BELLA VISTA MOTEL & COTTAGES **(517) 856-2650**
COTTAGES/EFFICIENCIES/MOTEL

1 bedroom efficiencies with kitchenettes, 2 bedroom cottages with full kitchens. Motel and cottages have lake views from picture windows and include screened porch, linens, tiled bath, CATV w/HBO. Heated outdoor pool, grills, picnic tables, sun deck, shuffleboard courts, swings, 400 ft. of beach.

Daily $65-$85 Weekly $395-$795

CARKNER HOUSE **(517) 856-3456**
BED & BREAKFAST

Built around 1865, President McKinley stayed in here while visiting the area. 4 rooms, A/C, king size beds with private entrance. An efficiency apartment with kitchen, private entrance and bath; and 2 rooms share a living room, full kitchen and bath. No pets. Major credit cards.

Daily $60-$125 (summer); $30-$75 (winter)

SURF-N-SAND **(517) 856-4400**
MOTEL/COTTAGES

Year around waterfront facility offers pool, A/C, and CATV. King and queen size beds available. Most major credit cards accepted.

Daily $68 (and up)

GRINDSTONE CITY

WHALEN'S GRINDSTONE SHORES **(517) 738-7664**
CABINS

Located on a harbor waterfront between mobile home and RV park site, this small and nicely wooded area features 11 units, 5 of them cabins with kitchen facilities. Beautiful Lake Huron view and good fishing. Handicap access. Major credit cards accepted.

Call for Rates

LEXINGTON

BEACHCOMBER MOTEL & APARTMENTS **(810) 359-8859**
COTTAGES/MOTEL

Spacious grounds feature motel, efficiencies, family units, cottages with fireplaces. Sandy beach, pool, fishing, tennis court, A/C, color TV. Beach house bed and breakfast offers continental breakfast served at your door. Open all year.

Daily $45 (and up)

COZMA'S COTTAGES **(810) 359-8150 • (313) 881-3313**
COTTAGES

A nice feature of this lodging is the location which is in a park-like setting along 200 ft. of sandy beach. Volleyball/badminton court, BBQ grill, shuffleboard, horseshoes on grounds. These small cottages (sleep 4-6) offer clean but limited kitchens. Two newer mobile homes (sleeps 5-6) are also available.

Weekly $315 (and up)

GLENVIEW **(810) 359-7837**
LINDA & CHUCK PHIPPS **COTTAGES**

Fully renovated and charmingly decorated cottage in quiet neighborhood. Private beach access across the street. Cottage features cedar interior, ceiling fan, fireplace, TV (no cable). Fully equipped kitchen. Webber grill and bicycles. Two bedrooms (sleeps 6). No pets. Open year around.

Weekly $500

Editor's Note: Appealing decor and good use of space make this small cottage a winner. No direct view of water, but beach access is available through a stairway just down the road. See our review.

Little White Cottages

(616) 669-5187
Two Private Cottages

Seadog: Charming, old-fashioned cottage right on Lake Huron, 50 ft. beach in quiet area. Two bedrooms with double beds (sleeps 6 comfortably), large furnished kitchen, dining room, bath and tub/shower, large screened porch and living room with fireplace. Bring own linens. Sorry, no pets. Open May-Oct.

Weekly $395-$575

Nymph: Cozy, old-fashioned cottage set 60 yards from lake Huron at the edge of the woods. 50 ft. beach in quiet residential area. Furnished kitchen, large screened porch, bath w/shower, 1 bedroom (sleeps 4 comfortably), living/dining room. Bring own linens. Sorry, no pets. Open May-Oct.

Exterior of *Nymph*

Weekly $295-$395

Editor's Note: On a small but quiet lot, several significant improvements which have added to the comfort and appearance of these older cottages. See our review.

Lusky's Lakefront Resort Cottages

(810) 327-6889
Cottages

The friendly owners of Lusky's have completely refurbished all cottages! Clean, cozy and comfortable, each comes w/ceiling fans, cable TV, picnic tables, BBQ grills, fully equipped kitchens, private toilets (most with private showers). Screened porches have good view of lake and play area. Play area features airplane swings, play boats, tire swirl, gymset with tube slide, large sandbox. Also volley ball, basketball, shuffle-board, paddle-boats and rowboats. Stop at our novelty store for candy, pop, ice cream and trinkets galore — at old fashioned prices! All this makes for a fun, relaxing and affordable family vacation place where memories are made and treasured. Rentals available daily-weekly. Pets allowed.

Daily $55-90 Weekly $375-$480

Editor's Note: The owners have done a very nice job maintaining this traditional resort. Cottages with cozy decor. Very nice beach.

The Powell House — **(810) 359-5533**
Nancy Powell — **Bed & Breakfast**

This charming B&B is located on beautifully landscaped grounds. Each of the four rooms offers their own separate charm and features king and queen size beds. Two rooms w/private baths, two rooms (suite) share a bath. Bicycles available for your leisurely tour of historic Lexington. Full breakfast included.

Daily $65-$75 (depending on room)

Marleen Wilson — **(517) 635-2911**
Vacation Home

Spacious 3,000 sq. ft. on 4 acres of wooded land with 250 ft. of beach front. Stairway (42 steps) leads to the beach. The home features 4 bedrooms (sleeps 8), is completely furnished with fully equipped kitchen including stove, refrigerator, coffee maker, washer, dryer, etc. Enjoy the scenic view of the Blue Water Bridge at night. Only 20 minutes north of Port Huron. Security deposit and payment required in advance.

Weekly $1,250

PORT AUSTIN

Garfield Inn — **(517) 738-5254**
Bed & Breakfast

Visited by President Garfield in 1860, the inn not only features period antiques but one of Michigan's premier restaurants! For that special occasion ask about the "Presidential Room"! Rooms feature double and queen size beds. Complementary bottle of champagne with each room and continental breakfasts. Six rooms.

Daily $85 (May-Oct); $65 (Cff-season)

Harbor Pines/North Shore Beach — **(810) 650-9888**
Condos

Two luxury condominiums, available year around, on 300 ft. of Lake Huron — tip of Michigan's thumb! Includes 2 bedrooms, 2 baths, sleep 6, fully furnished. Heat, air conditioning, CATV, VCR, and fireplaces. Playground area. Rental available weekly, monthly, or yearly. No pets.

Weekly $650 (Summer)

KREBS BEACHSIDE COTTAGES **(517) 856-2876**
MARV & SALLY KREBS **COTTAGES/EFFICIENCIES**

8 cottages (1-4 bedroom) sit on open, landscaped grounds with a scattering of trees. Lodgings are fully furnished with living area, private baths, equipped kitchens with microwaves. Cribs available. Large wooden deck overlooks 200 ft. of sandy beach and offers a great view of the Saginaw Bay. Open May-Nov. 15. Heated. Hunters welcome. Huron County now allows Sunday Hunting. Pets allowed in off-season.

Weekly $425 (and up) Reduced/daily rates spring/fall

Editor's Note: Simple, clean, comfortable cottages on spacious grounds, affordably priced with warm and caring owners make this a choice spot to stay — reserve early.

KREB'S LANE COTTAGES **(313) 886-5752 • (517) 738-8548**
COTTAGES/EFFICIENCIES

Set vertically to the water, these 5 clean, well maintained 2 bedroom cottages sit on a 300 ft. x 50 ft. lot with sandy beach on Saginaw Bay. Include equipped kitchens with microwaves. All are cable ready for your TV (TV's can be rented). Some cottages offer knotty pine interiors and lake views. Open May-September. Call for special holiday packages. No pets.

Weekly $465-$495

LAKE VISTA MOTEL & COTTAGE RESORT **(517) 738-8612**
RON & MARY GOTTSCHALK **MOTEL/COTTAGES**

On the shores of Lake Huron and Saginaw Bay. Motel units with CATV and A/C. Efficiencies with ceiling fans, two double beds and queen size sofa sleeper. Fully equipped kitchens include microwaves. Recreational area, heated pool, snack bar on premises. Bait and tackle. Fishing licenses. Major credit cards.

Weekly $480 (and up, for cottages)

LAKE STREET MANOR **(517) 738-7720**
BED & BREAKFAST

Built in 1875 by a lumber baron, it is furnished with antiques and features large bays, high peaked roof and gingerbread trim. Hot tub and in-room movies, private and shared baths. Brick BBQ's and bikes offered for guests' enjoyment. Fenced 1/2 acre. 5 rooms

Daily $55-$65

OSENTOSKI REALTY/LAKEFRONT CONDO'S **(888) 738-5251 • (517) 738-5251**
BRENDA **CONDOS**

Spacious condos located on the beautiful shores of Lake Huron. 1 and 2 bedroom units feature fireplaces, CATV, fully equipped kitchens and much, much more. Open all year.

Weekly $600 (and up)

THE CASTAWAYS BEACH RESORT & MOTOR INN — **(517) 738-5101**
MOTEL/COTTAGES

Located along 400' of Lake Huron shoreline, this resort offers 46 rooms, dining room and lounge. Also swimming pool, A/C, CATV, and handicap accessibility. MC/Visa accepted. Open all year. AAA rated.

Weekly $370-$510 Daily (motel) $60-$65 (call for off-season rates)

TOWN CENTER COTTAGES — **(800) 848-4184 • (517) 738-7223**
COTTAGES

In the heart of it all! Two bedroom cottages, full kitchens, CATV, screened front porch and a very private outdoor area for family fun. Major credit cards accepted.

Daily $55 Weekly $300

PORT HOPE

STAFFORD HOUSE — **(517) 428-4554**
BED & BREAKFAST

Only one block from Lake Huron, this nicely maintained B&B sits on an attractive open treed lot with a lovely backyard wildflower garden. Open year around. Full breakfasts served each morning. 4 rooms (one suite overlooks garden and is air conditioned).

Daily $50-$75

PORT SANILAC

RAYMOND HOUSE INN — **(800) 622-7229 • (810) 622-8800**
RAYMOND & SHIRLEY DENISON — **BED & BREAKFAST**

1871 Victorian home offers 7 large, high-ceiling bedrooms, private baths and central A/C. Rooms finished with period furniture, brightly colored bedspreads and lace curtains. Old-fashioned parlor/dining room, unchanged in a century, adds to the charm. Open mid-April through December. Antique shop/art gallery on premises. No smoking/pets.

Daily $65-$75

Editor's Note: Antiques and lovely decor highlight the Raymond House and make it a very nice choice for the area. Be sure to check out their art gallery for some original work completed by local artisans.

SEBEWAING

Rummels Tree Haven B&B **(517) 883-2450**
Carl & Erma Rummel, Jr. **Bed & Breakfast**
A 2 room bed & breakfast with full breakfast. Features private baths, cable TV, A/C, refrigerator and microwave. Fishing for perch and walleye. Very good area for hunting duck, goose, deer, and pheasant. Personal checks accepted. Open all year. Pets allowed in garage area.

Daily $30-$45

UNIONVILLE

Fish Point Lodge **(517) 674-2631**
Lodge
Located near Fish Point game reserve this lodge, built in 1902, offers 4 bedrooms, shared bath and a huge fireplace. Kitchen facilities are available. Lodging accommodates up to 20 people. Breakfast is included. Personal check OK. Open year around.

Call for Rates

BAY CITY • FRANKENMUTH • SAGINAW

Bay City, well known for its water sports, features a variety of events including speedboat and offshore power boat races. Tour the city's historical sites and view the many stately homes on Center Avenue, Wenonah and Veterans Memorial parks. Come south from Bay City and explore the historic district of **Saginaw**. Take a four-mile river walk, visit a museum or the zoo and stroll among the fragrant rose gardens in downtown parks.

Traveling south from Saginaw, you'll reach the historic town of **Frankenmuth.** The classic Bavarian stylings of its original settlers can be seen throughout the town's homes, buildings and craft shops. For many it has become a traditional yearly visit. They come to the more than 100 shops and attractions, stroll the streets, tour the wineries and brewery, sample traditional German cuisine or their famous *all you can eat* chicken dinners. While there are many good places to eat in the area, The *Bavarian Inn* and *Zehnder's* are still the most popular...and *beware* their bakeries are *too* tempting.

BAY CITY • FRANKENMUTH • SAGINAW

(continued...)

While you're in Frankenmuth, be sure to take a horse-drawn carriage ride or a river tour. And, of course, you must visit Bronner's Christmas Wonderland where holidays are celebrated 363 days a year. Spend the night, because you'll want to start shopping early the next morning at the areas largest designer outlet shopping mall located only a few minutes away in Birch Run.

BAY CITY

CLEMENTS INN — **(517) 894-4600**
KAREN HEPP — **BED & BREAKFAST**

1886 Victorian mansion offers 7 elaborately furnished rooms w/private baths. TV's and phones, 6 fireplaces, central A/C. Enjoy a romantic evening in 1 of 3 500-1200 sq. ft. whirlpool suites with in-room fireplaces.

Daily $70-$175

FRANKENMUTH

BED AND BREAKFAST AT THE PINES — **(517) 652-9019**
RICHARD & DONNA HODGE — **BED & BREAKFAST**

Welcome to our casual ranch-style home in a quiet residential neighborhood, within walking distance of famous restaurants and main tourist areas. Double and twin beds. Wholesome nutritious breakfast featuring homemade baked items, fresh fruit, jams and beverages. Open year around. 2 rooms. No smoking.

Daily $40-$50

Editor's Note: Charming owners create a real "homey" experience in this traditional, ranch-styled home. Small but very comfy rooms. See our review.

POINT OF VIEW — **(517) 652-9845**
ED AND BETTY GOYINGS — **PRIVATE COTTAGE**

Completely remodeled one-room cottage plus Florida Room has lots of history. It features open great room with original maple floors and paneled walls. Includes a fireplace, bar, dinette, furnished kitchen, private bath and very large Florida Room furnished in wicker. Also includes television, phone, AC , grill and picnic table. Linens included. No pets. Children under 12 FREE.

Daily $345 (dbl. occ. - $25 each add'l person)

Editor's Note: Betty has a talent for interior design and it shows in this delightfully cozy one room cottage. Lovely location. Very good value. See our review.

SAGINAW

BROCKWAY HOUSE BED & BREAKFAST (888) BROCWAY • (517) 792-0746
DICK & ZOE ZUEHLKES BED & BREAKFAST

On the National Register of Historic Homes, this 1864 B&B is built in the grand tradition of the old southern plantation. Near to excellent restaurants and antique shops. 4 rooms, private baths, A/C. Two-person Jucuzzi suite. Full gourmet breakfast served each morning.

Daily $85-$225

HEART HOUSE INN (517) 753-3145
KELLY ZURVALEC BED & BREAKFAST

This 8,000 sq. ft. mansion, built during the Civil War, features black walnut beams and lumber throughout. All 8 rooms with private bath, phones, TV, A/C, complimentary local daily paper. "Continental Plus Breakfast". Liquor License. Major credit cards accepted.

Daily $65-$75

REGION 2

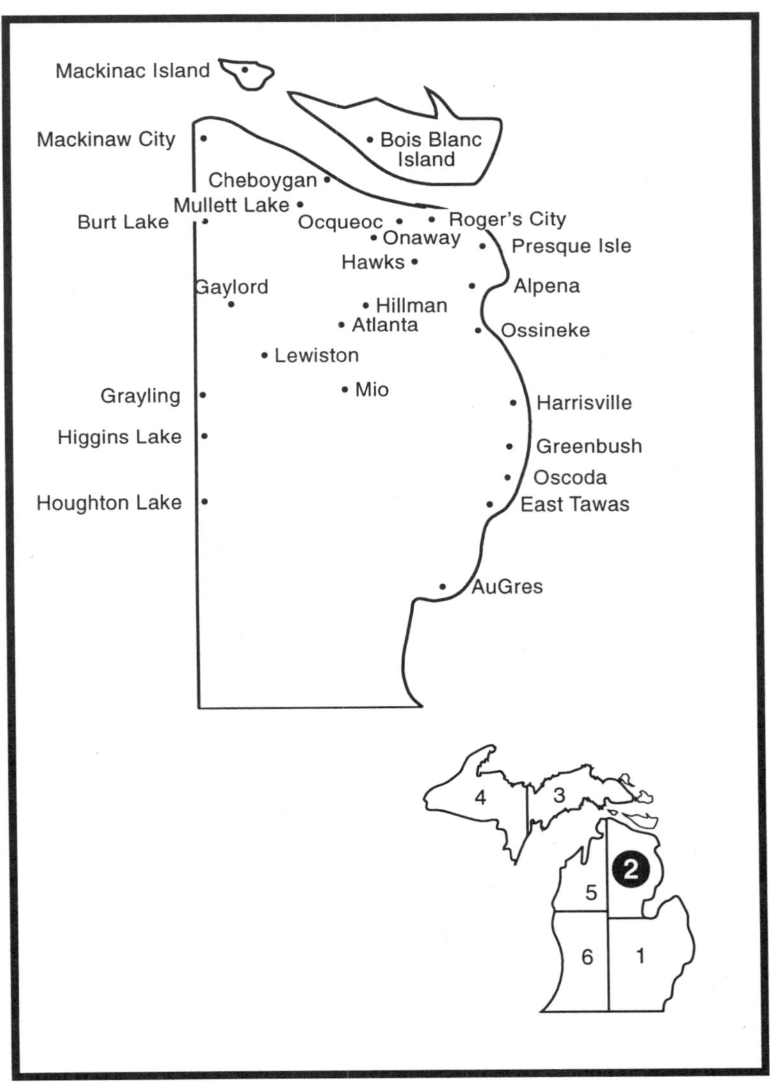

Mackinac Island
Mackinaw City
Bois Blanc
Island
Cheboygan
Mullett Lake
Burt Lake
Ocqueoc
Roger's City
Onaway
Presque Isle
Hawks
Gaylord
Alpena
Hillman
Atlanta
Ossineke
Lewiston
Grayling
Mio
Harrisville
Higgins Lake
Greenbush
Oscoda
Houghton Lake
East Tawas
AuGres
4
3
2
5
6
1

REGION 2

Progressing northward, the forest grows denser, filled with sparkling lakes and streams. Here is canoeing, skiing and abundant fishing, fine places to eat, festivals, art fairs and scenic beauty as far as the eye can see.

Going east, to Lake Huron, we enter the land where lumber once was *King*, the land of the *River Rat* and the *Legend of Paul Bunyan.* More money was made here on lumber than miners made in the Klondike during the Gold Rush. Stripped bare by the lumbering frenzy, in 1909 the reforestation began. Today the forests are tall and stately and the forest floors are deep again with pine needles and teaming with wild life. Throughout the forest there are lakes, trout streams and fishing at its best. In the winter, when the forests floor is covered by snow, you will see not only the markings of elk, deer and moose, but also those of snowshoe, snowmobile and ski trails.

The days along the Huron are filled with activities throughout the seasons — sandy beaches, good swimming, tournaments, museums, lighthouses, historic sights, but most of all the scenic beauty and wonders of nature. The morning is a gentle symphony as the sun rises, a golden globe, out of the Huron and the breezes whisper through the pines mingling with the sound of the birds.

Yes, here is the excitement, beauty, peace and tranquillity.

OSCODA & THE AUSABLE AREA

COVERS: AUGRES • EAST TAWAS • GREENBUSH • HARRISVILLE • MIO

Experience the open hospitality of **AuGres** as you continue to travel north on Michigan's east side. The restaurants and bake shops here are truly homey with freshly prepared meals. Considered the "Perch Capital", this small town has more than 1,000 boat docks and waters well stocked with perch, walleye and a large variety of pan fish. The best scenic views can be found along the lake shore roads, from Point AuGres and Point Lookout. Take your boat to Charity Island and explore its "most photographed" lighthouse. Excellent golf is available at Huron Breeze Golf & Country Club or, for the whole family, visit Lutz's Fun Land featuring waterslides, go-carts, and a variety of games and rides.

Settled where the AuSable River meets Lake Huron, these series of communities offer a variety of activities from canoeing and fishing to hiking, hunting, cross-country skiing, and snowmobiling. **Oscoda** is considered the gateway to the River Road National Scenic Byway that runs along the south bank of the AuSable River. **Tawas City** and nearby Huron National Forest offers lakes, beaches and great trails! During winter season, cross-country ski enthusiasts can enjoy the well-groomed trails at Corseair. In February, the Perchville U.S.A. Festival takes place — be there to enjoy the festivities!

The quaint harbor town of **Harrisville** offers terrific trout and salmon fishing. The Sturgeon Point Lighthouse Museum, a summer concert series, art and craft fairs, festivals, and the Harrisville State Park provide a variety of both summer and winter recreational fun.

Mio, the Heart of the AuSable River Valley, excels in canoeing and winter sport activities. In June they host the Championship Canoe Race and the Great Lakes Forestry Exposition in July. While there, tour the Kirtland warbler nesting area.

To sample some of the area's down home cooking, try *The Bear Track Inn* (AuGres) noted for outstanding breakfast buffets plus a diverse menu including, of course, excellent fish! *H&H Bakery* (AuGres) features excellent fresh baked goods daily...their specialty is pizza! *Charbonneau* (on the AuSable in Oscoda) for a diverse menu on the waterfront; *Wiltse's* (Oscoda) for some of the best blueberry pancakes around; and *Muehlbeck's* (Harrisville) for some freshly prepared German food. Also, we've heard the *Greenbush Tavern* offers up some pretty good pizza and "all you can eat" fish on Friday. If you happen to be in Tawas, stop by the *Tawas Bar* and tell them Bonnie sent you.

PT. AUGRES

THE GET-A-WAY — **(313) 389-1793**
TOM & KAREN WILSON — **PRIVATE COTTAGE**

Year round waterfront cottage, 70' landscaped lot. Beautiful vistas of Lake Huron/Saginaw Bay. Sleeps 6, 3 bedrooms, 1 bath, linens provided, fully equipped kitchen, modern appliances, patio, charcoal grill, play areas. TV/VCR. **No Pets**. Marina 1 mile, restaurant/bar walking distance.

Weekly $450 ($150 Security Deposit Required)

Editor Note: The best sunrise in town can be found at this well maintained and very comfortable cottage. On a quiet cottage lane it's a good value. See our review.

EAST TAWAS

RIPTIDE MOTEL & CABINS — **(517) 362-6562**
EMMA & LARRY, MANAGERS — **MOTEL & CABINS**

On Tawas Bay, this year around motel/cabin resort features large sandy beach, picnic tables, play area, CATV and BBQ grills. Cabins with 2 bedroom cabins , equipped kitchens, private baths, linens provided. No pets in summer.

Daily $41-$81 Weekly $486 (cabins, assumes 6 days/dbl. occ.)

GREENBUSH

SID'S RESORT — **(517) 739-7638 • (810) 781-3845**

COTTAGES

11, 1-3 bedroom cottages (sleep 2-8). Major renovations in 1993-95 including new interiors (custom draperies, dishes, etc.). Set on wooded grounds with excellent sandy swimming beach. Fully furnished lodgings offer equipped kitchen, CATV, and more. Gameroom, shuffleboard, badminton, playground and picnic area on premises. Water bicycles, paddle boards, kayak and wave runners rentals. Near many golf courses. Open May - Oct. No pets.

Weekly $450-$1,100 (Reduced off-season rates in spring and fall)

Editor's Note: A premiere resort — highly recommended. See our review

HARRISVILLE

Cedar Crest **(313) 202-7626 • (313) 881-7611**
Mr. & Mrs. Callas **Cottage**

Private cottage on Cedar Lake sits on 6 wooded acres. Includes canoe and rowboat. Private golf and beach club (2 courses) including Scottish Links. Cottage has 2 bedrooms, 1-1/2 baths, kitchen, den and living room with fireplace. Sleeps 8. Large screened front porch and rear deck overlooking the lake.

Weekly $400

MIO

Hinchman Acre Resort **(800) 438-0203 (MI) • (517) 826-3267**
Cottages

AAA Rated Family Resort. Summer family vacations or secluded getaway weekends. 1-2-3 bedroom cottages, CATV, A/C, fireplaces, phones, kitchens, cribs, baby-sitters, swimming beach, fishing. Enjoy campfires, gameroom, hiking and mountain bike trails. Canoe trips, canoe and tube rentals. Cross-country ski on groomed tracked trails, rentals. Golf, horseback riding nearby. Ask for brochure.

Daily $40-$95 Weekly $250-$475

Editor's Note: Spacious grounds in a natural setting. The resort offers diverse activities with very clean and well maintained lodgings. Good location for a very good price. See our review.

OSCODA

Anchorage Cottages **(517) 739-7843**
Peg Grice **Cottages**

Unpack & RELAX! On our sugar sand beach, Lake Huron. Six clean, comfortable, fully furnished cottages (2-4 bedrooms). CATV, grills, picnic tables,

ANCHORAGE COTTAGES (continued...)
shady backyard, fire pit, horseshoes, swing set. AuSable River nearby. Fish, golf, canoe, hunt, etc. Friendly atmosphere! Pet w/approval/Fee. April-Dec.

Weekly $385-$575

AUSABLE RIVER RESORT **(517) 739-5246**
COTTAGES
Two bedroom cottages w/kitchen and color TV, only 1/2 mile west of downtown Oscoda and five blocks from the lake. Boat dockage available. No pets.

Call for Rates

BAREFOOT BEACH COTTAGES **(517) 739-1818**
PAUL DAVIES **COTTAGES**
8 furnished, knotty pine cottages (sleep 4-6) w/private showers on 200 ft. of sandy beach along Lake Huron. Swimming is safe and fun. Resort features swings, loungers, rowboats, paddleboats, grills, bonfire pit, suffleboard and volleyball. Linens supplied. Gift shop. Bring towels. $100 deposit. No pets.

Weekly $400-$500 Daily $26-$70

EAST COAST SHORES RESORT **(517) 739-0123**
ROY WENNER **CABINS**
New Owner — major renovations completed in 1993-94. Resort rests on 200' of sandy beach, fully furnished, 2-4 bedroom beachfront cabins with equipped kitchens (includes microwave, automatic coffeemaker), CATV w/ HBO, ceiling fans and screened porch. Enjoy volleyball, badminton, horseshoes, bonfires and swimming. No pets.

Weekly $445-$705 Daily $60-$95

EL CORTEZ BEACH RESORT **(517) 739-7884**
COTTAGES
On Lake Huron, these 1-2 bedroom cottages offer equipped kitchens, gas heat, city water. Some cottages have CATV w/HBO. Linens provided. Enjoy the family fun area, BBQ's, picnic tables, and large sandy beach. Fish cleaning station on premises. Wave runner rentals. No pets.

Weekly $445-$1,000 Daily $40-$80

HURON HOUSE **(517) 739-9255**
BED & BREAKFAST
Located on a beautiful stretch of Lake Huron beach between Tawas and Oscoda. Accommodations feature panoramic views of Lake Huron, fireplaces, private outdoor hot tubs, in-room Jacuzzis and continental breakfast delivered to the room each morning. Glorious sunrises, romantic moonrises, lighted freighters passing in the night. Perfect for romantic getaways!

Daily $75-$145 dbl.

New AuSable Beach Resort **(800) 231-1875**
Ron Teasley **Condos • Cottages**

Located 2 miles south of Oscoda on Lake Huron, these 1-3 bedroom cottages and condos offer fully equipped kitchens, showers, carpeting. Some cottages w/fireplaces. Enjoy horseshoes, playground and sandy beach.

Weekly Condos $550-$650 Cottages $360-$750

Sand Castle **(517) 739-9881**
M/M Inglis **Cottages**

These 9, 1-2 bedroom cottages are located on the beach. Includes fully equipped kitchen (linens provided), CATV, shuffleboard, volleyball, fish cleaning area and more.

Weekly $375 (and up)

Shady Shores Resort **(810) 852-1103 • (810) 751-1835**
Kent & Jeanne Lang/Jim & Maryann Gross **Cottages**

Three miles south of Oscoda. On 200' of sandy beach, picnic tables, BBQ's, swings, horseshoe pits, basketball and shuffleboard courts. Furnished, 2 bedroom cottage with CATV. Kitchens include refrigerator, range and dishes. Linens provided (bring towels). Most have glassed-in porch. No pets.

Call for Rates

Shenandoah on the Lake Beach Resort **(517) 739-3997 • (941) 793-6173 (winter)**
Cottages

The resort, 2 miles south of Oscoda on Lake Huron w/300' sandy beach, has 1 and 2 bedroom cottages and 3 bedroom beachhouses. Each has fully equipped kitchen (some w/fireplaces), decks, CATV, recreation area, campfires. Open May-October.

Daily $45-$150 (call for weekly rates)

Thomas' Parkside Cottages **(517) 739-5607**
Cottages

On Lake Huron w/333 ft. of private beach, the cottages are near the AuSable River. Includes 2, 1 bedroom and 11, 2 bedroom cottages facing the lake with enclosed porches, kitchen w/stove and refrigerator, CATV. Bring radio and linens. $50 deposit. No pets.

Weekly $400-$500

ALPENA & THUNDER BAY

COVERS: ALPENA • ATLANTA • HAWKS • HILLMAN • OCQUEOC • ONAWAY • OSSINEKE • PRESQUE ISLE • ROGERS CITY

Located on the beautiful sunrise side of Michigan, visitors can enjoy a variety of activities — summer through winter. Explore **Thunder Bay's** underwater ruins of sunken ships from another era. Or, for something a little less exerting, enjoy **Alpena's** "live" theater which presents year around plays and musicals. The area also offers a wildfowl sanctuary, lighthouses, and excellent hunting, fishing, cross-country skiing, and golf. Don't miss July's Brown Trout Festival which lures (excuse the pun...) over 800 fishing contestants to this nine-day event featuring art, food concessions and nightly entertainment.

While in the area, don't forget to visit one of the Lower Peninsula's largest waterfalls, Ocqueoc Falls, in Rogers City.

ALPENA

JOE HASSETT **(517) 734-2066 (AFTER 4 P.M.)**
COTTAGE

One cottage located on US 23 South. It is south of Bluebird Restaurant (2 bedrooms) on Grand Lake.

Weekly $250

TRELAWNY RESORT **(517) 471-2347**
COTTAGES

Resort features 9 attractive, clean and comfortable cottage homes. They have 200 ft. of white sugar sand beach on Lake Huron's beautiful Thunder Bay with 3 acres of restful grounds and tall pines. On-site laundromat and game room. Cottages have fully furnished kitchens and shower bath.

Weekly $380-$460 Daily $55-$70

ATLANTA

BRILEY INN **(800) 824-7443 (RES.) • (517) 785-4784**
CARLA & BILL GARDNER **CABINS**

Elegant redwood inn with impressive windows overlooking Thunder Bay River. Rooms are decorated in Victorian Antique. Great Room, cozy den with

Briley Inn (continued...)

Fireplace, Jacuzzi, full country breakfast, afternoon tea. Canoes and boats available. Central AC, CATV. Minutes from Elk Ridge, Garland. Golf packages available. Private baths. 5 rooms.

Daily $55-$65

River Cabins **(517) 785-4123**

Cabins

One mile west of Atlanta on M32, 1/2 Mile south on McArthur and Thunder Bay River, these 5, 1-2 bedroom cabins offer furnace heat, cooking facilities, linens, plus a boat with each cabin. Bathhouse w/shower, picnic tables, games and fire ring on premises.

Daily $25-$35

HAWKS

NettieBay Lodge **(517) 734-4688**

Mark & Jackie Schuler **Cottages & Lodge**

Year around resort located on 2,000 acres of secluded private property by beautiful Lake Nettie. One to 4 bedrooms with full kitchens, living room, private baths (linens available), and lake views. Into bird watching? NettieBay is where you want to go! Mentioned in *Michigan-Out-of Doors* magazine and other media. Join them in classes, seminars and their birding walks. Also enjoy excellent fishing and x-country skiing. No pets.

Weekly $339-$498

Editor's Note: Excellent programs available on birding and other outdoor activities. Natural and picturesque setting. Accommodations basic, clean and comfortable. See our review.

HILLMAN

THUNDER BAY RESORT-BEST WESTERN **(800) 729-9375**

CONDOMINIUM/VILLAS

Golf resort featuring luxury suites, whirlpool suites and villas. Each includes bedroom(s), bathroom(s), kitchen, living room, and deck overlooking golf course. 2 restaurants on premises. During winter, Elk viewing sleight ride with gourmet dinner packages, cross-country skiing, snowmobiling, ice skating and romantic getaways.

Daily $41-$56 (and up)

Editor's Note: Premiere resort with unique golf course and interesting year around package programs. Wintertime Elk viewing/gourmet dinner program has become very popular. See our review.

OCQUEOC

SILVER ROCK RESORT ON OCQUEOC LAKE **(810) 694-3061**

STEVE & VICKI KELLAR **COTTAGE**

Ocqueoc Lake is a 132 acre lake twenty miles north of Rogers City and three miles west of Lake Huron. 2 bedroom cottage with boat, color TV. ORV trails nearby. Great fishing for bass, walleye, pike, trout and salmon. Open all year. Call for rates and reservations. No pets.

Call for Rates

ONAWAY

STILLMEADOW B & B **(517) 733-2882**

CAROL LATSCH **BED & BREAKFAST**

Flower beds, kitchen garden and berry patch add to the charm of this simple country home, nestled at woods edge, with deck for relaxing and enjoying the view. Four rooms, private baths, queen beds and a country breakfasts. Radios, CATV and stereo in public room. Smoke-free. Pets allowed leashed outside. Major credit cards.

Weekly $350* (and up) Daily $65* (and up) *Per Couple

Editor's Note: This charming B&B offers a comfortable and relaxing country atmosphere with freshly prepared, hearty breakfasts. Carol is truly knowledgeable about things to do and see in the area.

OSSINEKE

Fernwood Bed & Breakfast **(517) 471-5176**
Jay & Susan Anders **Bed & Breakfast**

Fernwood is located on Lake Huron's Thunder Bay and offers beautiful sunrises from their private, sandy beach. 2 uniquely decorated rooms, fieldstone fireplace in great room, wicker-filled sunporch, outdoor hot tub. 3 course full breakfast. No pets/smoking.

Daily $45-$55

PRESQUE ISLE

Fireside Inn **(517) 595-6369**
Cottages & Lodge

Densely wooded surroundings, built in 1908. 17 cottage/cabins and 7 lodge rooms. Some cottages are newly renovated, others maintain a "rustic" image. All with private baths. Some kitchens and fireplaces. Lodge offers small sleeping rooms, some with private baths. Tennis, volleyball, ping-pong, horseshoes, shuffleboard on premises. Price includes 2 meals per day. Open Spring through Fall. Pets allowed.

	Rooms	Cabins/Cottages
Daily*	$30-$40	$40-$75
Weekly*	$160-$210	$240-$350

* Price based per adult (children rates somewhat less)

Editor's Note: Historic resort located in a quiet, wooded setting. Cottages range in size with several maintained in rustic condition - sparse and basic furnishings. Several cottages have been renovated/updated.

ROGERS CITY

Manitou Shores Resort **(517) 734-7233**
Cottages/Cabins/Motel Units

Resting along 500 ft. of Lake Huron, this 12 acre resort features 4 cottages, 4 motel units, and 2 large log cabins — all with wood decks overlooking the lake. Cottages and cabins include fully equipped kitchens. Log cabins also feature microwave, dishwasher, fireplace with glass sliding doors. Evening campfires. Linens provided. No pets.

Daily $50-$150 Weekly $385-$700

MACKINAW CITY • MACKINAC ISLAND

Near the tip of the mitt, **Mackinaw City** is located at the southern end of the Mackinac Bridge and offers ferry service (May-October) to Mackinac Island. Known for its sparkling waters and natural beauty, it is visited by thousands of vacationers each year. While in the City, be sure to visit Fort Michilimackinaw. Built in 1715, the Fort was initially used as a trading post by early French settlers before becoming a British military outpost and fur-trading village. Today its costumed staff provide demonstrations and special programs.

Mackinaw City also offers a variety of other historical parks (several with archaeological excavations in progress), unique museums and souvenir shops.

Visit **Mackinac Island** and step back in time. This unhurried vacation land is a haven for any vacationer wishing a unique experience. Accessible by ferry, the Island allows only horse-drawn carriages and bicycles to be used as transportation. Historical and scenic, the Island is filled with natural beauty and boasts a colorful past. Explore Old Fort Mackinac where costumed staff perform period military reenactments and demonstrations. Take a carriage tour, visit nearby historic buildings and homes, browse the many shops, and dine at the many restaurants. Enjoy nightly entertainment, golfing, swimming, hiking, horseback riding, and just relaxing on this Michigan resort island. There are also many great restaurants on the island! For an elegant, fine dining experience, there's the 107 year old Grand Hotel's formal dining room. Or, on the northwest side of the island, *Woods* is the spot for a romantic, candlelight dinner located in Stonecliffe, a mansion built in 1905. For more casual dining with exceptional food, try the *Point Dining Room* at the Mission Point Resort. Hangout with the locals, and try the down-to-earth *Mustang Lounge* (one of the few places open year around). Enjoy your trip to the island ...oh, by the way, don't forget to bring home the fudge!

MACKINAW CITY

THE BEACH HOUSE **(800) 262-5353 • (616) 436-5353**

COTTAGES

Situated on 250' of Lake Huron frontage, view the Bridge and Island from these 1-3 bed cottages in Mackinaw City. Units include kitchenettes (no utensils), electric heat, A/C, CATV w/HBO. Coffee and homemade muffins available each morning! Playground, beach, indoor pool and spa on the premises. Small pets O.K.

Daily $32-$125

Editor's Note: Good, clean, comfortable accommodations.

CEDARS RESORT **(616) 537-4748**

COTTAGES

On Lake Huron, 5 miles from Mackinaw, these 1-2 bedroom cottages offer a great view of the Bridge and Island. Each unit offers full housekeeping and includes equipped kitchens, bathroom, fireplace (wood furnished), gas heat, and color TV. Sandy beach great for swimming - boat and docking included. Open year around. $75 deposit required.

Weekly $290 (and up)

CHIPPEWA MOTOR LODGE - ON THE LAKE **(800) 748-0124 • (616) 436-8661**

Motel and 2 bedroom cottage units (double/queen size beds) offered. Features sandy beach, CATV, direct dial phones, indoor pool/spa, sun deck, shuffleboard, picnic area. 1 block from ferry docks.

Daily $27-$88* Weekly $200-$525*

*Based on double occupancy. Rates will vary depending on season.

Editor's Note: Clean and very nicely maintained. Many rooms have cozy, paneled interiors.

LAKESHORE PARADISE **(616) 537-4779 • (810) 268-9119**

COTTAGES

Approximately 5 miles south of Mackinaw with 250' lake frontage, Featured are 6, 2 bedroom housekeeping cottages plus one studio with heat, stoves and refrigerators. Some tubs and TV's. Playground, picnic tables, grills on premises, raft in water, boats/dock facilities and bonfire on beach. May 15 to Sept. 15.

Call for Rates

MACKINAC ISLAND

BAY VIEW AT MACKINAC **(906) 847-3295**

DOUG YODER **BED & BREAKFAST**

This Victorian home offers grace and charm in romantic turn-of-the century tradition along with the comfort of today. It is the only facility of its type and style sitting at the water's edge. Deluxe continental breakfast served from harbor-view veranda. Private baths. Open May 1-Oct. 15. 17 rooms. Major credit cards.

Daily $95-$285

Editor Note: Located in a quiet section on the Island main road. This lovely B&B directly overlooks the water. All rooms have views. It's a bit of a walk from the docks...but that's Mackinac!

CLOGHAUN **(906) 847-3885 • WINTER (313) 331-7110**
JAMES BOND **BED & BREAKFAST**

This large Victorian home is convenient to shops, restaurants and ferry lines. Built in 1884, it was the home of Thomas and Bridgett Donnelly's large Irish family. Today guests enjoy the many fine antiques, ambiance and elegance of a bygone era. Open May-Nov. 10 rooms. Major credit cards.

Daily $80-$130

GREAT TURTLE LODGE **(800) 206-2124 • (906) 847-6237**
NORM BAUMAN **CONDOS/APARTMENTS**

Newly renovated in 1993, these two condo/apartments offer fully equipped kitchens, Jacuzzis (TV and VCR available). One bedroom sleeps 4-5, two bedroom sleeps 7-8. Located in a quiet wooded area of the Island — close to town. Minimum 2-3 night stay. Open year around.

	1 Bedroom	2 Bedroom
Daily	$180	$200
Weekly	$1,000	$1,200

HAAN'S 1830 INN **SUMMER (906) 847-6244 • WINTER (847) 526-2662**
NICHOLAS & NANCY HAAN **BED & BREAKFAST**

This Michigan historic home, built in Greek Revival style, is furnished in period antiques. The earliest building was used as an inn in both Michigan and Wisconsin. Enjoy continental breakfast on the wicker filled porch. Featured in Detroit Free Press, Chicago Tribune, Chicago Sun Times and Sears Discovery Magazine. Open May 21-Oct. 18. 7 rooms. 5 with private bath and 2 w/shared bath.

Daily $80-$130

ISLAND CONDO RENTALS **(906) 847-3260**
CONDOMINIUMS

15 vacation rentals available on the Island. Call for information on daily and weekly rates.

METIVIER INN **SUMMER (906) 847-6234 • WINTER (616) 627-2055**
GEORGE & ANGELA LEONARD **BED & BREAKFAST**

Originally built in 1877 and recently renovated, the Inn offers bedrooms with queen size beds and private baths. An efficiency unit is also available. Relax on the large wicker filled front porch and cozy living room with a wood burner. Deluxe continental breakfast served. Open May-October. 22 rooms.

Daily $115-$235

HOUGHTON LAKE TO CHEBOYGAN & BOIS BLANC ISLAND

COVERS: BURT LAKE • GAYLORD • GRAYLING • HIGGINS LAKE • LEWISTON • MULLETT LAKE

Houghton Lake, where hunters and vacationers thrive on one of Michigan's largest inland lakes. Enjoy hunting, boating, water skiing, cross-country skiing, and snowmobiling. Ice fishing for walleyes, bass and bluegill is so good it merits its own annual event. Each year, the Tip-Up-Town U.S.A. Festival (held mid to late January) offers a variety of events including contests, parades and games for the entire family.

Known as the "Alpine Village", **Gaylord** has more to offer than just great downhill and x-country skiing or groomed snowmobile trails! Try their championship golf courses or terrific year around fishing. Nearby, the largest elk herd roams, east of the Mississippi, in the Pigeon River State Forest.

Grayling's historical logging background is preserved at Crawford County Historical Museum and Hartwick Pines State Park. Grayling is also the area for canoeing and trout fishing enthusiasts. In fact, it is considered the Canoe Capital of Michigan. It is the spot for the internationally famous Weyerhaeuser Canoe Marathon which takes place the last week of July. During this event, up to 50 teams of paddlers attempt to finish a gruelling 120-mile course which can take up to 18 hours to complete. This event is considered one of the most demanding endurance races in any sporting event. Televised broadcasts reach over 150 countries worldwide. The popular AuSable River Festival takes place the week of the Marathon. The festival abounds with numerous activities which include a major parade, juried art shows, antique car shows, ice cream socials, special canoe tours, and several amateur and youth canoe races.

Cheboygan continues the chain of great year around fishing, skiing, snowmobiling, swimming and golf. Be sure to visit Cheboygan's Opera House built in 1877. This restored Victorian theater still offers great entertainment on the same stage that once welcomed Mary Pickford and Annie Oakley!

Seeking an island retreat — without all the bustling activities on Mackinac Island — **Bois Blanc Island** is your spot! Referred to as *Bob-lo* by the locals, this quiet, unspoiled island is only a short boat ride from Cheboygan and Mackinac Island. One main road (unpaved) takes you around the Island (cars are permitted). An excellent spot for nature hikes, private beaches, boating and relaxing. Here is a community of century homes and a remote lighthouse. While visiting, stop in for "eats" at the *Boathouse Restaurant* or the *Bois Blanc Tavern* and meet some of the warm and friendly year around residents!

The Island is accessible by two ferry boat services (runs several times per day). Be sure to call ahead and reserve a spot if you plan on bringing your car (Plaunt Transportation: (616) 627-2354 or The Island Ferry Service (616) 627-9445 or (616) 627-7878).

BOIS BLANC ISLAND

Bois Blanc Island Retreat **(616) 846-4391**
Gram/Linda McGeorge **Cottage**

Secluded, 4 bedroom, waterfront cottage on quiet protected bay. Surrounded by white pines and cedar forest. Beautiful view of Lake Huron and the Straits Channel. Cottage offers all the conveniences in a private setting — just bring groceries and fishing pole. Relax, fish, hike, explore, boat mooring. Mackinac Island 8 Miles. Open May-Nov. Car ferry. No pets.

Weekly $450-$650 *(Off-season weekend $250)*

Editor's Note: Comfortable, clean, newer cottage with all renovations completed in 1995. Great island retreat with natural grounds and sandy beach.

BURT LAKE

DiPietro Cottage **(517) 626-6682**
Robbe DiPietro **Cottage**

Private, wooded frontage on Burt Lake in the beautiful Maple Bay area. Cozy cottage with 4 bedrooms, complete modern kitchen, washer, dryer, dishwasher, wood stove, dock and boat hoist. Large deck. Provide your own linens. No smoking/pets!

Weekly $800 (July & August) $560 (off-season)

Miller's Guest House on Burt Lake **(616) 238-4492**
Jess & Pam Miller **Vacation Home**

One-of-a-kind spacious Burt Lake guest house. Recently built to exacting standards for our personal friends and family. Now available for up to 4 non-smoking guests. Includes complete kitchen, private sandy beach. Brilliant sunsets, quiet wooded atmosphere. Ideal for swimming, sailing, canoeing, bicycling. Friendly hosts. No pets. Open mid-June-August.

Weekly $560

SHARON PRESSEY **SUMMER (906) 643-7733 • WINTER (561) 229-1599**
COTTAGES/HOME

2 and 3 bedroom cottages. 150' water frontage. One with loft, one with fireplace, one with dishwasher. All have decks overlooking water, fully equipped kitchens, cable TV, gas grills & row boat. Bedding provided. Terrific walleye and bass fishing. Pets allowed. Open April-Oct.

Weekly $675-$775 ($375-$475 off-season)

CHEBOYGAN & MULLETT LAKE

LAKEWOOD COTTAGES **SUMMER (616) 238-7476 • WINTER (810) 887-5570**
KEITH R. PHILLIPS **COTTAGES**

Clean comfortable 2-3 bedroom cottages located on Mullett Lake, with 750' of lake frontage. Screened porches, CATV, carpeted, fully equipped kitchens, showers, picnic tables, grills, boats and motors for rent. Buoys for private boats, swimming, fishing, 24' pontoon boat, and evening bonfires. Pets allowed. Open May-Sept.

Weekly $330-$390 Daily $55-$60

THE PINES OF LONG LAKE **(616) 625-2121 • (616) 625-2145**
COTTAGES

Year around resort, 1-3 bedroom cottages. 2 bedroom cabins with 2 double beds face the lake, shared shower building. 1 & 3 bedroom cottages with private showers. All have stoves, refrigerators, limited utensils, gas heat, blankets/pillows (bring linens). Bar/restaurant on premises. Pets allowed ($10 add'l).

Weekly $225-$275 Daily $50-$60

VEERY POINTE RESORT ON MULLETT LAKE **(616) 627-7328 • (616) 627-4928**
FRED SMITH & DEBBIE SOCHA **COTTAGES/MOTEL - EFFICIENCIES**

I-75, EXT. 313 ON M-27 N. OF TOPINABEE • ON INLAND WATERWAY • AFFORDABLE AND VERY CLEAN.

Lakefront cottages, open year around, all face the water, docks. Fully furnished (except linens—linens available), includes microwave, CATV/HBO & Disney. Motel with efficiencies across from lake, beach privileges. Good fishing, x-country skiing, skating and snowmobiling. Ask about pets.

Weekly $250-$900

GAYLORD

BEAVER CREEK RESORT **(517) 732-2459**
LARRY BOWDEN **BED & BREAKFAST**

21 log cabins, sleeps 6, fully furnished with equipped kitchens, linens included. Clubhouse features CATV, Jacuzzi, sauna and indoor pool. Playground, picnic area, tennis and volleyball courts. Small lake on premises. 18-hole golf course, The Natural. Cross-country ski in winter. No pets.

Call for Rates

HERITAGE HOUSE B&B **(517) 732-1199**
BED & BREAKFAST

Come to relax and enjoy the collection of old and new in this 100 year old farmhouse featuring 5 guest rooms. Close to downtown Gaylord. Full breakfasts and homemade treats served in dining area overlooking backyard.

Daily $55-$75 (approx.)

MARSH RIDGE **(517) 732-6794**
HOTEL/TOWNHOUSES/CHALET(LODGE)

Unique decor and themes throughout. Some Jacuzzi rooms, king size beds, microwaves, refrigerators, and remote TV's. Townhouses with full kitchen, living room, bath, and bedroom downstairs (upstairs sleeping loft) and 2nd bath. Swimming pool, shops & more on premises. No pets.

	Hotel/Suites	Townhouses/Lodge
Weekend	$60-$150 (Dbl. Occ..)	$165-$425

POINTES NORTH **(517) 732-4493**
BETSY BERRY **PRIVATE VACATION HOMES**

6 private, lakefront vacation homes for day, week or month rental. Sizes vary from 3 to 4 bedrooms. Properties vary from sophisticated country to cozy, log cabin and chalet styling. All are set in secluded locations and come fully furnished and equipped including rowboat, CATV and telephone. No pets.

Weekly $700-$1,200

Editor's Note: All of Betsy's lodgings are very comfortable with good locations.

TREETOPS SYLVAN RESORT **(888) TREETOPS • (517) 732-6711**
HOTEL/CHALET/EFFICIENCY

Standard, deluxe accommodations, efficiencies and chalets. 63 holes of championship golf, 19 downhill ski runs and 20 km. of groomed, x-country trails. Dining room, grill and sports bar on premises. Plus indoor/outdoor pools, spas, fitness center, state licensed daycare, Edelweiss Ski and Sports Shop.

Daily $69 (and up)

GRAYLING

BORCHERS BED & BREAKFAST **(517) 348-4921**
TINK & SHIRLEY HENRY/MARK & CHERI HUNTER **BED & BREAKFAST**

The friendly hosts at Borchers invite you to enjoy a unique riverfront experience. On the banks of the AuSable. Built in the early 1900's and now fully restored. 6 rooms, twin/double beds (shared baths) and queen beds (private baths). Full breakfasts. Canoe rentals. Smoking permitted on porch. Open year around. No pets.

Daily $49-$62 (shared bath); $59-$82 (private bath)

Editor's Note: This delightful retreat will make a great place to begin your AuSable river vacation. See our review.

HIGGINS LAKE

BIRCH LODGE
(517) 821-6261
COTTAGE RESORT

This 50 year old resort rests along the shores of Higgins Lake. The 17 cottages (1-3 bedroom/no kitchens) are simply furnished, maintained in good condition and sit in a semi-circle facing the water. Sandy beach. Gathering room features TV w/VCR. Meals are included in price. Open May-Oct.

Daily $82 (approx. - per adult; children less)
Weekly $485 (approx. - per adult; children less)

Editor's Note: The Lodge has developed a great reputation for preparing very tasty meals.

MORELL'S HIGGINS LAKE COTTAGE
(517) 821-6885 • (810) 733-0420
COTTAGE

Overlooking the south end of beautiful Higgins Lake, this immaculate, cozy cottage sits on a nicely wooded lot and is fully furnished w/equipped kitchen, two bedrooms and nursery. Cottage sleeps 5-6. Includes use of rowboat and a 4000 lb. hoist. No pets.

Weekly (Summer) $700 (After Labor Day thru June 17 — special rates.)

REZNICH'S COTTAGES
(517) 821-9282
COTTAGES

Clean, comfortable 3, 2 bedroom cottages on Higgins. Tiled floors, private bath, gas heat and equipped kitchen. BBQ, picnic table and rowboat included in rental price. All cottages are close to the water, one directly overlooks the lake and features knotty pine interior.

Weekly $425-$500

HOUGHTON LAKE

BAY BREEZE RESORT & MOTEL
(517) 366-7721
MANFRED & DIANE BOEHMER
COTTAGES

2 large cottages (sleep 6) and spacious kitchenette motel rooms with 2 double beds on Houghton Lake. Private sandy beach, CATV, picnic tables, BBQ grills, horseshoes, boat dockage. Linens provided. Pontoon, boat/motor, wave runners and bicycle rentals available. Open year around. Pets allowed.

Weekly $315-$485 Daily $50-$75

BEECHWOOD RESORT **(517) 366-5512**

COTTAGES

2-3 bedroom, fully furnished, log cabins with fireplaces (wood provided), equipped kitchens (linens provided), private baths. Boat included with each cabin. Trampoline, shuffleboard, horseshoes, swings. Good swimming beach—great fishing.

Weekly $350 Daily $50

THE CREST **(517) 366-7758 • (810) 363-9485**

COTTAGES/EFFICIENCIES

Lakefront lodgings (3 cottages/3 efficiencies) feature nicely maintained, very clean facilities inside and out! Furnishings in good condition and comfortable. Complete kitchens, picnic table and grill. Ping pong, horseshoes, basketball, paddlewheeler and swim raft. No pets.

Weekly $300-$475

DIETERICH'S RESORT **(517) 366-7655**

COTTAGES/EFFICIENCIES

These 2-3 bedroom cottages (sleeps 4-8) and efficiency units are completely furnished w/equipped kitchens, gas heat, private bathrooms w/showers. Most offer paneled walls, tile floors and include double bed, w/hide-a-bed or studio couch. Linens provided (bring your own towels). Swings, picnic tables, grills, fish cleaning house, shuffleboard, badminton, horseshoes on premises.

Weekly $390 (and up)

DRIFTWOOD RESORT **RESERVATIONS: (800) 442-8316 • (517) 422-5229**

BOB & SHEILA BLESSING **CABINS**

Modern lakefront resort on 2 quite wooded acres on the north shore with 7 housekeeping cabins. 4 are log cabins with fireplaces and microwaves. Cabins include porches with swings, color TV, full kitchens, electric coffee-makers, carpeting. 14' aluminum boat, picnic table and grill. We have the ultimate playground with basket-ball, volleyball, horse shoes, swings, etc. Motor and paddle boat rental. Open all year. No pets.

Weekly $335-$550 (Call for daily rates.)

HIDEAWAY RESORT **(517) 366-9142**
MARYANN PRZYTULSKI **COTTAGES**

A clean and well kept resort on Houghton Lake features 4 cottages (2 bedrooms) with full kitchens. 3 cottages directly face the water. Sandy swimming beach. Rowboat included, dock available. Pets allowed.

Weekly $400-$425

LAGOON RESORT & MOTEL **(517) 422-5761**
DON & ELLEN THOMAS **MOTEL/COTTAGES**

The resort offers motel units plus 2 and 3 bedroom cottages with full kitchens and double beds. It features 260' water frontage with a sandy beach, water slide, boat ramp, lighted playground, shuffleboard, and horseshoes court. Handicap access. Ice shanty, pontoon and water bike rentals available. Open all year. Daily rates available. No pets.

Weekly $230-$490

LAZY DAYS ASSOC. COTTAGES **(810) 979-2819**
COTTAGES

Near Tip-Up-Town site on the shores of Houghton Lake. Features 100 ft. sandy beach with 124 ft. dock. Cottages fully furnished and equipped. Kitchens include microwaves. Queen size beds, CATV. Boats available.

Call for Rates

MILLER'S LAKESHORE RESORT **(810) 652-4240**
DOUG MILLER **COTTAGES/CHALET**

Open all year. Good swimming, fishing, hunting, snowmobiling and ice fishing! New chalet with fireplace. Modern lakefront housekeeping cottages. Large unit with fireplace. Boats with cottages. Motor rentals. Dockage. Safe sandy beach. Large playground. Grill and picnic tables. Ice shanty. On snowmobile trails. Located at Tip-Up-Town, Zone 10. 306 Festival Drive. Visitors by approval. No pets.

Call for Rates

MORELL'S MAPLE LEAF RESORT **(517) 821-6885**
SANDY & DON MORELL **COTTAGES**

A large 3 bedroom and 2, 2 bedroom cottages located on north shore of Houghton Lake — are fully furnished w/equipped kitchens and baths. Cottages are heated and immaculate. Includes row boat. No pets.

Call for Rates

MORRIS'S NORTHERNAIRE RESORT — **(517) 422-6644**
WES & MARY MORRIS — **COTTAGES**

1 and 2 bedroom housekeeping cabins on the largest inland lake in Michigan. Lake frontage with dock and 14' boat included. Cabins feature microwave, drip coffeemaker and CATV. Open all year. Hunting, fishing, cross-country skiing, water activities. No pets. Winter and summer rates available.

Weekly $250-$550 Daily $50-$100 (Call for special Holiday rates)

NORTH STAR RESORT — **(517) 422-4618**
COTTAGES

On the north shore of the lake, in a relaxed wooded setting, these 6 cottages are open year around. Each sleeps 6 and features gas heat and equipped kitchens.

Call for Rates

SHADY VALLEY RESORT — **(517) 366-5403**
COTTAGES

These fully furnished cottages feature equipped kitchens, color TV, carpeting and paneling in the bedrooms and living rooms. Some cottages offer screened porches. Newly built cottages available. Boat included in rental. Motors, pontoons, canoes, snowmobile rentals available. Playground, grills, lawn furniture, fire pit on beach. Handicap access. Laundry facilities. Opean all year. Pets allowed.

Weekly $450-$550 Daily $60-$100

Editor's Note: Clean and well maintained cabins on the water.

SONGER'S LOG CABINS — **(517) 366-5540**
AL & PAULINE SONGER — **COTTAGES**

Open year around, these clean and well maintained log cabins, located on the north shore of Houghton Lake with 150' lake frontage. Each two bedroom cabin features fully equipped kitchens, cable TV, private baths, screened porches and use of 14' boat. Several have natural fireplaces. Paddle boat, pontoon boat, tether ball, swimming and more! No pets (except for fall).

Weekly *$475-$570 (summer) Daily $65-$85 (winter)
*Rates reduced in winter

Editor's Note: Clean and cozy log cabins by the water — very nice.

TRADEWINDS RESORT — **(517) 422-5277**
PAUL & KIM CARRICK — **COTTAGES**

This year around resort, offers carpeted, fully furnished cottages with equipped kitchens, private bath/showers, double beds, color CATV. Boats included with rentals. Motors and pontoon boats available. Facilities set on spacious grounds with sandy beach. Horseshoes, volleyball, shuffleboard, playground on premises. Provide your own linens and paper products.

Weekly $450-$500 (off-season rates available)

WEST SHORE RESORT **(517) 422-3117**

COTTAGES

Nicely maintained, clean and comfortable, these small 2 bedroom (sleep up to 6) cottages are fully furnished w/equipped kitchens. The cottage closest to the water is more spacious and offers comfortable furnishings and nice view. Provide your own linens/ towels during prime season (June-Aug.). $150 deposit. No pets.

Weekly $385-$676

Editor's Note: Mostly smaller but well maintained, clean cottages. The cottage nearest to the lake was good sized, comfortable and had a great view of the lake.

THE WOODBINE VILLA **(517) 422-5349**

COTTAGES

On 300' of sandy beach, these 2 bedroom log cottages are gas heated offer CATV, and are fully furnished with equipped kitchens. Includes use of playground and paddle boats. Modern baths and saunas. Visit our new game room.

Weekly $325-$625

LEWISTON

LAKEVIEW HILLS COUNTRY INN RESORT & NORDIC SKI CENTER **(517) 786-2000**

COUNTY INN/B&B

14 rooms furnished in authentic antiques feature different eras in American history. Private baths, CATV and individually controlled heating and A/C. Enjoy the beautifully groomed pro-croquet court, fitness center w/whirlpool, sauna and exercise equipment. Full breakfast served with kitchen privileges. Relax in the great room, observatory, library or 165 foot porch. In the winter, enjoy 20 km. of groomed cross-country ski trails.

Daily $89-$135

Editor's Note: Contemporary country styling, beautiful views in a secluded wooded setting. A professional croquet court adds an interesting touch.

REGION 3

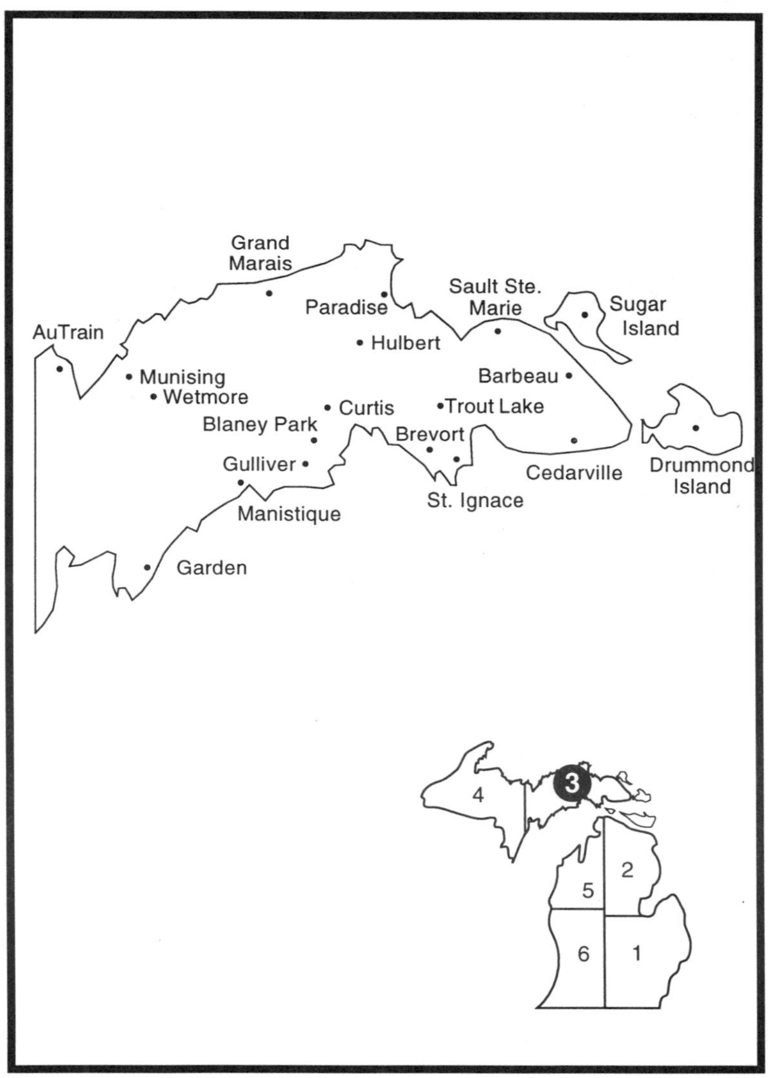
Grand
Marais
Paradise
Sault Ste.
Marie
Sugar
Island
AuTrain
Hulbert
Munising
Wetmore
Barbeau
Curtis
Trout Lake
Blaney Park
Brevort
Gulliver
Cedarville
Drummond
Island
St. Ignace
Manistique
Garden
4
3
2
5
6
1

REGION 3

After crossing the "Big Mac's" five mile span, you will see a place of remote beauty where the interstate highways are nonexistent and fast food restaurants and motel chains are hard to find. In their place are roads "off the beaten path" surrounded by natural beauty, family-run cottages, inns and cafes.

You will walk in the footsteps of our Forefathers and view the marvels of their ingenuity. You are entering a land of a unique combination of dense, unspoiled wilderness, wildlife of all types, streams and waterfalls, yet unnamed mountains and rock formations millions of years old.

You are entering the land of Hiawatha and Gitche Gumee.

ST. IGNACE TO SAULT STE. MARIE

COVERS: BARBEAU • CEDARVILLE • DRUMMOND ISLAND • SUGAR ISLAND

St. Ignace is a community established in 1671 by the Ojibwa, Huron, and Ottawa tribes. The French Father, Jacques Marquette, was the first priest at the Mission of St. Ignace and became famous for his travels of the Great Lakes and Mississippi River. He is buried outside a 150 year old church which is now a museum in the Father Marquette State Park, located at the base of the Mackinac Bridge. Native American pow-wows are still held outside the mission church. Some are open to the public with the most popular being held Labor Day Weekend. Be sure to see the Marquette Mission Park and the Museum of Ojibwa Culture where you'll learn about Native Americans at the Straits of Mackinac.

Of course, you may want to take one of the ferry rides to Mackinac Island for a day of exploration. If you're a walker, don't forget the famous Bridge Walk on Labor Day. Join in the joy and celebrations with Michigan's Governor and thousands of others who walk the world's longest total suspension bridge.

An hour's drive north is **Sault Ste. Marie** (meaning the Rapids of St. Mary), the oldest community in Michigan. The Indians once considered this area their summer gathering and fishing place and the first Jesuit missionaries arrived in 1641. It is often referred to as the Gateway to the North.

Starting at the Sault, you will see the Great Rapids white waters as Lake Superior feeds into Lake Huron. The Soo Locks, an engineering marvel, were built in 1855 to raise or lower vessels up to 1,000 ft. in length through these white waters. Take a boat tour through the Locks, experience the feeling and wonder at the ingenuity of man. Afterwards, walk the path to historic churches and homes and visit the Tower of History. Of course, you must take time to relax and enjoy one of Lake Superior's many sandy beaches. For all those wanting to give Lady Luck a try, this is also the home of The Kewadin Casino, one of the largest casinos in this region. In winter, this region becomes a snowmobilers' heaven. It's also the spot for many winter festivals and outdoor events.

There are several good restaurants in the Sault St. Marie area. *Antler's* has been a favorite among vacationers for years. The atmosphere here is fun and laid back and the decor a taxidermist's fantasy with numerous stuffed wildlife found throughout. Expect loud whistles, bells and plenty of good hamburgers (the menu is a fun read, too!). If you have a taste for Mexican, try *The Palace Restaurant* or, for an Upper Peninsula flavor, *Abner's Restaurant* is the spot for a traditional "Yooper's" menu which includes, of course, their special pasty. A quieter atmosphere, with good Italian food can be found at *Ang-gio's Restaurant.*

BARBEAU

CHANNEL VIEW RESORT **(906) 647-7915**
RICHARD COX **APARTMENTS**

Located 20 miles southeast of Sault Ste. Marie on the St. Mary's River, the resort offers spectacular views of long ships, and has excellent fishing. Cottages feature 2 bedrooms, double beds, heater, stove w/cookware, refrigerator, and TV. For more information write: Hi 51, Box 17A, Barbeau, MI 49710.

Weekly $165

RIVERVIEW TAXIDERMY & MARINE **(906) 647-7211**
CABINS

Located 23 miles southeast of the Soo Locks, all units overlook the St. Mary's River. Four housekeeping cabins include complete kitchen, 2 bedrooms (linens included). TV and screened porch, dock and boat ramp. Boat and motor rentals available. Great fishing. Smoking allowed. Pets allowed on a leash.

Weekly $170-$180 ($5 additional for each person)

CEDARVILLE

ISLAND VIEW RESORT, INC. **(906) 484-2252**
LARRY & JACKIE **COTTAGES**

2 and 3 bedroom cottages with carpeting, showers, gas heat and ranges, refrigerators, dishes and cooking utensils. Linens furnished except towels and wash cloths. Fish cleaning house and freezer. Children's playground. Good swimming area. Great fishing. Boats and pontoon available.

Weekly $400-$575

DRUMMOND ISLAND

BRETT'S HIDE-A-WAY **(508) 533-6087**
BRETT DAVIS **PRIVATE COTTAGE**

Newly constructed log cottage, built in 1993, with water view. Located in a quiet wooded lot 300' from the road. Fully equipped and furnished for comfort. CATV, VCR, ceiling fan, 16' Sea Nymph boat with 30 HP motor ($100 add'l. weekly), boat dock across the road. New hot tub.

Weekly $500 Daily $90

Captains Cove Resort **(906) 493-5344**
Trish Brugger **Cottages**

These 9, 1 and 2 bedroom cottages sit in a wooded area on Gold Coast Shores in the heart of Potagannissing Bay. Newly remodeled, some are lakefront cabins w/fireplaces. All are completely furnished light housekeeping cottages with automatic heat, and bathroom w/showers. Boat included with each cabin. $100 refundable deposit required. No pets.

Weekly $300-$350 (based on 4 people)

Wa-Wen Resort **(906) 493-5445 • (602) 746-2244**
Phil & Marcia Stites **Cabins**

10 acre resort on a sheltered bay near the mouth of the Potagannissing River. Housekeeping cabins have 1-4 bedrooms. Equipped kitchens, electric stoves, bed linens and towels. Aluminum boat, fish cleaning house, electric scaler and freezer available. Tackle shop. Enjoy shuffleboard court, fire-pit, basketball/badminton court, picnic tables, charcoal grills and outdoor pool.

Weekly $330-$530 (off-season rates available)

Woodmoor **(800) 999-6343**
Homes and Lodge

From family reunions to corporate retreats, Woodmoor offers privacy and comfort on 2,000 acres of beautiful woods and waters. Challenging golf at the "Rock" - considered one of the best courses in the Midwest. 8 homes have stone fireplaces, full kitchens and 1-5 bedrooms. The Lodge offers 40 rooms. Restaurant on premises. Boats, pontoon rentals. Island Botanical Trips offered throughout the seasons.

Weekly $750-$2,500 Daily $59-$500

Editor's Note: Former Domino's Pizza's executive retreat. Luxury accommodations with a rustic ambiance. Excellent golf and vacation resort.

ST. IGNACE

Balsam's Resort **(906) 643-9121**
Betty **Cottages/Motel**

At the Straits of Mackinac, 5 miles west of Big Mac, these "real log" cabins have fireplaces and are completely furnished with all kitchen equipment and linens (sorry, no heat). Private sandy beach, safe swimming, night bonfires, picnic, playground, shuffleboard, horseshoes, volleyball and badminton/croquet court. Nearby, there are 40 acres of woods full of beautiful gardens. Have served guests for over 65 years.

Weekly $425-$450 Daily $50-$80

COTTAGE ON THE STRAITS **(612) 645-7423 • (612) 690-0590**
JIM & DIANNE MASTERS **COTTAGE**

Old world charm, modern amenities, and a spectacular view of the Mackinac Bridge and Island from 100' of private lakeshore. Spacious cottage, newly renovated. Antiques, wicker, quilts, fireplace, screened porch. Sleeps 6. Close to shops, restaurants, ferry. Open year around. No pets/no smoking.

Weekly $650 July/Aug. (Call for other rates/times)

SAULT STE. MARIE

RIVER COVE CONDOMINIUMS **(906) 632-7075**
AL TIPTON **CONDOS**

Waterfront, two bedroom condos completely furnished in nautical themes. CATV, VCR and radios. Docks available. Handicap access. Great view of lake freighters. Two miles from Kewadin casinos, Locks and boat. Casino package available. Open April-December. No pets.

Weekly $600-$800 Daily $99-$149 (2 night min.)

Editor's Note: New, nicely decorated and very comfortable condos. Great spot to watch the big freighters pass. Highly recommended. See our review.

THE WATER STREET INN **(800) 236-1904 • (906) 632-1900**
PHYLLIS & GREG WALKER **BED & BREAKFAST**

1900's Queen Anne home overlooking the St. Mary's River has stained glass windows, Italian marble fireplaces, and original woodwork. A wide wraparound porch for watching passing freighters promises a special visit whatever the season. North country breakfast served in an elegant dining room. Only B&B in Sault Ste. Marie. Emphasis is on hospitality and tranquillity. Walking distance from the locks and fine restaurants. 4 rooms.

Daily $75-$105

SUGAR ISLAND

BENNETT'S LANDING **(906) 632-2987**
CABINS

This fishing resort located on the shores of Big Lake George, has been newly remodeled including a new general store. The cabins offer linens, and have a full kitchen, heat, handicap access and a boat. They rent boats, motors, bait and also have propane for RVs. Open April 1-Oct. 15.

Weekly $250 Daily $60

BREVORT • PARADISE

Covers: Hulbert • Trout Lake

As you travel along M 123, stop at **Hulbert** and plan a trip on the Tom Sawyer River Boat and Paul Bunyon Timber Train, or the Toonerville Trolley and River Boat. Both offer 4-1/2 hour round trips to the Tahquamenon Falls with commentary on fauna, flora, points of interest and wildlife. Then on to **Paradise**, only 10 miles from the second largest waterfall east of the Mississippi River. It is sometimes called Little Niagara, for here lies Tahquamenon Falls in all its glory. Not far away is Whitefish Point, site of an Audubon Bird Observatory. When you're in the area, be sure to tour the Great Lakes Shipwreck Museum. This is where you will find the "Graveyard of the Great Lakes" and the first Lighthouse of Lake Superior.

BREVORT

Clearwater Resort Hotel and Condominium — **(800) 638-6371 • (906) 292-5506**
Condo & Hotel

Just 22 miles west of the Mackinac Bridge. These beautiful, clean and quiet condos face Lake Michigan. Only a few years old, they offer 2-3 bedrooms w/fully equipped kitchens and walkout decks Most offer dishwasher, microwaves, and phone. Towels and sheets provided. Resort includes indoor pool, racquetball, sauna, dining room, and lounge.

Daily $45-$75 (hotel); $155 (condos - 4 people/3 night min.)

HULBERT

Hulbert Lake Lodge — **(906) 876-2324**
Greg & Marge Curtis — **Cabins**

Five heated log cabins plus 8 duplexes situated 1/4 mile into the forest have 1-3 bedrooms (one w/fireplace). Furnished but no kitchen facilities. Main lodge offers hearty home cooked breakfasts and dinners. Boats, motors, bait available. Come see the beautiful fall colors. While you are here, do some fantastic snowmobiling, ice fishing and x-country skiing.

Weekly $315-$630 (Daily rates available)

SNO-SHU INN (906) 876-2324
GREG & MARGE CURTIS CABINS/INN

Cozy housekeeping cabins and apartments are fully furnished with kitchen and private bath/showers. Lodging at the Inn accommodates up to 20 people. Fantastic snowmobiling from your door. Heated workshops. Bring your horse and ride miles of wooded trails—stabling available.

Daily $55-$85 (cottage/efficiency units) and $250 (inn)

PARADISE

BIRCHWOOD LODGE (906) 492-3320
STEVE AND CATHY HARMON CABINS

8 modern but rustic log cabins. Lakefront cabins with fireplaces, satellite TV/VCR and movie rentals. Grills. Free use of bikes. Safe, sandy beach, inner tubes, beachhouse, playground. Open year around. Located on Whitefish Point Rd. in a private wooded setting. No pets.

Weekly $325-$425 (2 people) Daily $38-$78 (2 people/3 night min.)

MILE CREEK CABINS (906) 492-3211
DAN & LINDA SMYKOWSKI CABINS

Modern, authentic log cabins (1-2 bedrooms) are clean, carpeted, comfortable and fully furnished including linens. All cabins overlook Lake Superior and provide a magnificent view in a white birch setting. Each features color TV, fireplace (wood provided). Great swimming on private beach. Centrally located to Tahquamenon Falls and Whitefish Point. X-country ski and snowmobile right from your door. Open year around. Pets allowed but must be kept under control.

Daily* $40-$50 (Based on 2 people) $3 ea. add'l. person

TROUT LAKE

TROUT LAKE RESORT (906) 569-3810
CABINS

Just 45 minutes from the Mackinac Bridge, these clean comfortable cabins overlook Trout Lake. Each cabin has a fully equipped kitchenette with microwave, and color TV. Fishing boat is included. Open year around.

Daily $65 (July & August, 7 day minimum stay)

Twin Cedars Resort **(906) 569-3209**

Cottages/Motel

The resort provides a private setting. Located in the Upper Peninsula—a 35 minute drive from St. Ignace, on beautiful Frenchman's Lake. Cozy, two bedroom cottages and plush motel accommodations. Well established. Extras too numerous to list! For complete information, please phone/write. Well established, modest rates. Address: 95 Trout Lake, Michigan 49793

Call for Rates

Editor's Note: Nice location, friendly owners. Cottages in good condition. The two hotel-type accommodations compare to some of the nicer motel rooms we've seen. See our review.

GRAND MARAIS TO GULLIVER

Covers: Blaney Park • Curtis

Grand Marais is the Eastern Gateway to the Pictured Rocks National Lakeshore. This lovely, unspoiled village offers it all — ladyslippers and trillium, white-tailed deer, black bear, Canadian lynx, moose and — even our own bald eagle resides in this beautiful Upper Peninsula wilderness. As might be expected, boating, fishing, hunting, skiing, and snowmobiling are the thing to do in this area. The Grand Marais Historical Museum, Pictured Rocks Maritime Museum, and the AuSable Lighthouse are some of its attractions. But, of course while you are here, you must be sure to explore their many scenic overlooks including the Log Slide, Munising Falls, Sable Falls and don't forget the unforgettable Tahquamenon Falls and the beautiful Pictured Rocks along Gitche Gumee (Lake Superior). This area is a photographer's dream—bring your camera!

If you're in the **Gulliver** area, enjoy a casual meal at *Fisher's Old Deerfield Inn* which features an informal log cabin atmosphere and quaint dining room!

BLANEY PARK

Celibeth House **(906) 283-3409**

Elsa R. Strom **Bed & Breakfast**

This lovely home on 85 acres overlooks Lake Anne Louise. Rooms are clean, spacious, and comfortably furnished. Guests may enjoy the cozy living room, a quiet reading room, a comfortably furnished front porch, and a spacious deck. Continental breakfast. No smoking. 8 rooms.

Daily $48-$78

BLANEY COTTAGES **(906) 283-3163**

COTTAGES

11 cottages, 1-3 bedrooms with fireplace, gas heat and color TV (no kitchens). Continental breakfast. Smoking/non-smoking cabins, picnic areas with gas grills and tables. On 40 acres, bike and snowmobile trails at your door. Seney National Wildlife Refuse nearby. Open all year. Pets O.K.

Daily $35-$120

CURTIS

MANILAK RESORT **(906) 586-6690 • (800) 587-3285**

CHALETS & RANCHES

2 miles N. of Curtis. Chalet and ranch style homes (sleep 1-12), carpeted, fireplaces, full baths, fully equipped kitchens, linens, charcoal grills, picnic tables and decks overlooking Manistique Lake. Includes rowboat. Activity area with basketball, volleyball, horseshoes, recreation room and laundry. Open year around. No pets.

Weekly $450-$1,100

SUNSET PINES RESORT **(906) 586-3199**

KAY **CABINS**

Cozy, romantic cabins in a lovely woodland/lakeside setting. Spacious, well-kept grounds, secluded and quiet. Small playground. Safe swim area. Comfortable, very clean, attractively furnished 1-4 bedroom cabins. Fireplace, TV, laundromat, recreation room, gas grills, posturepedic beds, carpeted. Heated snowmobile repair area. M.S.A. member. Snowmobile, x-country ski from your door. Guide service for hunting/fishing. Open year around.

Weekly $350-$615 (Off-season rates available)

SUNSET POINTE RESORT **(906) 586-9531 • (906) 586-9527**

MIKE SODER **CABINS**

Manistique Lake, 3 miles north of Curtis. 4 spacious cottages on 260' of lake frontage. 2-3 bedroom cottages, fully equipped kitchens, color TV, outdoor cooker. Winter packages include cottages *and* snowmobile. Outboard motor, pontoon, paddleboat and snowmobile rentals available.

Weekly $400-$500 (June-Aug.); $300-$350 (Fall); $400-$475 (Winter)

GRAND MARAIS

HILLTOP MOTEL & CABINS **(906) 494-2331**

CABINS/MOTEL

Five cozy motel units (2 with kitchenettes), 5 completely furnished housekeeping cabins. All include gas heaters, showers and TV. Outdoor fireplace, grills, picnic and play area. Also includes 9 hole mini golf.

Weekly $240 (and up) Daily $35-$95 (Off-season rates available)

THE RAINBOW LODGE **(906) 658-3357**
RICHARD AND CATHY **CABINS/MOTEL**
All new, modern cabins. Full housekeeping services. Each cabin sleeps up to 6 and features a complete kitchen. Linens are furnished — all you need to do is come! Three day minimum stay required. Call to confirm rates.

Weekly $210-$315

GULLIVER

FISCHER'S OLD DEERFIELD **(906) 283-3169**
MARILYN **COTTAGES**
On 101 acres of tall pines and the shore of Gulliver Lake, these 21 up-to-date lakeside motel units and housekeeping cottages feature pine paneled walls, bath w/shower, and automatic heat. Enjoy the private, shallow, sandy beach, stroll among the well groomed grounds and wooded nature trails. Restaurant, lounge, gift shop, fish cleaning on premises. Eat at Fisher's Old Deerfield Inn, with informal log cabin atmosphere and two quaint dinning rooms. Open May through November. No pets.

Weekly $294-$470 Daily $30-$36

AUTRAIN • GARDEN • MANISTIQUE MUNISING • WETMORE

Just north of **Manistique** you will find Palms Books State Park where you will see one of the most unusual water sites in the Upper Peninsula. Take a wooden raft out to the middle of crystal clear Kitch-iti-kipi (Bring Spring) and watch as more than 23 million gallons of water daily erupt from the lake's bottom.

While in **Garden,** visit the Gayette Historical Townsite and take a walking tour through the well preserved example of a 19th century company town. For you fishermen, stop at either Big Bay de Noc or Little Bay de Noc. Why? Because it is rated in USA Today as one of the top ten walleye fishing spots in the country. With nearly 200 miles of shoreline, the bay hosts perch, smallmouth bass, northern pike, rainbow trout, salmon, and fishing tournaments. Here also are uncongested golf courses and golf tournaments. Even a Las Vegas style gambling casino called "Chip-in-Casino" is found here. In the winter there are pow wows and sled dog races. In **Munising**, take a cruise along the shores of the world famous Pictured Rocks — Miner's Castle, Battleship Rock, Indian Head, Lovers' Leap, Colored Caves, Rainbow Cave and

AUTRAIN • GARDEN • MANISTIQUE MUNISING • WETMORE

(continued...)

Chapel Rock, for these can only be seen from the water. Visiting **Au Train,** you will walk in the footsteps of Hiawatha for, according to Longfellow, here lies his home. Es'ca'naw'ba, from the Indian Eshkonabang, means flat rock. Longfellow's Hiawatha tells of the rushing Escanaba River, sometimes referred to as the land of the Red Buck.

While in the Munising/Au Train area, for good family dining at very reasonable prices, check out *Dog Patch Restaurant* or the *Forest Inn.* Another excellent restaurant is the *Camel Riders* restaurant (2 miles east of county highway 450, reservations are recommended. Just west of Manistique at Highway 2 and 13, *Maxie's* provides a simple but homey Yooper's atmosphere with pretty good steaks.

AUTRAIN

Coleman's Paradise Resort **(906) 892-8390**
Bill & Michelle Coleman **Cottages**

Located on the west side of AuTrain Lake, this resort offers 1-3 bedroom cottages. Each private cottage is completely furnished. Three bedroom cottages have fireplaces. Large deck overlooks sandy beach. Great swimming. Playground, w/horseshoes, volleyball, badminton, basketball. General store & bait shop. Boats included (motors available).

Weekly $280-$600

Dana's Lakeside Resort **(906) 892-8333**
Barry & Linda Cleary **Cottages**

Heated 2-3 bedroom housekeeping cottages are 3 miles S. of M-28 on the west side of AuTrain Lake. The resort offers sandy beach, fiberglass boats (motors available), lighted boat dock, screened in fish cleaning house. Shuffleboard and horseshoes. Recreation building offers pool table, pinball, video games, air hockey, juke box and more. Washer and dryer are available.

Call for Rates

NORTHERN NIGHTS **(906) 892-8225**
HERB & DEBBIE BLACKSTOCK **COTTAGES**

On the west side of AuTrain, enjoy excellent fishing in Lake Superior. 7 completely furnished, 2-3 bedroom, housekeeping cottages (3 bedroom w/ fireplace). Laundry facilities, sauna, recreation room, large play area. Boat included (motors available). Sandy beach, nightly campfires, easy access to trails for mountain biking, hiking and x-country skiing on well groomed trails. Snowmobile from your door. No pets.

Call for Rates

NORTHWOODS RESORT **(906) 892-8114**
ED & PAM **COTTAGES**

Located in Hiawatha National Forest, 2 miles from Lake Superior, with easy access to all major highways, a paved roadway brings you to the resort. Set on Au Train Lake, the resort offers good walleye, northern pike, and perch fishing. These 1-4 bedroom cottages, with housekeeping, are fully equipped, and heated. Open year around. Pets allowed.

Weekly $295-$650

PINEWOOD LODGE BED & BREAKFAST **(906) 892-8300**
JERRY & JENNY KRIEG **BED & BREAKFAST**

Massive log home overlooking Lake Superior. Relax on decks, gazebo, atrium, great room. Enjoy the sauna and stop at our craft store. Walk miles on the sandy beach. Tour Pictured Rocks, Hiawatha National Forest, Song Bird Trail, water falls and Seney Wildlife Refuge. Cross country ski. Enjoy year around. 7 rooms. Private and shared baths.

Daily $75-$125

Editor's Note: On M-28. Country-styled rooms give a rustic, woodsy feel with all the modern conveniences. Many of the crafts decorating the rooms are made with Jenny's skillful hands.

GARDEN

THE SUMMER HOUSE **(906) 644-2457**
JAN MCCOTTER **BED & BREAKFAST**

Built in 1880, this two-story Colonial Revival home has been restored and decorated in Victorian style. It is located on the picturesque Garden Peninsula, just 7 miles from Fayette State Historical Park. Enjoy swimming, hunting, fishing, hiking and snowmobile trails. Explore area antique shops or just relax! 5 rooms.

Daily $35-$75

MANISTIQUE

Mountain Ash Resort **(906) 341-5658**

Cottages

4 miles from Manistique on Indian Lake. Waterfront housekeeping cabins, screened porches, fully furnished (bring bath towels). Cable hook-up. Boats included. Picnic tables, BBQ grills and lawn chairs. Individual fire pits by all lakefront cabins. Nice, safe and sandy beach. Private dock, enclosed fish cleaning house/freezing facilities. Boat motor and heated shanty rentals. New and extensive children's play ground. Open all year. Senior discounts. Visa accepted.

Weekly $210-$506 Daily $35-$75

Whispering Pines Resort **(906) 573-2480**

Mike Holm **Cabins**

On Thunder Lake, 5 lake front cabins with 1 *plus* or 2 bedrooms, fireplace. Boat included. All kitchens fully equipped. Bed linens included. Sportman's paradise for fishing and hunting. Near to many attractions. Open May-Dec.

Weekly $275-$350

MUNISING

Camel Riders Resort **(906) 573-2319**

Cabins

Four carpeted, heated, fully furnished housekeeping cabins (2-3 bedrooms) open all year, on the "Chain of Lakes" in a wilderness setting. All bathrooms with modular showers, glass doors and vanities. Knotty pine interiors. Bring towels. Great sandy swimming beach, 2 docks, and 14' aluminum boat. Motors, gas, oil, paddle boat, and canoe available. Log cabin restaurant overlooks the lake rated one of best in the U.P. Full menu.

Call for Rates

Sturgeon River Cabins **(906) 249-3821**

Cabins

Year around, new, rustic log cabins in the Hiawatha National Forest. Birdwatcher's paradise, songbird trails, hiking and nature trail. Great snowmobiling and cross-country skiing, fishing and hunting. Full bathroom and kitchen facilities, modern appliances including microwave. CATV. 2 bedrooms (sleep up to 8).

Daily $65-$75 (May-Oct.); $75-$95 (Nov.-April)

White Fawn Lodge **(906) 573-2949**
Sandra & Scott Butler **Cabins/Lodge**

In the heart of Hiawatha National Forest, lakeside and wooded area cabins. Rooms, suites or apartment units. All have microwaves, refrigerator, coffee makers and color TV's. Community building. Enjoy ATV, hiking and snowmobile trails, hunting, fishing, canoeing and waterfalls. Located 2 hours from Mackinac Bridge/3 hours from Green Bay,

Weekly $375-$450 Daily $50-$125

WETMORE

Cabin Fever Resort **(906) 573-2372**
Rick & Colleen Johnson **Log Cabins**

On 30 acres, these log cabins are fully carpeted and completely furnished with log furniture. Each has housekeeping facilities for 1-6 people (1-3 bedrooms), with fully equipped kitchen and private bath w/shower. Game room. Use of boat included. Excellent snowshoeing, x-country ski and snowmobile trails.

Daily (summer) $11 per person; (winter) $13 per person
(based on 3 night minimum; 4-5 person per cabin)

REGION 4

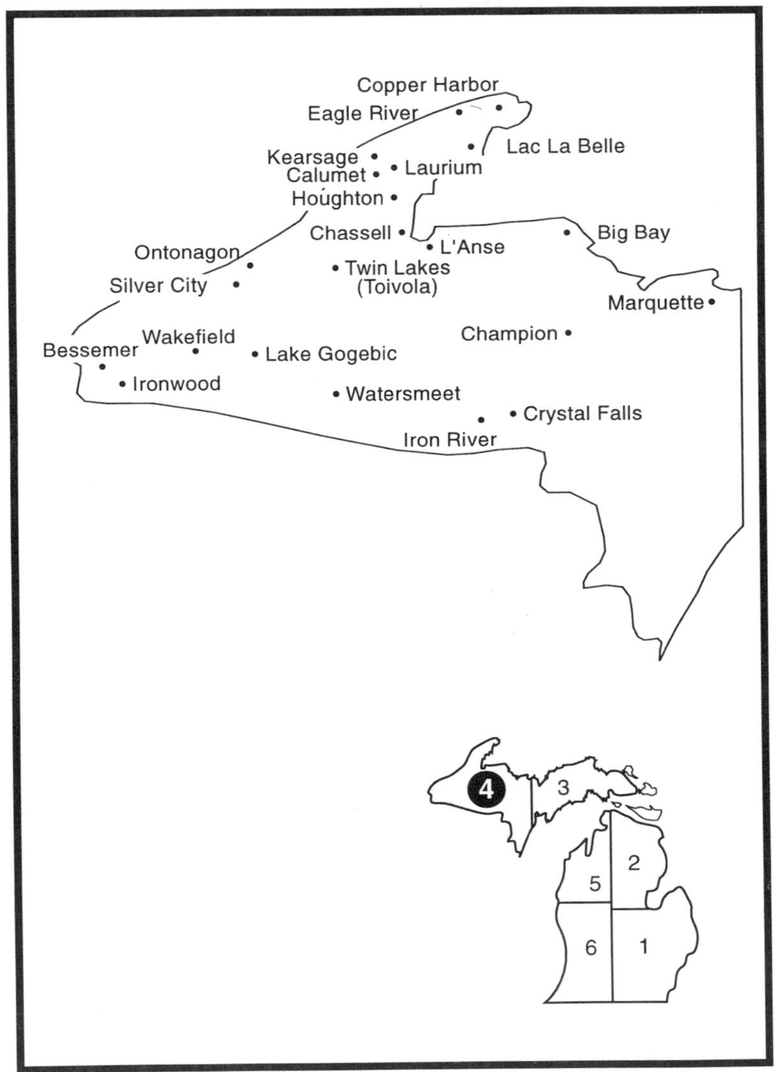
Copper Harbor
Eagle River
Lac La Belle
Kearsage
Calumet
Laurium
Houghton
Chassell
Big Bay
L'Anse
Ontonagon
Twin Lakes
(Toivola)
Silver City
Marquette
Champion
Wakefield
Bessemer
Lake Gogebic
Ironwood
Watersmeet
Crystal Falls
Iron River
4
3
2
5
6
1

REGION 4

Welcome to this region of deep wilderness. Here is the beauty of nature, cascading waterfalls, panoramas of forest wilderness. A lake set in a sea of red, yellow and orange painted by fall leaves, set deep between and surrounded by mountains. A narrow peninsula that jets into Lake Superior and dares its mighty force and yet so lovely that the wealthy have built their summer homes here. A wilderness so complete that some areas can only be reached by hiking, biking or backpacking. You will see hues of red in the sand as Lake Superior sculptures the dunes along its shores. An area so breathtaking, poets have written about it. Lakes so crystal clear you can see the fish in their leisurely swim.

Take a fishing cruise on Lake Superior and catch that "big one". Salmon fishing here is comparable only to fishing in the ocean. Take any tour by boat or by land to see the mines and the wonder of this area. Stop and eat at one of their many fine restaurants.

In the winter, all you skiers, come to the mountain ranges that receive 250 inches of snow yearly. And, if you dare — go *ski flying*. Ski flying is ski jumping but much higher, much longer and definitely more challenging.

You have now seen Michigan's Upper Peninsula.
You will long remember it — and you will soon return.

MARQUETTE THROUGH KEWEENAW PENINSULA TO SILVER CITY

COVERS: BIG BAY • CALUMET • CHAMPION • CHASSELL • COPPER HARBOR EAGLE RIVER • HOUGHTON • KEARSARGE • LAC LA BELLE • L'ANSE • LAURIUM • ONTONAGON (PORCUPINE MTNS. & LAKE OF THE CLOUDS) • TWIN LAKES (TOIVOLAS)

M**arquette**, one of the oldest cities in the Upper Peninsula, was initially founded in the 1840's by French settlers to serve the iron-ore mining and lumber industries. Visitors to the area will enjoy the 328-acre Presque Isle Park with its extensive cross country and hiking trails or its International Food Festival in July, hosted by Northern Michigan University. There are plenty of historic sites and outdoor activities to fill your day. As you leave Marquette for Copper Country, you'll want to stop at the *Mt. Shasta Restaurant* in the **Champion/Michigamme** area where several scenes from the 1950's movie, *Anatomy of a Murder,* were filmed. Here you'll find pictures of Jimmy Stewart, Lee Remick and other cast members adorning the walls.

Thrill to a genuine underground adventure—The Arcadian Copper Mines not far from **Houghton/Hancock**. Take a tour and see the geological wonders created eons ago deep inside the earth. Here, too, is a mecca for rock hounds. Then on to the Quincy Mine Hoist (the Nordberg Hoist), the largest steam-powered mine hoist ever manufactured. Not only is the hoist of great interest, but so is the lore of the Quincy Mining Company. You'll have to visit the area to learn more about it.

In **Calumet,** visit Coppertown USA's Visitor Center. It tells the story of mines, communities and the people of the Keweenaw Peninsula. Visit Fort Wilkins located on the shores of the Lake Superior. Comb through the gemstone strewn beaches to Jacob's Falls. In **Kearsarge,** stop at the "Last Place on Earth" and see the unusual but elegant spoons hand carved from local woods. Theater buffs must stop at the Calumet Theatre and walk with the "Greats" — Bernhardt, Fairbanks, and Sousa. While visiting the area, you'll want to stop at *The Old Country House* just two miles north of Calumet known for its fresh Lake Superior fish, prime rib and homemade bread.

Copper Harbor, at the tip of the peninsula, is a village where everything is less than four blocks away. Stop at the Laughing Loon Gift Shop and from there take a tour into the countryside to view the untouched, towering Estivant Pines. Before the tour, stop for breakfast at the *Pines Restaurant* and taste one of "Red" Twardzik's cinnamon rolls—a local institution — or *Johnson's Bakery* for great rolls and coffee. The aroma alone from these tasty places will add 10 lbs.! Of course, your trip to Copper Harbor is not complete until you dine at the *Keweenaw Mountain Lodge*. Here in this wilderness setting you will find cuisine at its finest. Take a boat trip to Isle Royale National

MARQUETTE THROUGH KEWEENAW PENINSULA TO SILVER CITY

(continued...)

Park, a roadless land of wildlife, unspoiled forests, refreshing lakes, and rugged scenic shores. You will find massive waves exploding on a rugged coastline, lighthouses, rolling hills, thimbleberries, vast pines and hardwood forests, a unique culture and accent. Best of all, you can view both the spectacular sunset and sunrise no matter where you are. Here is vacation land at its very best.

BIG BAY

Big Bay Point Lighthouse B&B — **(906) 345-9957**
Jeff & Linda Gamble — **Bed & Breakfast**

A secluded retreat from modern life, 7 rooms all with private baths. Living room with fireplace, sauna, 1/2 mile of lakeshore and 50 wooded acres for walking. Ideal area for hiking, mountain biking, snowmobiling, cross-country skiing and more. Open year around. Full breakfasts.

Daily (May-Oct.) $115-$155; (Nov./Apr.) $85-$115

Editor's Note: This B&B represents one of the few surviving resident lighthouses in the country. Very secluded — a truly unique experience for guests.

Thunder Bay Inn — **(906) 345-9376 • (800) 732-0714**
Darryl & Eileen Small — **Inn**

Built in 1911 and renovated by Henry Ford in the 1940's. Pub added in 1959 for the filming of "Anatomy of a Murder". 15 rooms furnished with antiques, large lobby with fireplace. Full liquor bar, menu including burgers, soups and pizza. Facilities for conferences, seminars and small weddings. Gift Shop. Open year around. Private and shared baths. Breakfast not included in price.

Daily $49-$85

Editor's Note: This is a classic inn with well maintained rooms which definitely reflect an earlier time. See our review.

CALUMET

Bostrom-Johnson House — **(906) 337-4651**
Curt & Pat Johnson — **Bed & Breakfast**

A large Victorian era residence features 4 spacious guest rooms furnished in antiques. Guests will find a friendly, cheerful home within walking

Bostrom-Johnson House
(continued...)
distance of Calumet. Cross-country ski and groomed snowmobile trails nearby. Children welcome. 4 rms/2 baths. Library open for reading or visiting at all times. There is tea and coffee available all day and a full breakfast every morning.

Daily $50

Calumet House B&B **(906) 337-1936**
George & Rose Chivses **Bed & Breakfast**
In the Keweenaw Peninsula, built in 1895, B&B features original woodwork, upright piano and antique furniture. Breakfast served in the formal dining room which has an original butler's pantry. Guests can view television in the drawing room by a cozy fire with their evening tea. No smoking or pets. Adults only.

Daily $30-$35

CHAMPION

Michigamme Lake Lodge Cottage **(906) 228-0028**
Frank & Linda Stabile **Cottage**
Owners of the former Michigamme Lake Lodge B&B now offer a private cottage on the bluff of Lake Michigamme, fronting 1200 ft. of sandy beach. Canoe with cabin. Sauna by the lake. Cottage features two-bedrooms (sleeps 4), with all the extras including fully equipped kitchen, newly remodeled bathroom, living room with TV, screened porch. Very private. Cottage is furnished with antiques from the Lodge. Swim, bike, fish or canoe. No pets.

Weekly $500

CHASSELL

The Hamar House **(906) 523-4670**
Bed & Breakfast

Built in circa 1903, this turn-of-the-century Victorian, set on spacious grounds, features 2 rooms with adjoining sunroom and 3 rooms with shared bath. Children welcome. Enjoy the 3/5 size playhouse. Parking for snowmobiles and trailers. Close to shops, lakefront, ski/snowmobile trails. Open year around. Check or cash only.

Daily $38 (single) $58-$68 (double)

Helmick's Log Cabins **(906) 523-4591**
Maryann Helmick **Cabins**
3 heated, lakeside cabins. One large room (sleeps 4). Private baths. Equipped kitchen includes refrigerator, stove, pots/pans, dishes, utensils. Porches face the lake. Linens provided (bring towels). Boats available. Open May 15-Oct. 1. No pets.

Weekly $200

MANNINEN'S CABINS **(906) 523-4135 (W) • (906) 334-2518 (S)**
CABINS

The 7 housekeeping cabins, located on 60 acres of land, are very accessible. The cabins, on Otter Lake (well known for outstanding fishing), come with boats. Freezer service. Open May thru Labor Day.

Call for Rates

NORTHERN LIGHT COTTAGES **(906) 523-4131**
GARY & MARGE WICKSTROM **COTTAGES**

Three fully furnished cottages on Chassell Bay. Two bedrooms sleep up to 6, bed linens provided. Sandy beach, swimming, fishing, docking space. Boats, sauna and campfire site are available. Rent weekly - Saturday to Saturday.

Weekly $238 and up

PALOSAARI'S ROLLING ACRES B&B **(906) 523-4947**
CLIFF & EVEY PALOSAARI **BED & BREAKFAST**

Operating Dairy Farm since the 1920's! Visit the barn and watch the milking or help feed the baby calves. It is centrally located and offers three comfortable, cozy rooms with shared bath. Enjoy a full country breakfast in this "home away from home." Open year round. No smoking/pets. Snowmobile trails, swimming and hiking nearby.

Daily $45

Editor's Note: Operating dairy farm B&B. Rooms are very comfy. A great place to bring the kids. They'll enjoy the farm and so will you.

COPPER HARBOR

BELLA VISTA MOTEL & COTTAGES **(906) 289-4213**
DEAN & TODD LAMPPA **COTTAGES/MOTEL**

Eight cottages in Copper Harbor. Motel rooms overlook Lake Superior with cottages one block away. Cottages feature kitchens or kitchenettes, color satellite TV, some with fireplaces. Fish off the dock or, if you prefer, boats are available. Open May to mid-October. Pets allowed.

Weekly $234-$360 Daily $39-$60

BERGH'S WATERFRONT RESORT **(906) 289-4234**
HOWARD & PHYLLIS BERGH **COTTAGES**

These comfortable housekeeping cottages are fully equipped. They include showers, dishes and linens, also boat w/dock available. Resort overlooks harbor near Copper Harbor Marina. Open May 15-Oct. 15. Pets allowed.

Call for Rates

LAKE FANNY HOOE RESORT — **(906) 289-4451 • (800) 426-4451**
ALAN & GRACE CATRON — **COTTAGES/MOTEL**

14 units on the lake with 2, 1-2 bedroom cottages and a lakefront motel. Units have private balconies, kitchenettes, private baths, CATV and some gas fireplaces. Sandy swimming beach. Wooded campsites w/ trout stream. Laundromat, clubhouse, sauna on premises. Boats/canoes available.

Weekly $410-$450

HARBOR LANE COTTAGES — **(906) 289-4211 • (407) 639-2676**
JIM & JANET SHEA — **COTTAGES**

Four log cabins, a century old, offer natural surroundings on Lake Superior. Completely furnished, including linens. Cozy fireplaces w/firewood, and lakeside decks. You can fish off your deck or boat. Fishing guide service, motor and canoe rental available. Within walking distance from Copper Harbor. 50% non-refundable deposit. Pets allowed for an additional $10.

Call for Rates

KEWEENAW MOUNTAIN LODGE — **(906) 289-4403**
CABINS/LODGE

Surrounded by acres of primeval forest land, this framed mountain lodge is located in the Keweenaw Peninsula. Lodge features gracious dining room, cocktail lounge and golf course. Most cabins offer fireplaces, comfortable living areas with private baths and 1-3 bedrooms (no kitchens).

Daily $60-$82

Editor's Note: Picturesque comfort in a wilderness setting ... and all the modern conveniences. The restaurant serves well prepared meals.

EAGLE RIVER

EAGLE RIVER'S SUPERIOR VIEW — **(906) 337-5110**
PAUL — **VACATION HOME**

Three bedroom vacation home overlooking Lake Superior and the Sand Dunes. Sleeps 9 comfortably, 1-1/2 baths, fully equipped kitchen, modern decor. Linens provided. Fireplace, washer/dryer. Full screened porch. Excellent snowmobiling, skiing, swimming beach and play area. Pets and smoking allowed. Call for free brochure.

Weekly $475 (winter/summer) Daily $75 (winter only)

HOUGHTON

CHARLESTON HISTORIC INN **(800) 482-7404 • (906) 482-7790**
JOHN & HELEN SULLIVAN **BED & BREAKFAST**

Circa 1900 Georgian architecture. Ornate woodwork, library with fireplace, grand interior staircase, antique and reproduction 18th Century furniture. Posturpedic king canopy beds. All rooms with private baths, TV's, telephones A/C, sitting areas. Suites, some with fireplace, private verandas or Jacuzzi. Full breakfast. Major credit cards. Smoking limited. Children welcome. No pets.

Daily: $78-$140

KEARSARGE

BELKNAP'S GARNET HOUSE **(906) 337-5607**
BED & BREAKFAST

Enjoy the huge porch and 3 acres of this beautiful mining captain's Victorian home. Unchanged throughout the 1900's, it still has the original fireplaces, fur room, leaded/beveled glass pantries, fixtures, woodwork, and servants quarters. Each room is decorated with Victorian theme. 5 rooms/2 shared baths. Full breakfast. Private/shared baths. Open mid-June through mid-September. Adults only. VISA/MC accepted.

Daily $50-$90

LAC LA BELLE

LAC LA BELLE RESORT **(906) 289-4293**
SANDY **CABINS**

A quiet place at the end of the road. Basic fishing/snowmobiling camp 35 miles from anywhere! Five cabins (3 on water) 1 and 2 bedrooms. Gas heat, showers, fully equipped kitchens, linens, dock space. Rental boats available. Convenience store and gift shop with limited groceries, beer and wine. Gas on dock and road. Access to Lake Superior via Mendota Canal.

Weekly $225 and up Daily $45 and up

L'ANSE

FORD BUNGALOW **(906) 524-7595**

VACATION HOME

Spacious retreat sitting 40 ft. above the shores of Lake Superior in a densely wooded area. It was Henry Ford's summer home where he entertained many visitors including Thomas Edison and Harvey Firestone. Now, fully restored to its 1920's splendor, it's ideal for family or recreational groups of up to 16 people. Features more than 5,000 sq. ft. of living area, 9 bedrooms /6 full baths. Fireplace, linens provided, rocky/pebble beach area. No pets/restricted smoking.

Weekly $1,800 2 Days $800

LAURIUM

LAURIUM LACE GUEST HOUSE **(906) 337-2549**

BED & BREAKFAST

Southern antebellum style home built in 1907. Features 6 fireplaces, 2 porches, regal foyers, library, oak and maple woodwork and staircase. In-ground pool, tennis court and basketball hoop. Near x-country skiing and snowmobile trails. Two rooms shared or private, with queen brass and wicker beds, CATV and overhead lighted fans. Continental or full breakfast. Open year around. No smoking/pets. Visa/MasterCard.

Call for Rates

LAURIUM MANOR INN **(906) 337-2549**

BED & BREAKFAST

Built in 1905, this opulent 13,000 sq ft. antebellum style mansion has 41 rooms (including a ballroom), 5 fireplaces, hand painted murals and gilded leather wall covering. This elegant mansion offers 10 bedrooms (8 private bath, 2 shared bath), king and queen size beds. Take a tour of this mansion and relive the unforgettable wealth that once was Copper Country. No smoking. No pets.

	Winter	Summer
Daily	$64-$94 pvt. bath	$79-$109 pvt. bath
	$49 sh. bath	$54 sh. bath

Editor's Note: Elegant and inviting, this is a premiere Victorian styled B&B.

WONDERLAND MOTEL & CABINS **(906) 337-4511**

CABINS/MOTEL

These lodgings offer 10 units, 6 housekeeping cabins & 4 motel units. Clean quiet and comfortable.

Call for Rates

MARQUETTE

Whitefish Lodge **(906) 343-6762**
Karen Hart & Steve Pawielski **Lodge/Cottages**

A quiet retreat in the U.P. northwoods on the picturesque Laughing Whitefish River. All new, 2 and 3 bedroom lodgings, each completely furnished throughout including kitchens, bedrooms (queen beds) and baths. Enjoy our outdoor decks, grills, mountain bikes, excellent walking and biking trails from door. Great fall colors! Five minutes from Lake Superior and close to Pictured Rocks. Open year-round — on the snowmobile trail and close to x-country ski trails. Gas available on property. 17 miles east of Marquette and 21 miles west of Munising, off M28.

Weekly $350-$675 Nightly $60-$130

Editor's Note: This new lodging is squeaky clean and in very secluded, scenic location. See our review.

ONTONAGON & SILVER CITY (PORCUPINE MTNS. & LAKE OF THE CLOUDS)

Lake of the Clouds Lodging **(906) 885-5412**
Cabins/Motel/Vacation Homes

Only 1 mile from Porcupine Mtn. State Park, on Trail #1, cabins sleep up to 10 and feature fully equipped kitchens, fireplace, TV, VCR, movies. Restaurant within walking distance. The snowmobile trail is 1/2 mile away and alpine and x-country ski areas are two miles away. No pets.

Daily $52-$237

Lake Shore Cabins **(906) 885-5318**
Cabins

Two miles from the Porcupine Mtns., with 500 ft. frontage on beautiful Lake Superior, experience nature with the calm and comfort of home. Private sandy beach. Fish, hunt, bike, ski, snowmobile, and snowshoe right from your door. All cabins offer housekeeping and include sauna bath and screened porch.

Daily $39-$59 (based on 2 people)

Editor's Note: Well maintained log cabins with a beautiful, large sandy beach!

LAMBERTS CHALET COTTAGES & VACATION HOMES **(906) 884-4230**
RICHARD LAMBERT **CHALETS/HOMES**

On the sandy shore of Lake Superior, these 13 chalets come with kitchenettes (some with fireplaces) and vacation homes features TV's, phone in room, sauna/whirlpool. Enjoy the sandy beaches, grills, picnic tables and Porcupine Mountain; gift shop on premises. Major credit cards. Open all year. Some non-smoking units available. No pets.

Daily (cottages) $52-$82 (dbl.) (Homes) $225 (6 people)

Editor's Note: Each lodging varies in style and amenities from small to large size homes and chalets. All are well maintained and comfortable...something for everyone.

MOUNTAIN VIEW LODGE **(906) 885-5256 • (800) 435-5256**
CURT **COTTAGES**

Contemporary lakeside cottages 1 mile from Porcupine Mtns. Ski hill 2 miles. Snowmobile trail 300 ft. 300 ft. sandy beach. Two bedroom with queen beds, fully equipped kitchen w/dishwasher and microwave. CATV w/ videoplayer, fireplace. All lodges w/view of Lake Superior. New 1994. No pets. Email address: mtnview@up.net • URL:http://visit-usa.com/mi/mtnview

Daily $79-$189

TOMLINSON'S RAINBOW MOTEL & CHALET **(906) 885-5348**
CHALETS/MOTEL

Overlooking Lake Superior and 5 min. from the Porcupine Mtns. large chalets sleep 10 and are furnished (including linens) w/fully equipped kitchens. Enjoy Jacuzzi, sauna, free in-room phone and coffee. New unit with hot tub in room. Restaurant on premises. Credit cards accepted. Open all year. Smoking/pets allowed. New in 1996, 2 bedroom beach front home on Lake Superior.

Daily $45-$116 (double occupancy)

Editor's Note: Chalets and motel look very attractive, well maintained and new.

TWIN LAKES (TOIVOLA)

KRUPP'S ALL SEASON RESORT **(906) 288-3404**
COTTAGES

Six units, 1-3 bedroom housekeeping cottages with full kitchens, TV and more. Located on the lake - boating, fishing and swimming. Near golf course, state park, bakery and restaurant. Open year round. Gasoline on premises. Major credit cards accepted.

Weekly $150-$350

Twin Lakes Resort **(906) 288-3666**

Cottages

8 units, semi-rustic cabins, 2-3 bedrooms with kitchens, sandy beach, private tub and showers. Safe swimming. Boat included. Located near a golf course and state park. Reservations recommended. Open mid-May thru mid-October. Brochure available.

Call for Rates

IRONWOOD & SURROUNDING AREAS

Covers: Bessemer • Crystal Falls • Iron River • Lake Gogebic • Wakefield • Watersmeet

Ironwood is known as *"The Big Snow Country"*. But don't let that fool you, it is more than just winter fun. Here among unspoiled forest and mountains are miles of trout streams and hundreds of spring fed lakes. Visitors will enjoy their vacation on the famous Cisco Chain of Lakes, in Bergland/Marenisco. Bring your camera! Here stands "The World's Tallest Indian"—*HIAWATHA.* He towers 150 feet over downtown Ironwood. Also, don't miss the Copper Peak Ski Flying Hill in the Black River Recreation Area, 10 miles northeast of Ironwood.

Lake Gogebic is the area's largest lake, with 13,000 acres of prime fishing water. In June, September and throughout the season, fishing tournaments are held. Families will enjoy all sorts of summer fun, sightseeing, hiking and water sports. Further northeast we come to the Porcupine Mountains Wilderness State Park (15 miles west of Ontonagon). The Park's 63,000 acres is one of the few remaining large wilderness areas in the Midwest and it features the beautiful Lake of the Clouds. Backpacking the "Porkies" is a challenge reserved only for the strong of heart. The Department of Natural Resources maintains over 90 miles of foot trails and more than a dozen rustic trail side cabins.

BESSEMER

Blackjack Ski Resort **(800) 848-1125**

Condos/Chalets

Trailside lodging units offer ski-in, ski-out convenience. Cozy fireplaces, new TV systems, complete kitchens, and saunas in every building. Longest run over 1 mile. PSIA Ski School, Kinderkamp and nursery. Lodgings range from studio to 1-3 bedroom. Special package rates available.

Daily $65-$100 (and up- assumes 2 nights) Call for special package rates

Big Powderhorn Lodging (800) 222-3131 • (906) 932-3100
Condos/Chalets

Luxury chalets to budget conscious private chalets and condos provide a wide selection of accommodations. Ice rink, horse-driven sleigh rides, x-country skiing, pool, special events, trailside decks, and live entertainment. NASTAR, ski school, ski shop, rentals, kinderschool, and cafeteria. 3 restaurants and lounges, sauna/whirlpool, and fireplace. Credit cards accepted.

Call for Rates

Hedgerow Lodging (800) 421-4995 • (906) 663-6950
Jeff & Sue Shepherd **Chalets**

Ski and snowmobile right out your door! These cozy, clean, comfortable units (sleeps 6-10) come with furnished kitchenettes and microwaves. CATV, linens and towels provided. Only 5 min. to Indianhead and 10 min. to Big Powderhorn. Special ski packages available. Major credit cards accepted.

Daily $108-$138 (and up)

CRYSTAL FALLS

Birchwood Cabins (906) 875-3637
Cabins

On Swan Lake in a park-like setting, these 5 (1-2 bedroom) cabins are completely furnished (linens included) and offer equipped kitchens, showers and gas heat. Boat included. Excellent hunting/fishing (walleye and perch), plus easy access to miles of snowmobile, x-country ski trails. Pets allowed.

Call for Rates

Whispering Pines Resort (906) 875-6151
Roy & Jeanne Brown **Cottages**

7, 1-3 bedroom units completely furnished. Nestled in a wooded area and located on 450' of Lake Mary. Sandy swimming beach. Only 7 miles from Crystal Falls. Boat with each cabin. Area noted for fishing, particularly walleye.

Weekly (May-Sept.) $200-$285 (Off-season rates slightly higher)

IRON RIVER

Cataldo's Cabin (906) 265-3991
Phil & June Cataldo **Chalets**

2 chalet units (3 bedrooms each) on 150 acres of quiet forest land on Stanley Lake. Heated, 1-1/2 baths, linens provided (bring towels). There is abundant wildlife on the property, with plenty of muskie and bass in the Lake. Includes use of boat. 5 min. from Ski Brule Ski Area. Pets allowed.

Weekly $325 (summer) Weekends $160 (winter)

LAC O'SEASONS RESORT — **(906) 265-4881**
RANDY & NANCY SCHAUWECKER — **COTTAGES**

10 min. from downtown Iron River on Stanley Lake, close to groomed x-country ski and snowmobile trails. Facilities feature indoor swimming pool sauna and whirlpool. Newly constructed 2-3 bedroom cottages, some log styled, are fully carpeted w/electric heat and appliances. Some units w/fireplaces. Porch w/grills with each unit. Boat, canoe, paddle boats and pontoon rentals.

Call for Rates

IRONWOOD

BEAR TRACK INN — **(906) 932-2144**
CABINS

On the western end of Hiawatha National Forest, adjacent to a designated National scenic river. Each cabin is set apart from each other. All include complete kitchen, bath, shower, wood burning stoves, and linens. Finnish style wood sauna on premise. Minutes from Lake Superior, waterfalls, hiking/ bike trails and more.

Daily $50-$125 (Off-season rates available)

BLACK RIVER LODGE — **(800) 666-9916 • (906) 932-3857**
TOWNHOUSES/MOTEL/CONDOS

Located 2 miles from Big Powderhorn Mtn., near Copper Peak Ski Flying Hill w/7 waterfalls and Black River Harbor. The lodge offers accommodations to fit all pocketbooks, from motel rooms to spacious townhouses and condominiums. Indoor swimming pool, restaurant, lounge, and game room.

Call for Rates

RIVER ROCK RETREAT — **(906) 932-5638**
LOG CABIN

Massive log cabin that sets the highest standard for log cabin construction with many special features including hand-hewn red pine logs. Snowmobile right outside your door and snowshoeing. Fully equipped and furnished, 3 fireplaces, 3 baths, 3 living areas, complete kitchen, jacuzzi, sauna, phone, BBQ. Open year around.

Call for Rates

LAKE GOGEBIC

The Fisherman Resort **(906) 842-3366**
Cottages/Lodge

Well maintained cottages on Lake Gogebic. Boats available for rent—or bring your own! Fully furnished with equipped kitchens, private baths. Some fireplaces. Bring towels. Cabins sleep 2-8. Gift shop features handcrafted items. Lodge rooms also available.

Weekly $390 (and up, winter); $375 (and up, summer)

Editor's Note: Well landscaped resort on the shores of Lake Gogebic. Clean and comfortable lodgings — great fishing area.

Gogebic Lodge **(906) 842-3321**
Don/Chris/Brian Berquist **Chalet/Motel/Cottages**

West side of Lake Gogebic, motel, cottage and chalet accommodations. Cottages feature private bath, CATV, equipped kitchens, and more! The Lodge includes sauna/whirlpool, dining room/lounge. Boat and motor rentals available. Enjoy hunting, fishing, swimming, snowmobiling and skiing. Credit cards accepted. Pets allowed, extra charge.

Weekly $260-$950 Daily $55 (for 2)-$175 (for 6)

Editor's Note: Their resort has established a good reputation on the lake. Book reservations early. The three new chalets built in 1994 looked great.

The West Shore Resort **(906) 842-3336**
Cottages

450 ft. on Lake Gogebic. Great fishing for walleye or hunting for bear and deer. All cabins are 2 bedrooms, sleep 7, bath (towels and linens provided). Boat launch on site, docks and hoist available. Boat and motor rentals. Pets welcome May-Oct.

Weekly $280 (dbl. occ. - $25 each add'l person) Summer Rates
Daily $50 (dbl. occ. - $5 each add'l person) Summer Rates

Editor's Note: Small but very clean, comfortable accommodations — reasonable prices make this a good choice.

MALLARD COVE & TEAL WING **(800) 876-9751**
SNOW COUNTRY CONTRACTING, INC. **2 PRIVATE VACATION HOMES**
TOM & ARLENE SCHNELLER

Mallard Cove: Spacious 4 bedroom, furnished in Duck motif and features cedar sauna. Accommodates 8. Features phone, fireplace, Weber grill, fully equipped kitchen with dishwasher, linens, towels. Excellent waterfront view. Boat dock (boat and motor available). Groomed snow-mobile trails and skiing nearby.

Teal Wing: Contemporary, spacious home on Lake Gogebic, accented in teal and light oak. 4 bedrooms (sleeps 8). Fully furnished and equipped including microwave, phone, TV/VCR, stereo. Includes use of boat dock (boat and motor available). Also overlooks Lake Gogebic and is located on snowmobile route. Both properties available year around. Pets O.K.

TEAL WING

Weekly $895

Editor's Note: The Schneller's have designed and decorated these homes with comfortable elegance. We highly recommend both Mallard Cove & Teal Wing.

NINE PINE RESORT **(906) 842-3361**
RON & JOANN MONTIE **COTTAGES**

A family resort, centrally located in "Big Snow Country". Snowmobile right to your door. Modern, carpeted housekeeping units (sleep 2-8) with TV. Boats and motors available for rent. 1 cottage with fireplace. Linens provided. Restaurants nearby. Open year around. Major credit cards. Pets allowed.

Weekly $335-$700

SOUTHWINDS COTTAGE **(906) 575-3397**
MARLIN & PAT HANSON **COTTAGE**

Very cozy, clean 2 bedroom cottage on Lake Gogebic with 220 ft. of sandy beach. Private dock. Sleeps 6. All new carpet and furnishings. Fully equipped kitchen with microwave and grill. Private, very quiet. New wood deck overlooking the lake. Rent year around. No pets.

Weekly $400

SUNNYSIDE CABINS **(906) 842-3371**
SUE GROOMS **CABINS**

Set along 300 ft. of Lake Gogebic, these 8 well maintained, comfortably furnished lodgings feature fully equipped kitchens including microwaves, knotty pine interiors, satellite TV, private baths, bedrooms with 1 to 2 full size beds. Doorwalls lead to private deck. Linens provided.

Call for Rates

Editor's Note: Spotless cabins with a "luxurious" feel. We were very impressed.

TIMBERLINE SPORTS COTTAGES & CHALETS **(906) 575-3542**
COTTAGES

New owners completed major renovations in 1995. Waterfront resort on Lake Gogebic midway between Porcupine, Indianhead and Powderhorn Mountains. Featured are 6 cottages and 7 chalets fully furnished with equipped kitchens and private baths. Enjoy hunting, fishing, snowmobiling and skiing. Boat and snowmobile rentals available. No pets.

Daily $45-$125

WHITETAIL LODGING **(906) 842-3589**
COTTAGES

2 bedroom cottages (2-8 people) on the east shore of Lake Gogebic. Furnished and equipped, knotty pine interiors, cedar exteriors, tiled bath/shower. Individually controlled electric baseboards. Boats available. Great fishing for walleye, bass, perch. Snowmobile trail to the Porcupine Mountains.

Weekly $295-$355 Daily $45-$55 (double occupancy)

WAKEFIELD

INDIANHEAD BEAR CREEK **(800) 3-INDIAN**
CONDOS/CHALETS

Chalets tucked into the woods, condos on or adjacent to the slopes and Main Lodge, an authentic barn converted to a complete and cozy hotel - all are featured at Indianhead. Accommodations include phones, color TV's, VCR's. Lodge rooms with CATV. Some units with dishwashers, washers/dryers, some with Jacuzzi or sauna. Facilities offer 2 restaurants, 2 cafeterias, 5 cocktail lounges, indoor pool and spa, health/racquet club, full service ski shop, child care, Kinder Country children's programs (kids 12 and under sleep free w/ parents). Golfing packages, bicycle tours and races, auto show, kite festival, and more — call for special package rates. Pets allowed in some units.

Daily $65-$595 (from basic lodge room to 6 bedroom chalet)

TULA HAUS **(906) 575-3296**

VACATION HOME

Located along the Big Presque Isle River on almost 3 acres of land, only 4 miles from Lake Gogebic, this all season home is completely furnished with equipped kitchen, microwave, TV, VCR, stereo, fireplace, sauna, phone and garage. Located right on Trail 8.

Daily $55-$108

WATERSMEET

THE ARROWS **(906) 358-4390**

COTTAGES/HOMES

Modern/ultra-modern cottages, luxury vacation homes with fireplaces, TV, dishwashers, whirlpools, microwaves, washers, and dryers. On Thousand Island Lake (Cisco Chain). Sleeps up to 15 per home. General store, gift shop, boats, motors, bait, tackle, licenses. Access to snowmobile trails, x-country trails. One hour to downhill skiing.

Weekly $575-$1,280

Editor's Note: The interiors of these cottages are well maintained. The newer cottages are very nice. Beautiful, natural setting. Excellent fishing and boating.

CROOKED LAKE RESORT **(906) 358-4421**

COTTAGES

On Crooked Lake, located directly on the water in Sylvania Perimeter/ Wilderness Area. Motors allowed. Six modern (3 newer) 2 and 3 bedroom housekeeping cottages. Everything furnished except personal towels. Each cottage comes with a boat or canoe. Motor rental, bait, gas also available. Open May 15-November. Pets allowed.

Weekly $412-$624

JAY'S RESORT **(906) 358-4300**

COTTAGES

Lakefront cottages surrounded by woods on Thousand Island Lake. 9 beautiful and inviting 1-4 bedroom housekeeping cottages (new or totally refurbished), many with fireplaces. Complete kitchens, color TV's, sleeps up to 12. New Lund boats; deluxe boats and pontoons available. Spacious grounds with play area. Seasonal discounts. Call to inquire. Pets with permission, extra charge. Handicap access.

Weekly $400-$950

Editor's Note: Cottage exteriors new — the natural grounds were well groomed. Cute play area for children.

LAC LA BELLE RESORT **(906) 358-4396**
SKIP & CARYL BUCHANAN **CABINS**

These well maintained year around cottages are nestled on Thousand Island Lake and each unit has a view of the water. These heated, 1-2 bedroom units have knotty pine interiors, fully equipped kitchens, linens and blankets are provided (bring your own towels). On the grounds they have a fire pit, fish cleaning station and freezer. Boats, guide service, gas and oil are available.

Weekly $400 *plus*

Editor's Note: Comfortable and affordable lodgings. Much of the woodworking here has been done by Skip.

VACATIONLAND RESORT **(906) 358-4380**
BILL & JAN SMET **COTTAGES**

Housekeeping cottages, 2-3 bedrooms, some w/fireplaces, on Thousand Island Lake. Linens furnished (bring towels). Boat included (motors extra). Safe swimming beach. Dock and raft, tennis, volleyball, basketball, fishing and boating. Great x-country skiing, snowmobiling and ice fishing!

Weekly $300-$900 Daily $60-$180

REGION 5

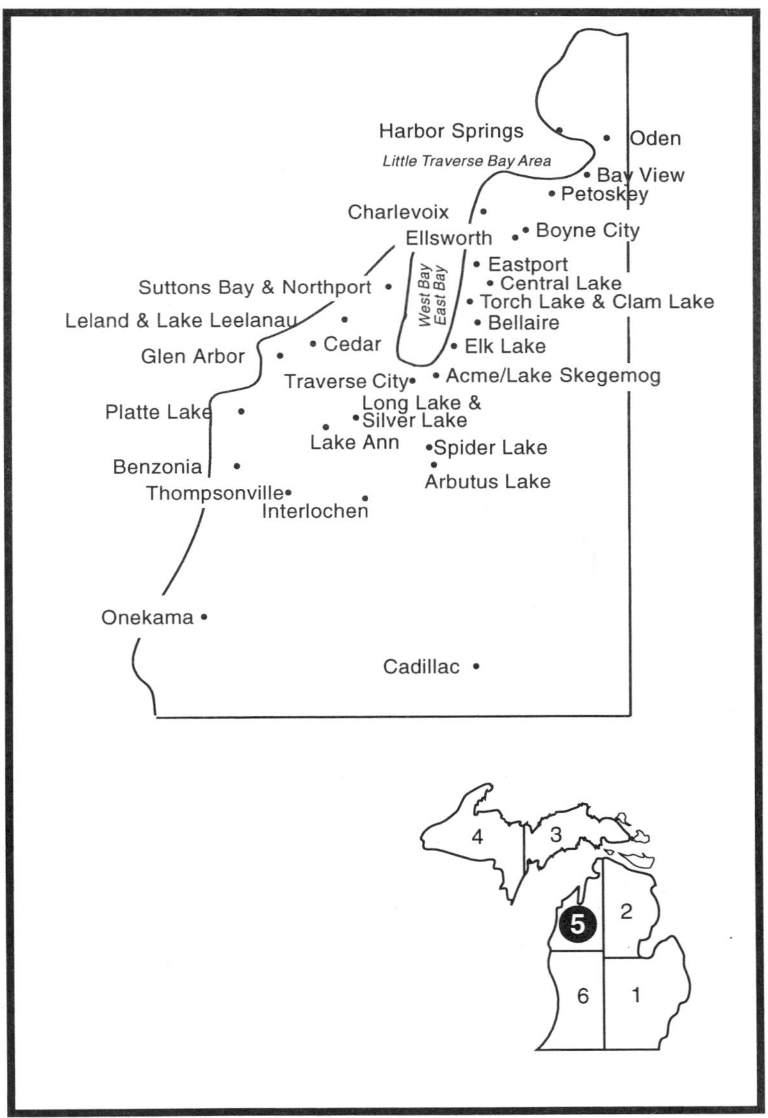
Harbor Springs
Oden
Little Traverse Bay Area
Bay View
Petoskey
Charlevoix
Ellsworth
Boyne City
West Bay
East Bay
Eastport
Central Lake
Suttons Bay & Northport
Torch Lake & Clam Lake
Leland & Lake Leelanau
Bellaire
Cedar
Glen Arbor
Elk Lake
Traverse City
Acme/Lake Skegemog
Long Lake &
Silver Lake
Platte Lake
Lake Ann
Spider Lake
Benzonia
Arbutus Lake
Thompsonville
Interlochen
Onekama
Cadillac
4
3
5
2
6
1

REGION 5

There's more to this area than just relaxing on the pure, sandy beaches and watching the sun as it sets on Lake Michigan. It offers miles of scenic drives, wilderness, acres of sand dunes and nature preserves, hundred of lakes, and more varieties of trees than you're likely to find anywhere else. In this area you will also find some of the best salmon, trout and bass fishing in the U.S.A. Within Region 5 lies the Cherry Capital and Summer Golf Capital with many designer golf courses.

If you want things to do, try the festivals, art shows, summer theaters, museums, 19th Century communities and some of the best shopping, gourmet restaurants and winery's around.

The shimmering white snow of winter is broken not only by pine trees, deer and elk, but miles of groomed snowmobile trails, cross-country ski trails and some of the Midwest's finest downhill ski runs. Our lake-effect snow is denser, heavier and more durable than mountain snow.

Nature at its most natural, civilization at its most refined.
The perfect blend in any season.

BOYNE CITY • CHARLEVOIX • PETOSKEY

COVERS: BAY VIEW • EASTPORT • ELLSWORTH • HARBOR SPRINGS • LITTLE TRAVERSE BAY • ODEN

The scenic area of **Boyne, Charlevoix, Harbor Springs, and Petoskey** offers superb sight-seeing, unique shops, fishing, sailing, and some of the best downhill and cross country skiing in Lower Michigan!

Five linear miles of flower-lined streets, a drawbridge, and two lakes have earned **"Charlevoix the Beautiful"** its name. The village has become the center for the arts complete with galleries and shops. The spring offers Petoskey Stone and other fossil collectors hours of treasure hunting along its many sandy beaches. Don't forget to visit **Petoskey's** unique shops in the historic Gaslight District, and **Harbor Springs'** scenic beauty compares to few which includes the very scenic, 31 mile route to Cross Village, through the Tunnel of Trees. Harbor Springs also features several interesting shops that you'll want to take time and browse. Of course we can't overlook **Boyne's** high peaked hills which provide the scene for some of lower Michigan's finest downhill skiing during winter months.

Some outstanding restaurants in the area include *The Rowe Inn* (Ellsworth), *Tapawingo* (on St. Clair Lake) and *Pete and Mickey's at the Edgewater* (Charlevoix). For other good fixin's in Charlevoix, try homestyle cooking at *Darlene's*, dine on the lake at *Round Table Restaurant* or, for a Friday night fishfry, tasty hamburgers, pasties, or Mexican there's the *Lumberjack Saloon.*

BAY VIEW

THE GINGERBREAD HOUSE — **(616) 347-3538**
MARY GRULER — **BED & BREAKFAST**

Pastel hues, white wicker and floral gardens provide a romantic setting for this 1881 renovated Victorian cottage situated in the heart of Bay View, a National Historic Landmark. All rooms with view of Little Traverse Bay, private entrances and baths. Deluxe continental breakfast. No smoking/pets. Open May-October. 4 rooms.

Daily $80-$120

BOYNE CITY

ATRIUM CONDOS/DILWORTH INN (800) 748-0160 • (616) 582-6220
MAIN RENTAL OFFICE CONDOS/INN

Built in 1912 and renovated in 1993, the Dilworth Inn has 26 rooms with A/C. Private baths, suites (multi-rooms), phone and cable TV's in room. Porch surrounds building. Continental breakfast served daily. Excellent dining and lounge with entertainment on weekends. Open year around. Atrium condominium units feature 1-3 bedrooms. Each fully furnished with equipped kitchens (1 bedrooms w/limited kitchens) and fireplaces. Some w/Jacuzzis.

Daily (Inn) $49-$99 Daily (Condos) $79-$199

DEER LAKE BED & BREAKFAST (616) 582-9039
SHIRLEY & GLENN PIEPENBURG BED & BREAKFAST

Contemporary waterfront B&B on Deer Lake in quiet country setting. An all season resort area near Boyne Mountain. Features five rooms with private baths, individual heat and A/C. Enjoy full breakfast by candle-light on china and crystal. Personalized classes to make your own 24kt. Gold or Sterling Silver rings are offered by the experts!

Daily $80-$95 (dbl.); $60-$75 (sgl.)

HARBORAGE CONDOMINIUMS (800) 456-4313 • (616) 582-3000
MAIN RENTAL OFFICE CONDOS

2-3 bedroom units on the shores of Lake Charlevoix near a full-service marina. Completely equipped and beautifully decorated. Prices exclude holidays.

Weekly $1,325-$1,950 2 Day Pkg. $395-$525

THE LANDINGS (616) 547-1222
VACATION PROPERTY RENTAL AND MGT. CO. CONDOS

2 and 3 bedroom condominiums on the shores of Lake Charlevoix in the heart of northwest Michigan's recreational playground! Sandy beach, heated pool, boat slips. Only minutes from Boyne Country Championship Golf. An excellent rental value, located in Boyne City. Call early for best availability.

Weekly $1,200

JOHN C. SCHADE (313) 675-2452 • (313) 262-3048
CONDO

Spacious, 3-level condo overlooks Lake Charlevoix. Completely furnished (w/linens), sleeps 6. Features king/queen size beds, full kitchen, microwave, dishwasher, Jenn-Aire grill, 4 baths, fireplace, sauna, private beach and dock,

JOHN C. SCHADE (continued...)

balcony, patio, CATV, VCR, washer/dryer. In Boyne City — walking distance to shops. Minimum 1 week rental. $675 non-refundable deposit per week. No pets. References please.

Weekly $ 1,350 ($75 cleaning fee)

NANCY SERRA **(810) 625-8705**

CHALET

In prime golf area. Deck overlooks a panoramic view of Lake Charlevoix. Only steps to beach and conveniently located 2 blocks from marina. Chalet features 3 bedrooms (4 twin, 1 full, 1 queen and queen hide-a-bed). All amenities including CATV and linens. Weekly rentals. $250 deposit. No pets.

Weekly $650

WATER STREET INN **(800) 456-4313 • (616) 582-3000**

MAIN RENTAL OFFICE **CONDOS**

On the shores of Lake Charlevoix, these units are set along the sandy beach front near a full-service marina. All 27 bedroom suites have a Turn-of-the-Century antique decor, Jacuzzi/whirlpool tubs, complete kitchen, gas fireplaces, queen beds. Overnight or weekly packages available. Prices exclude holidays.

Weekly $1,000 Daily $145-$165 (summer); $80-$120 (off-season)

Editor's Note: Good location and well decorated rooms make this a nice choice.

CHARLEVOIX

AARON'S WINDY HILL GUEST LODGE **(616) 547-6100 • (616) 547-2804**

BED AND BREAKFAST

Beautiful Victorian home with a huge riverstone porch where you can relax, visit with friends and enjoy a homemade buffet breakfast. 8 spacious rooms have private bathrooms. 2 rooms can accommodate up to 5. One block north of drawbridge, one block east of Lake Michigan. Children welcome. Open May - Oct.

Daily $65-$120

GARY & CATHERINE BARNES **(810) 370-0674(S) • (313) 876-9201(W)**

CONDO

On Lake Charlevoix, pool, marina, and beach, steps away. Sleep 4 + (bedroom loft and 1st floor bedroom). Deck, skylight, A/C, fireplace, beamed Cathedral ceiling, microwave, 3 CATV's, 2 VCR's, CD-cassette, phones, ice maker, laundry. Great for family or 2 couples. No pets.

Weekly $800

BOULDER PARK COTTAGES **(810) 354-1636 • (616) 547-6480**
JOAN CHODAK **COTTAGES**

STONE COTTAGES IN A PARK-LIKE SETTING

2 charming stone cottages (1 and 3 bedroom) are located in Earl Young's Boulder Park on 2 acres of land in a park-like setting. Only 800 ft. to Lake Michigan. Includes: bed linens, dishwashers, microwaves, CATV and fireplaces. 50% deposit. Pets allowed.

Weekly $800 (1 bedroom); $1,200 (3 bedroom) Off-season rates available)

Editor's Note: Part of Charlevoix's history. These 2 cottages are built in the style of Earl Young's boulder homes and are located on a quiet side street.

THE BRIDGE STREET INN **(616) 547-6606**
BED & BREAKFAST

Built in 1895, this Colonial Revival home retains all the charm of yesteryear. Relax on its sweeping porch with view of Lake Michigan or in the bright living room. 9 guest rooms attired with old floral rugs on wooden floors, antique furnishings and plush beds. Breakfast and coffee served in the dining room.

Daily $65-$115 (In-season—May to October)

CHARLEVOIX COUNTRY INN **(616) 547-5134**
BED & BREAKFAST

Visitors will feel welcomed in this 1896 country decor inn. Relax and get acquainted in the common room, balcony or on the porch while watching boats and colorful sunsets on Lake Michigan. 8 bedrooms and 2 suites, all with private baths. Continental breakfast buffet and late afternoon beverage, wine and cheese social.

Daily $70-$130

HIDDEN VALLEY RESORT **(616) 547-9905 • (616) 547-4580**
COTTAGES

Quiet, unspoiled resort on 620 ft. of Nowland Lake w/natural shoreline. Though rustic atmosphere, each cottage has been renovated to retain knotty pine charm and modern conveniences. 1-2 bedrooms, private bath, equipped kitchen, TV, screened porch. Sandy beach, excellent fishing lake. Linens not provided. Brochure available.

Weekly $350-$500 (Call for availability of 3 and 4 night rentals & rates)

SUE HUMMEL **(810) 855-3300 • (810) 363-3885**
CONDOS

Lakefront condos sleep 2-12 with 1-3 baths, A/C, fireplace, 2 person Jacuzzi, and CATV. Designer furnished! Includes linens and laundry. Within walking distance to Charlevoix, marinas, beach. Heated pool. Lots of skiing within 1/2 hours. Available year around. 50% deposit.

Weekly $400-$1,000 Daily $75-$150 (summer rates)

DR. DEBORAH JEAN OR PAM **(810) 545-8900**
COTTAGES

2 log cottages on Lake Michigan, approximately 12 miles from Charlevoix. First sleeps up to 6 and features full kitchen with wood burning stove. Wide sandy beach. Second offers 2 bedrooms with loft, sleeps 8, includes washer/dryer and microwave. Near golf and Michigan's finest gourmet restaurants. Pets allowed.

Weekly $700-$1,100 (June-Aug.); $450-$800 (Sept.-Oct.)

LARRY KISH **(517) 349-5474 HOME • (517) 482-7058 WORK**
VACATION HOME

Built in 1993, home features 4 bedrooms/2 baths, 128 ft. water frontage, 600 sq. ft. deck, dock, raft, 5 sliding glass doors and lots of windows. Dishwasher, washer/dryer, TV/VCR and stereo. Vaulted ceiling. Fabulous view. Available year around.

	Sept.-June	July/Aug.	Xmas/New Years
Weekly	$1,200	$1,700	$1,700

LAKE CHARLEVOIX **(616) 536-7343**
MARIE YETTAW **COTTAGES**

Lake Charlevoix Cottages: 4, 2 bedroom, sleep 2-6. Furnished with equipped kitchens. Linens included. CATV, picnic table, lawn chairs, barbecue, boat dock, sandy beach. Overlooks the south arm of Lake Charlevoix, 130 ft. of beach. Open all year. Weekly (summer) $430

Lakefront Home: Beautiful 3 bedroom home (sleeps 12) with sandy beach, dock and lawn on Lake Charlevoix. 130' frontage, large decks with BBQ and furniture. Large kitchen, washer, dryer, 6 walkouts, completely furnished, turnkey. Weekly (summer) $1,680

Cape Victorian: 1890's style Victorian home, 2,500 sq. ft., 4 bedroom, on 1+2 acre with large trees. Quiet setting. Country kitchen, formal dining room, den library, large living room w/wood burning fireplace. 2 full baths. Open all year. Daily $35 per night/per adult (min. $95)

Smuggler's Cove Condos: Contemporary, 1-2 bedroom units. Furnished with linens, full kitchen, washer/dryer. Fireplace, gas grill, patio furniture, CATV, some with A/C. Boat wells. On southarm of Lake Charlevoix. Open all year. No pets. Weekly: $764-$1.275

Editor's Note: Diverse range of properties - you're sure to find one to suite your needs and pocketbook. See our review.

LAKEFRONT LOG LODGE **(616) 536-2851**
SHARON & AL FROST **VACATION HOME**

PERFECT FOR FAMILY REUNIONS AND GROUPS — NEAR SKIING AND GOLF

These 2 spacious, 7 bedroom vacation homes with serene setting offer a spectacular view of Lake Charlevoix. Features 3 full baths, large modern kitchen, CATV, fireplace, dock, campfire area and swing set. 3 decks and 200 ft. of sandy beach. Sleeps up to 25 — great for 3 or 4 families. Only 50 ft. from Lake Charlevoix and 5 minutes from town. Great swimming and fishing. Available year around. 50% deposit. No pets.

Weekly (summer) $3,300 ea. (winter $975 long weekends)

POINTES NORTH INN **(616) 547-0055 • (800) 968-5433**
CONDOMINIUMS

1-2 bedroom suites with lofts and full or partial kitchens. Indoor/outdoor pool. CATV, A/C, VCR and Jacuzzi whirlpools in all units. Located in downtown Charlevoix. No pets.

Daily (summer) $147-$192; (spring/fall) $67-$107; (winter) $57-$97

MCREYNOLD'S LOG CABIN **(313) 761-2043 • (313) 663-8056**
LAURA MCREYNOLDS **LOG HOME**

Charming, lodge-like 1920's log home on Lake Michigan outside Charlevoix with massive stone fireplace, hardwood floors, beamed ceiling, sunroom with gorgeous sunset views, updated master bedroom and bath, washer-dryer, fenced yard and private beach. 2 bedroom plus sleeping loft (sleeps 8). Open year around.

Weekly $1,200 (June-August — off-season rates avail. Sept.-May)

DUANE TAYLOR **(616) 537-2687**
VACATION HOME

Near downtown and beaches (7 blocks to Lake Charlevoix and 5 blocks to Lake Michigan), this lovely 5 bedroom home is fully furnished (linens included) with large, comfortable deck and warming fireplace. CATV, VCR, stereo. Available June 22-Sept. 2. 50% deposit. No pets.

Weekly $1,200 (assumes 4 adults)

UHRICK'S LINCOLN LOG **(616) 547-4881**
COTTAGES/MOTEL/CAMPGROUNDS

24 cottages (1, 2 and 3 bedrooms) include full kitchens, CATV and linens. 2 blocks to beach and 1 mile to town. Open April to November. Pets allowed.

Daily $48-$150 (July/Aug.); $30-80 (off-season)

EASTPORT

EDEN SHORES **(616) 547-5316 • (616) 547-5583**
MARILYN & CHARLES WILMOT **COTTAGE**

Eastport cottage sits in a secluded wooded area. Quiet, clean. Bright sunroom with lots of windows. 5 minute walk to Lake Michigan beach. Recently redone — new carpeting, tile, walls, bathroom. Full kitchen. Linens provided. No pets/smoking.

Weekly $350 Daily (weekends) $100

ELLSWORTH

HOUSE ON THE HILL **(616) 588-6304**
JULIE & BUSTER ARNIM **BED & BREAKFAST**

"Our 13th Season" featured in Detroit Free Press, Chicago Tribune, and Midwest Living. Elegantly furnished Victorian farmhouse. Picture postcard lake views from the veranda. Enjoy a delicious Texas Breakfast and walk to two world class restaurants: **Tapawingo** and **Rowe Inn**. 7 rooms w/private baths, some fireplaces.

Daily $85-$115

HARBOR SPRINGS

HAMLET VILLAGE **(616) 526-2641**
c/o LAND MASTERS **HOMES & CONDOS**

Contemporary country styling located in the secluded, rolling hills of Harbor Springs. Slope side condos features ski-in/ski-out access to Nubs Nob. Condos offer 1-3 bedroom + loft. Homes/chalets (between Boyne Highlands and Nubs Nob) vary in size and sleep from 6-12, 1-3 baths. A few miles to beaches/marinas/golf. Prices vary based on season and size of accommodation. Call for special package prices.

	Condos	Homes
Weekly	$798-$1,190	$637-$1,176
Weekend Pkgs.	$260-$1,096	$440-$960

Editor's Note: Scenic locations and very well maintained properties make Hamlet Village accommodations a nice choice. You Nubs Nob fans will love the ski-in/out privileges available at their condos.

KIMBERLY COUNTRY ESTATE **(616) 526-7646**
RONN & BILLIE KIMBERLY **BED & BREAKFAST**

This colonial plantation style B & B welcomes its guests with a lovely veranda and terrace overlooking the swimming pool and Wequetonsing Golf Course. On several secluded acres. Features 6 exquisitely decorated rooms, one w/ wood burning fireplace, sitting area, and four poster bed. 4 min. to Boyne Highlands or Nubs Nobs! 6 rooms.

Daily $135-$225

THE VERANDA BED & BREAKFAST **(616) 526-7782**
DOUG YODER **BED & BREAKFAST**

This delightful B&B is as warm and inviting as a Norman Rockwell painting. All guests are treated to a full country breakfast on the wrap around enclosed porch which overlooks the Bay. Conveniently located to shops, restaurants, tennis courts, and beaches. Open year around. 4 rooms.

Daily $95-$195

TROUT CREEK CONDOMINIUM RESORT **(800) 748-0245 • (616) 526-2148**
CONDOS

Family resort with beautifully furnished units (accommodate 2-12) with full kitchens and fireplaces. 2 outdoor pools, spas, fitness center, indoor pool, tennis courts, trout ponds, nature trails. Nearby skiing with on-site cross-country trails and sleigh rides during winter. Nearby golf, beaches, on-site children's programs during summer. No pets.

Weekly $780-$1,365 Daily $70-$110

Editor's Note: Contemporary and comfortable setting with plenty to do for couples or families.

LITTLE TRAVERSE BAY

HOLIDAY ACCOMMODATIONS **(800) 968-4353 • (616) 348-2765**
CHRIS HOWSE **CONDOS/CHALETS/COTTAGES**

A variety of cottages, chalets and condos are offers throughout the Little Traverse Bay area. From 1 bedroom log styled chalets to 4 bedroom homes and condos. Prices to fit all budgets.

Weekly $625-$1,395 (June-Aug.); $285-$725 (Off-season)

ODEN

WINDJAMMER MARINA & CRAFT VILLAGE **(616) 347-6103**

HOUSEBOATS

Located on Crooked Lake, the Windjammer Marina offers an unusual vacation lodging allowing you to cruise the water ways of scenic Northern Michigan. The 40 ft. Royal Capri sleeps 8 and includes head with hot water and shower, refrigerator with freezer, gas stove/oven, dishes and utensils. The 28 ft. Riviera Cruiser sleeps 4 and has 3-burner gas stove, ice box, porta potty, hand pump water system, dishes and utensils. Deposit required. Rates do not include gas. No linens. Visa/MasterCard accepted.

Weekly $1500 (50 ft.); $750 (28 ft.)
3 Day Weekend or 4 Day Weekday Pkgs: $500-$900

PETOSKEY (WALLOON LAKE)

BEAR RIVER VALLEY BED & BREAKFAST **(616) 348-2046**
RUSS & SANDRA BARKMAN **BED & BREAKFAST**

A north woods retreat in the heart of northern lower Michigan. Comfort and luxury in a spectacular, sylvan setting. Close to lakes, beaches, shops, galleries, gourmet restaurants, ski hills, and trails. Three rooms share 2 baths. Authentic Finnish sauna, healthy Gourmet Continental Breakfast. No smoking. No pets.

Daily $65-$75

BENSON HOUSE BED & BREAKFAST **(616) 347-1338**
RUTH BELLISSIMO & DIANE GILLETTE **BED & BREAKFAST**

1878 Victorian, formerly the Ozark Hotel. Located 3 blocks from Petoskey's famed Gaslight Shopping District. Large rooms, private baths; 80' veranda overlooks Little Traverse Bay. Full breakfast — wine and snacks in afternoon. Close to golf, beaches, boating, downhill and x-country skiing. No pets/smoking.

Daily $95-$135

BARBARA MOYERS **(810) 668-8507 (W) • (616) 347-4043 (S)**

COTTAGE

Spacious, multi-level cottage on Walloon Lake. 4 bedrooms, 2 full baths, 2 kitchens, plus extra sleeping area (can sleep 10). Fully furnished, wood burning cast iron fireplace, electric heat. Bring your own linens. Features lounge deck and fire pit. Aluminum boat. Swimming deck. Prefer 2 weeks rental but will except 1 week. No pets/smoking please.

Weekly $1,400 (May-Aug.); $600 (winter)

WILDWOOD ON WALLOON **(800) 632-8903 • (616) 582-9616**
MAIN OFFICE - RESERVATIONS **CONDOS**

Lovely townhouse community near the borders of Walloon Lake. Enjoy 3 professionally designed holes of golf and two carefully sited tennis courts. Units vary in interior design but maintain a contemporary theme. Units sleep from 6-12 and features up to five bedrooms with 2 baths and fully equipped kitchens. Amenities frequently include fireplace, TV/VCR. No pets.

Weekly (summer) $1, 125-$1,425; 2 Night Pkgs. (spring-fall-winter) $350- $600

Editor's Note: Located on well groomed grounds surrounded by trees, the units we visited varied in decor but maintained a very comfortable, contemporary theme.

WILDWOOD ON WALLOON - RENTERGHEM UNIT **(616) 754-8380**
JOANNE/LEE RENTERGHEM **PRIVATE CONDO UNIT**

2 bedroom condo overlooking golf area. Features fully equipped kitchen, fireplace, TV/VCR. Access to Wildwood's tennis, volleyball courts, beach and dock located on Walloon Lake at Wildwood Harbor, near Walloon Village. No pets.

Call for Rates

TRAVERSE CITY & SURROUNDING AREAS

COVERS:

ACME • ARBUTUS LAKE • BELLAIRE • BENZONIA • CEDAR • CENTRAL LAKE • CLAM LAKE • EAST BAY • ELK LAKE • GLEN ARBOR • GRAND TRAVERSE BAY • INTERLOCHEN • LAKE ANN • LAKE LEELANAU • LAKE SKEGEMOG • LELAND • LONG LAKE • NORTHPORT • PLATTE LAKE • SILVER LAKE • SPIDER LAKE SUTTONS BAY • THOMPSONVILLE • TORCH LAKE • WEST BAY

From beautiful sunsets and lazy days on a sandy beach to the rush of downhill skiing—**Traverse City** and the surrounding areas have a variety of fun and excitement in a setting of blue waters, rolling hills, and natural beauty. Dining, shopping, entertainment, and even gambling will fill your days and nights.

Just a few of the many excellent restaurants include: *Hattie's Grill* or *Boone's Prime Time Pub* (Sutton's Bay) , *The Trillium*, *Papparazzi* or *Orchard Room* (Grand Traverse Resort), *Boone's Long Lake Inn*, , *Sweitzer's by the Bay* (Traverse City), or *Scott's Harbor Grill* (M-22 on Sleeping Bear Bay beach), or *LeBea*r (M-22 in Glen Arbor). *Windows* (on M-22, N. of Traverse City), though pricey, has developed a reputation for preparing some of the area's finest cuisine. We also understand that *Spencer Creek Fine Dining* in the **Torch Lake/Alden** area, though also rather pricey, prepares creative and diverse fare with a very distinctive Italian flavor and, being on

TRAVERSE CITY & SURROUNDING AREAS

(continued...)

Torch Lake, the view is wonderful. For tasty and inexpensive "eats" give *Art's Tavern* a try (**Glen Arbor**) for breakfast, lunch or dinner. We've heard their special 1/3 pound ground chuck burger with bacon, blue cheese along with their homemade chili (not too spicy) is quite good.

For good pizzas and burgers in a country-styled family restaurant, try *Pegos Restaurant* in the **Spider Lake** area. For a fun 50's deco atmosphere and to re-discover the taste of good old-fashioned hamburgers, *Don's Drive-In* is definitely a good choice.

Take a ride on the Malabar, a two-masted schooner, or tour the Bay in a hot air balloon. Be sure to visit the Big Red Barn Music House north of Traverse. Your trip to this area would not be complete unless you visit the many wineries and sample some of Michigan's finest made wines.

ACME

GRAND TRAVERSE RESORT **(800) 748-0303 • (616) 938-2100**

CONDOS

Luxury condos — some w/wet bars, whirlpool baths, and fireplaces. Grand Traverse offers casual to fine dining in a variety of restaurants and lounges. Also featured are shopping galleries, indoor-outdoor tennis, weight room, indoor-outdoor pools, and aerobic studio. Children's activities center. Well groomed x-country ski trails and 36 holes of championship golf including *The Bear*.

Call for Rates

Editor's Note: Premier resort. Excellent accommodations with abundant amenities.

ARBUTUS LAKE

GEORGE CZANSTKE **(810) 373-0005 • (616) 947-0039**

VACATION HOME

Situated on Arbutus Lake with 200 ft. of private sandy beach, this 5 room, 2 bedroom and 1 bath, log cottage is furnished w/fireplace and a fully equipped kitchen. It also offers dock, pontoon boat and raft. Sleeps 5. No pets.

Weekly $900

Mac's Landing Resort (616) 947-6895

Cottages

14 cottages (1-3 bedrooms, sleeps 2-8) on 700 ft. of beautiful lakefront property offers a scenic setting and sandy beach. Features docks, great swimming, raft, boats and motors, campfire pits, playground, volleyball, and horseshoes. Bring linens. Open June-Sept. Pets allowed.

Weekly $275-$620

Pineview Resort (616) 947-6792

Cottages/Apts.

12 cottages and apartments on the lake (some fireplaces). Fire pit on beach, lounge deck and dock on lake. Enjoy volleyball, shuffleboard, horseshoes, and playground area. Boats, motors, pedal boats, and pontoons available for rental. 2-3 bedrooms (sleeps 5-8).

Weekly $470-$560

Shadycrest Resort (616) 947-9855

Cottages

These 9 cottages, 1-2 bedrooms (sleep 4-8). Includes use of boat. Provide your own linens and towels. All sports lake and sandy beach. Boats included, motors available for rent. Open April-Nov. Pets allowed.

Weekly $325-$525 (Based on 2 adults w/children. Reduced rates Sept.-May)

BELLAIRE

Grand Victorian B&B Inn (800) 336-3860

Jill & George Watson **Bed & Breakfast**

1895 Victorian mansion built by lumber barons. On National Register. Inn features antiques, 3 fireplaces, etched glass and wicker-filled porch/balconies overlooking park. Elegant breakfast. Close to golf and skiing. 4 rooms w/ private baths. No smoking.

Daily $95-$135

Shanty Creek/Schuss Mountain Club Resort (800) 678-4111

Rooms/Chalets/Condos

Four season resort on the lake. 3 championship golf courses including *The Legend* by Arnold Palmer. 29 downhill ski slopes, 31 km of x-country trails, ski school. Other amenities include tennis, mountain biking, health club, hiking, beach club and indoor/outdoor pools. Fine dining, live entertainment. 600 rooms, condos and chalets some with full to partial kitchens, fireplaces, Jacuzzis. Great swimming. No pets.

Golf Plus Packages (Beginning at) $760 - 3days/2 nights

Call for Ski Season Rate Packages.

Richard & Jo-Ann Socha **(313) 663-3766**

Chalet

This 3 bedroom, 2 bath, year around chalet sleeps 8 and offers a secluded setting. Completely furnished, TV/VCR, fireplace (wood provided), dishes, linen and maid service. It sits at the top of Schuss Mt. and offers ski-in, ski-out. A mecca for golfers, swimming pools in village. No pets/smoking.

Weekly $650 Daily $200

Clare Taylor **(517) 394-4162**

Condominium & Chalet

Two privately owned properties are available for daily or weekly rental:

Condo: New 2 bedroom/1 bath condo is located on the 1st fairway of Schuss Mountain's golf course. Features deck, telephone, A/C, CATV, fireplace fully equipped kitchen w/microwave and dishwasher. Linens provided. Use of hot tub, pool and sauna at Schuss Lodge. Available year around. No pets.

Weekly $350-$500 Daily $100-$180

Chalet: Located on a secluded lot in the wooded, rolling hills area of Schuss Mountain has 3 bedrooms/2 baths. Lodging features a fully equipped kitchen w/microwave, ski storage area, electric heat, CATV w/remote control, and telephone. Linens provided. Use of hot tub, pool and sauna at Schuss Lodge. Available year around.

Weekly $350-$500 Daily $100-$180

BENZONIA

Hanmer's Riverside Resort (800) 252-4286 Reserv. • (616) 882-7783

John & Barbara Hanmer **Cottages**

On the Betsie River, located near the Sleeping Bear Dunes National Lakeshore. 2 bedroom housekeeping units completely furnished with equipped kitchens, A/C, CATV, phone. Decks overlook the river. Enjoy the pool and Jacuzzi. Open year around. Summer fun, winter skiing and snowmobiling, fall/spring steelhead/ salmon fishing. No pets.

Weekly $315-$490 Daily $55-$85

CEDAR

Sugar Loaf Resort **Res: (800) 968-0576**

Chalet/Townhouse

Amenities include golfing, Lake Michigan beach, 3 swimming pools, tennis, casino, biking and hiking. New Palmer golf course. Nursery, kids camp, new water slide, miniature golf.

Daily $89-$109
Special Golf Pkgs. $72-$118 (dbl. occ.- includes golf/cart/breakfast/dinner)

CENTRAL LAKE

BOB & BETTY KACZMAREK **(810) 363-8814 • FAX (810) 363-7777**
COTTAGES

These 2 cottages with 2 bedrooms sleeps 6. Fully furnished. Kitchens with refrigerators, stoves, microwaves, breadmakers cooking and eating utensils, TV's and VCR's, gas grills, fire pit, picnic table and patio furniture. Includes use of pontoon and fishing boat. Properties include:

River's Edge—Attractive, modern cottage on Hanley Lake. Features bath/tub shower, screened porch. Short walk to town, beach, park.

Weekly $600 Weekend $275

Editor's Note: Quiet setting with a relaxing view of the river from the newly tiled screened porch make River's Edge a favorite of ours.

Lakeside— Attractive, modern cottage on Hanley Lake. Features private bath with shower stall and screened porch. Short distance to town, beach and park.

Weekly $600 Weekend $275

CLAM LAKE

NORTHAIRE RESORT **(616) 347-1250**
MIKE & HELEN LAMBERT **COTTAGES**

6 furnished cottages (2-3 bedrooms) on Clam Lake. Great fishing! Docks, boats, paddle boat, grills and picnic tables. Cable-ready for your TV. Serene setting, sandy lake bottom, near nature preserve and marina. Open April 1-Nov. 1. Pets allowed.

Weekly (in-season) $395-$595 Daily (off-season) $50-$60

Editor's Note: Traditional resort with 1950's "look". Located in a quiet, lakeside setting. Some newly completed renovations are very nice. See our review.

EAST BAY

BAYSIDE RESORT **(616) 943-4128**
TOM BRADY **COTTAGES & HOME**

Three private cottages (2 or 4 bedroom) each with 100 ft. lake frontage. Well decorated, fully furnished and equipped. Includes microwaves, dishwashers, washers/dryers, cable TV, grill, dock and use of fishing boat. Larger home also features whirlpool with view of bay from all rooms. Linens provided. No pets.

Weekly $600-$1,650 (July -Aug.) $300-$850 (June/Sept./Oct.)

THE BEACH CONDOMINIUMS **(616) 938-2228**
CONDOS

These 30 luxury condos on Grand Traverse Bay feature private sun decks (sleeps 4), whirlpool baths, complete kitchen and 27" stereo CATV. Beautiful sandy beach, outdoor heated pool and hot tub, and daily housekeeping. Adjacent boat launch and close to championship golf. AAA discount, daily rentals, getaway and ski packages.

Call for Rates

NORTH SHORE INN **(800) 968-2365 • (616) 938-2365**
CONDOS

Set on 200 ft. of private sandy beach on East Bay, these 26 luxury condos offer 1 and 2 bedrooms. Spectacular views of bay from front decks and balconies. Outdoor pool, sun deck. Full-size kitchens, dishwashers, microwaves, queen-size beds, remote TV w/HBO, VCR. Special fall, winter and spring weekend packages. Open year around.

Daily $179-$199 (prime season); $129-$139 (off-season)

Editor's Note: Well maintained, attractively decorated. All rooms provide waterfront views. Very nice beach area.

STONEWALL INN **(616) 223-7800**
COTTAGE

Privately owned log cottage built in 1986 situated on Old Mission Harbor. Has fully equipped kitchen, fireplace, 2 full baths, private beach, washer/dryer, porch overlooking the water. No pets.

Weekly $700 (May-Nov. 1st) Daily $100

TRAVERSE BAY INN **(616) 938-2646**
CONDOS

All units are furnished with equipped kitchens including microwaves. A/C, CATV. Some rooms with whirlpool tubs and fireplace. Pool, hot tub, gas grills, and complementary bicycles. Swimming beach less than 1 mile away road. No pets. Major credit cards accepted.

Weekly $175-$1,175 Daily $35-$165

Editor's Note: Clean, contemporary, well maintained units. Sizes vary significantly.

WINTERWOOD ON THE BAY **(616) 929-1009**
R. SCHERMERHORN **COTTAGE**

Recently built beach house, located on East Bay. Sleeps 4 (2 bedrooms), bath, kitchen, living/dining room, fireplace, hot tub on outside deck. Dishwasher, microwave, VCR and cable TV. Fully furnished kitchen. Linens provided. Private dock. No pets.

Weekly $725

ELK LAKE

CEDARS END ON ELK LAKE **(972) 424-2858 • (616) 322-6286**
DEAN & SHARON GINTHER **VACATION HOME**

Spacious 3 bedroom, 2 bath home on 450 ft. of private east Elk Lake frontage. Furnished, dishwasher, microwave, cookware, 2 fireplaces, dock with boat mooring. 50 acres of woodland attached. Excellent swimming, hiking, boating and fishing. No linens. No pets. Available July-October.

Weekly $1,500 (off-season $1,000)

KEWADIN LAKESHORE LODGE **(616) 264-8340**
COTTAGES/EFFICIENCIES/MOTEL

With Elk Lake frontage, this resort offers cottages, efficiencies and motel type accommodations. Four units offer full kitchens and color TV. Boats, picnic tables and gas grills included. Sandy beach, paddle boats and two docks available. Recreation room features pool table, ping pong and more. Bring linens. No pets.

Weekly $415-$550

WANDAWOOD RESORT & RETREAT CENTER **(616) 264-8122**
COTTAGES/DUPLEXES

On Elk Lake, 13 cottages with lakefront and orchard settings. Each varies in size from small 1 bedroom cottage to duplex and 5 bedroom homes. Full kitchen/bath facilities. 9 beach areas with docks plus 2 swimming rafts. Boats, canoes and paddle boards available. Area for field sports and a paperback book library for those quiet times. Open Memorial Day to mid-November.

Weekly $380-$1,165

WHISPERING PINES **(616) 264-5424**
JERRY MCKIMMY **LAKEFRONT HOME**

3 bedroom ranch, walkout lower level on the west side of Elk Lake (100 ft). Summer rental max. 10 people. Furnished and equipped with C/A, washer/dryer, microwave, dishwasher, cable TV and VCR. Linens provided. Excellent sandy beach. Bonfires allowed. Grill, volleyball, ping pong. Boat lift. No smoking/pets, please.

Weekly $1,500

WHITE BIRCH LODGE **(616) 264-8271 • (616) 264-5823**
RESORT

Year around resort on Elk Lake. Packages offer 3 meals a day plus water-skiing, wind surfing, sailing, tennis, children's programs and more. Accommodations range from simple lodge rooms to deluxe condominiums. Children 2-12 half price. Call for brochure

Weekly $465-$855 (per person)

GLEN ARBOR

Elk Rapids Beach Resort **(800) 748-0049**

Condos

Luxury condos overlooking Grand Traverse Bay, just minutes from Traverse City. Heated pool (in the summer), in room Jacuzzi and full size kitchen. No pets. Special off-season rates available.

Weekly $1,088 (dbl. occ., summer) Daily $155 (dbl. occ.)

The Homestead **(616) 334-5000**

Main Office Rentals **Condos**

1 mile of frontage on Lake Michigan, 3 miles on Crystal River, surrounded by the Sleeping Bear Dunes. Shops, golf academy, tennis, pools, restaurants, x-country and downhill skiing, conference centers, lodge rooms, suites and condos ranging from studio to 4 bedrooms. Closed late Oct.-Christmas; mid-March-May (open winter weekends). Contact the rental office for special package prices.

Weekends $145-$466 Weekly $825-$3,260

Editor's Note: Secluded location in a scenic setting... a favorite of our staff for years.

White Gull Inn **(616) 334-4486**

S. W. Thompson **Bed & Breakfast**

Older 2 story home on a lovely wooded lot in Glen Arbor. Nestled between Sleeping Bear Sand Dunes and the lake shore of Sleeping Bear Bay. Walking distance to shops, restaurants, tennis courts, hiking trails. Short drive to golf courses and Glen Lakes. 5 rooms. Major credit cards accepted.

Daily $65-$75

GRAND TRAVERSE BAY

Roger & Phyllis Browne **(517) 792-8290**

Vacation Home

Built in 1989, this luxury home features 7 bedrooms (sleeps 14), 4 full and 2 half baths, wrap around deck, 150 ft. of sandy beach on Lake Michigan. Indoor swimming pool, Jacuzzi, sauna, washer, dryer, dishwasher, 2 conventional ovens, microwave/convection, TV/VCR. No smoking/pets. Deposit $1,000.

Weekly $3,800

Traverse Beach Motel • Condo **(800) 634-6113 • (616) 946-5262**

Motel/Condos

This all season resort is located on 700 ft. of sugar sand beach on the East Arm of Grand Traverse Bay. Most units face the water and include double or queen size beds and refrigerator. Some include kitchen, microwave, whirlpool tubs, wetbar, and /or patios/balconies, CATV. Sleeps 2-6 people. No pets.

Daily $48-$198

INTERLOCHEN

BROOKSIDE COTTAGES — **(616) 276-9581**
JOE & NANCY MAREK — **COTTAGES**

Located in the Traverse City/Interlochen area, with 250 ft. lake frontage, these 13 cottages vary in size (studio - 3 bedrooms) and sleeps 6. Includes fully equipped kitchens. Motor rentals available. $200 deposit required. Open year around. No pets.

Weekly $315-$500 (Off-season rates available)

ELLIS LAKE RESORT — **(616) 276-9502**
GEORGE & TERESA HILL — **LOG CABINS**

Log cabins and rooms on secluded lake surrounded by forest. Retreat-like atmosphere. Kitchen facilities, some with Franklin firestoves. Includes private outdoor hot tub, boats, canoes, more. Linens included. Open year around. X-C skiing in winter. Resort featured in *Midwest Living Magazine.* Pets allowed.

Weekly $435-$550 Daily $54-$99

JUDY'S PLACE — **(616) 275-6561 • (810) 626-2464**
LOG HOME

Log ranch-style home, built in 1992 on 1.12 wooded acres with sandy beach area on small, clean spring-fed lake. 5 miles to Interlochen, 20 miles SW of Traverse City. 4 bedrooms, 3 full baths, can sleep 10. Full kitchen, stacked, full-size washer/dryer. Private outdoor hot tub. Well behaved pets O.K. with extra refundable deposit. Prefer non-smokers. Photos available. Open year around. Everything provided except food, clothing and guaranteed good weather!

Weekly $1,200 Daily $200

Editor's Note: Wonderful location and home. Highly recommended. See our review.

MARY MUELLER & MARK PAYNE **(616) 276-6756**
CABIN

Cozy cabin on 1-1/2 wooded acres with 125' Green Lake frontage. One bedroom with additional set of bunk beds. Sleeps 2-4. Fully equipped kitchen with microwave. Provide your own linens/towels. Large wood deck. Private dock and 10' rowboat included. Open May-Sept. Non-smoking. Pets allowed.

Weekly $295

LAKE ANN

BIRCH GLEN RESORT **(616) 275-7340**
VIRGINIA CULLEN **CABINS**

Open year around. Cabins with screened porch/fishing boat. Sandy beach, fire pit, kids' playhouse. Motor rentals available, bait sold. Two bedroom cabins sleep 4. Three bedroom cabins sleep 8. Family-oriented resort on quiet, dead-end street.

Weekly $550-$650 (Nightly and off-season rates available)

LAKE LEELANAU

GREAT ESCAPE RESORT **(810) 375-0425**
MARK & RENEE SMITH **VACATION HOME**

Three bedroom home (sleeps 8), 2 full baths — great sunsets. Redwood deck overlooks trees/lawn and leads to beach. Home features fireplace, attached garage, microwave, CATV, stereo, grill, and more! 10 min. from Traverse City & 15 min. from Sugar Loaf. Open year around. No pets.

Weekly $1,200 (Off-season $650)

JOLLI LODGE **(616) 256-9291**
Cottages/Apts./Lodge

This homey retreat offers a great view of Lake Michigan from their 5 cottages, 11 apartments and 6 lodge rooms. Apartments (1-3 bedrooms) are newer. Cottages and lodge simply furnished but clean. Several steps down leads to pebbled beach. Tennis, rowboat, kayaking, volleyball and shuffleboard. Open May-Oct.

Weekly $600-$950

MIMI'S RETREAT **(616) 941-1663 • (616) 256-7602**
MARLENE VANVOORST **VACATION HOME**

Lakefront home on east shore, 2 bedrooms plus loft (can sleep 6). Screened porch. Furnished except linens. Includes use of rowboat. Safe swimming. No pets. No maid service available - guests are requested to leave the cottage in clean condition for the next renters.

Weekly $525 (and up)

West Wind Resort **(616) 946-9457**

Cottages

10 cottages feature 2 to 4 bedrooms (sleeps 4-10) some with fireplaces. Facilities have children's playground, hot tub. Paddle boards, kayaks and canoe rentals. Protected harbor. Open year around. No pets.

Weekly $725-$1,675 (Call for special off-season rates)

LAKE SKEGEMOG

John King **(810) 349-4716**

Home

Lakefront home on 200 ft. of sandy beach near Traverse City. 4 bedrooms, 2 baths, fully furnished with fireplace. Spacious deck overlooking Lake Skegemog which is part of Elk-Torch chain of 5 lakes. Rowboat. Very clean. One family limit. No smoking/pets.

Weekly $1,200 (June-Aug); $700 (Off-season)

LELAND

Manitou Manor **(616) 256-7712**

Bed & Breakfast

Beautifully restored 1900 farmhouse surrounded by cherry orchards and woods. Queen size beds, private baths, on the main floor in the wing of the home. Huge parlor with fieldstone fireplace and TV. Breakfast features **Leelanau County** specialties. Near sand dunes, bike trails, beaches, golf, x-country and downhill skiing. Non-smoking. No pets. Open all years. 4 rooms.

Daily $75-$110

LONG LAKE

Ron Jones or Fred Jones **(616) 946-5119 • (810) 286-1582**

Cottage

Two bedroom log cottage w/knotty pine interior features fireplace (wood provided), color TV and full kitchen with microwave. Private beach, dock, 12' aluminum boat, gas BBQ grill, picnic table, lawn furniture. Bring linens. Located 6 miles from Traverse City. Available year around. Pets allowed.

Weekly $575

Linden Lea on Long Lake **(616) 943-9182**
Bed & Breakfast

"Enchanting spot on a crystal-clear lake...reminiscent of on Golden Pond," Fodor's B&B Guide. Lakeside bedrooms with window seats, antiques and treasures. Relax by the fire, listen for the loons. Peaceful sandy beach with row boat, paddle boat. Private baths. Full breakfast. Central A/C. 2 rooms.

Daily $80-$95

Editor's Note: Peaceful, picturesque surroundings and charming hosts make Linden Lea an excellent choice. See our review.

NORTHPORT

North Shore Inn **(616) 386-7111**
Susan Hammersley **Bed & Breakfast**

A great sunrise over Grand Traverse Bay from luxurious waterfront rooms in this elegant, spacious home built in 1946 in the colonial tradition. Private baths, fireplaces, sandy beach, porches and decks. Join your hosts for afternoon appetizers and a gourmet breakfast. Excellent golf nearby. Closed November to May. 4 rooms.

Daily $145 (Ea. additional guest $25); $135 (Spring & Fall)

PLATTE LAKE

Platte Lake Resort I **(616) 325-6723**
Cottages

On beautiful Big Platte Lake. These 1-3 bedroom cottages are completely furnished and carpeted with kitchenettes. All include linens, dishes, cable TV, picnic tables and grills. Fishermen and hunters welcome. Open April-November. Daily and weekly rentals. No pets.

Daily $45 and up (based on number of people)

Riverside **(616) 325-2121**
Cottage

All season fun! Fish, swim, canoe, hike, snowmobile, ski, sightsee...be "Up North". Newer home, built in 1990, located on the Platte River in Honor, MI, 30 miles from Traverse City; 10 minutes from Lake Michigan. 4 bedrooms, 2 baths, fully equipped kitchen, CATV. No pets. Available year around.

Weekly $300 Daily $65

SILVER LAKE

TOM BRADY **(616) 943-4128**

COTTAGES

Two private cottages, each with 2 bedrooms, with 100 ft. of lake frontage. All lodgings well decorated, fully furnished and equipped with microwave, dishwasher, CATV and deck. Dock and use of fishing boat included. Newer cottage features 2 baths and fireplace. Linens provided. No pets.

Weekly $600-$700 (July/Aug.); $300-$350 (June/Sept./Oct.)

GERALD NIEZGODA **(616) 943-9630**

COTTAGE

Furnished vacation cottage on Silver Lake offers 80 ft. private frontage, 2 bedrooms (sleeps 4-6), sandy beach, swimming, fishing, sailing, skiing, outstanding view. Only 2 miles from new mall and 4 miles to Traverse City. Includes CATV, VCR, microwave, boat and dock. Bring towels. Open all year. No pets/smoking.

Weekly $625 (Based on occupancy of 4)

RAYMOND PADDOCK & JILL HINDS **(616) 943-8506**

COTTAGE

Fully furnished 3 bedroom cottage accommodates 8 people and features full kitchen, fireplace, stereo, TV, grill, and 2 decks. Also features dock, swim raft, canoe and rowboat. Open June-Sept. Pets allowed.

Weekly $500

SPIDER LAKE

BEACH HOUSE @ SPIDER LAKE **(616) 946-5219**

ROLF & KATHY SCHLIESS **COTTAGE**

Lots of fun & sun! This 2 bedroom, 1 bath home also includes a bunk house, large family room with a huge brick fireplace, full kitchen with microwave, sandy beach and dock. Pontoon boat included. Available year around. No pets.

Weekly (summer) $925 (6-8 people)

HAROLD'S RESORT **(616) 946-5219**

ROLF & KATHY SCHLIESS **COTTAGES**

7 log-style cabins sit on a private peninsula overlooking Spider Lake and offer a terrific sandy beach. Open year around. Weekends, romance, bed & breakfast package rates available. Each feature wonderful views, kitchens, carpet. No pets.

Weekly (summer) $320 (2 people); $600-$625 (6 people)

L' Da Ru Lakeside Resort, Inc. (616) 946-8999
Danny & Jill Rye Cottages

With 455' lake frontage, this lodge, built in 1923, was once the hideout for Al Capone. Come see how the notorious lived. The 17 cottages, added in the mid-1950's, have all been updated. Each is complete with eating and cooking utensils, coffee maker and toaster + 20" CATV's. Linens and bedding are provided. Boats included — motors available. Good swimming beach! Towels are $8 per person for a week. Open year around. No pets.

Weekly $445-$800 (June-Aug.); $280-$675 (off-season)

Editor's Note: Very nice beach, private locations and nicely maintained, traditional cottages make L'Da'Ru a good choice. See our review.

Jack & Rosemary Miller (616) 947-6352
Cottage

Attractive lakefront log cottage on Spider Lake. Offers knotty pine interior, 2 bedrooms (w/linens), fireplace, electric heat, TV and complete kitchen including microwave. This quiet, quaint hide-away is furnished with antiques, oak dining set, china cabinet, brass bed, and marble top dresser. 13 miles from Traverse City. No pets.

Weekly $365 (May-Oct.)

Moonlight Bay Resort (800) 253-2853 • (616) 946-5967
Roger & Nancy Hendrickson Cottages

Beautiful wooded setting surrounds our private 8 cottage resort with direct frontage on Spider Lake. 1-3 bedroom cottages are furnished with fully equipped kitchens. Rowboats, canoes, pedal boat included. Motor and pontoon boat rental available. Open year around. No pets. Call for brochure.

	1 Bedroom	2 Bedroom	3 Bedroom
Weekly (Summer) *	$430-$570	$620-$655	$810

* Off-season rates lower

Red Ranch (616) 946-3909
Harold Myers Cottage

3 bedrooms, ranch-style cottage with kitchen, dining area, living room with fireplace, enclosed porch facing the lake, 2 car attached garage. Located in a quiet, private area. Includes bedding, towels, microwave, washer, dryer, CATV, rowboat and dock. Good fishing/swimming, x-county skiing/snowmobile trails nearby. $150 non-refundable deposit after May 1st. Pets allowed.

Weekly $575 (Seasonal rates) Daily $75 (2 day min.)

WILKINS LANDING (616) 946-5219
ROLF & KATHY SCHLIESS COTTAGE

Quiet, private, secluded, this private residence enjoys 225 ft. of beautiful Spider Lake frontage with dock, paddle boat and pontoon boat. Fully furnished (except linens) with fieldstone fireplace, equipped kitchen and more! Available year around. 4 bedrooms, 2 baths, sleeps 10.

Weekly (summer) $1,100 (10 people)

WINDJAMMER RESORT (616) 946-8466
COTTAGES

Clean, comfortable, rustic cottages are completely furnished for housekeeping. These 7 cottages have 1-3 bedrooms, bathroom with shower, kitchen, living room and outside deck. Kitchen fully equipped. All newly carpeted and painted. Pillows and blankets are provided (bring your own linens and towels). Sandy beach, 160 ft. frontage. Boats/canoe available. No pets.

Weekly $410-$545

SUTTONS BAY

THE COUNTRY HOUSE (616) 271-4478 • (616) 941-1010
VACATION HOME

Fully furnished house in Suttons Bay offers A/C and 2 bedrooms (sleeps up to 4). It is centrally located to Lake Michigan and Lake Leelanau.

Weekly $550 (June-Aug.); $375 (off-season)

OPEN WINDOWS BED AND BREAKFAST (616) 271-4300 • (800) 520-3722
DON & NORMA BLUMENSCHINE BED & BREAKFAST

A charming, century-old home with lovely gardens, decks and old-fashioned front porch for relaxing. This warm, inviting home is decorated with your comfort in mind. Enjoy our hearty homemade breakfast and our friendly atmosphere. The village with its beaches, shops and restaurants is just a short walk away. 3 rooms (private/shared baths).

Daily $90-$105

THOMPSONVILLE

BETSIE VUE (888) 834-0380 • (616) 834-0380
COTTAGE

Year around cottage on Betsie River, 1-1/2 miles from Crystal Mountain. 2 bedrooms (sleeps 9), 2 baths. Features new furnishings, TV, VCR, CD player. Fully equipped kitchen. Linens provided. Large deck overlooking river. Enjoy skiing, biking, hiking, shopping, canoeing, golf, snowmobiling. No pets.

Weekly $600 Daily $100 (2 night min.)

Crystal Mountain Resort **(800) 968-7686 • (616) 378-200**
Main Office Rentals **Condos/Resort Homes**

Deluxe condos/resort home. Enjoy in-room Jacuzzi, full service dining room, live entertainment, indoor and outdoor pools, fitness center, 27-hole golf course and tennis courts. Ski 25 downhill ski slopes and 30 kms. x-country ski trails, night skiing, rentals, lessons. Summer/winter children's programs. 28 miles from Traverse City. No pets.

Daily from $65 (low season - assumes 2 people)

TORCH LAKE

Jane Blizman **(810) 644-7288 • (616) 264-5228**
Cottages

2 cottages offered, on 800 ft. of Torch Lake amid 25 acres of woods and fields. Features antique furnishings and snooker table. Each cottage has fireplace, color TV, stereo, dishwasher, microwave, washer/dryer, all linens and cookware. Also includes dock w/lift, picnic table, grill and swim raft. No pets.

Weekly* $1,200 (2 bedroom); $1,500 (5 bedroom) * Based on up to 4 people

Rich & Jane Carlson **(614) 761-3533**
Vacation Home

Spacious, well-decorated, 3 bedroom, 2 bath home on 1 acre of beautifully landscaped land on 100' of Torch Lake Frontage. Set high and back from the water, it is very clean and well maintained. The living/dining area provides spectacular views of Torch Lake. Kitchen fully equipped including dishwasher and microwave. Linens provided (including bath). Bright, airy sunroom leads to a large deck with patio furniture and gas grill. A private dock is also provided. Additional features include fireplace, 3 CATV's w/remote control, VCR, washer, dryer, ceiling fans and garage. Off-season rates for golf and ski enthusiasts may vary.

Weekly $900 (June/Sept.); $1,400 (July/Aug.)

Editor's Note: Spacious and well landscaped lot — a real home-away-from home. Sloping grounds take you to a pebbled beach and a great view of Torch Lake.

TORCHLIGHT RESORT **(616) 544-8263**
ROBERT & GLENDA KNOTT **COTTAGES**

Six cottages w/150 ft. frontage on Torch Lake (part of the Chain of Lakes). Features sandy beach, playground, excellent boat harbor, beautiful sunsets. Located between Traverse City and Charlevoix. Near excellent golf courses and fine restaurants. Open May thru October. No pets.

Weekly $440-$600 (Off-season rates available)

Editor's Note: Friendly owners, clean, traditional cottages in a lovely setting make this one a nice choice.

TRAVERSE CITY

BOWERS HARBOR BED & BREAKFAST **(616) 223-7869**
BED & BREAKFAST

1870 fully remodeled country farmhouse with private sandy beach is located in the Old Mission Peninsula. Open year around. Enjoy a gourmet breakfast in the dining room overlooking the Harbor. 3 rooms w/private baths.

Daily $100-$130

CHÂTEAU CHANTAL BED & BREAKFAST **(616) 223-4110**
BED & BREAKFAST

Retreat to the Old World in this *new*, fully operational vineyard, winery and B&B. Set on a beautifully landscaped, scenic hill in the Old Mission Peninsula, this grand estate features an opulent wine tasting room and 3 delightful guest rooms (includes 2 suites) with private baths. Handicap accessible. Full breakfast.

Daily $95-$125 (assumes 2 people - $25 for each additional person)

Editor's Note: Grand estate with a spectacular view of Old Mission Peninsula. You'll enjoy their "Jazz at Sunset" ($8.50 extra) program, too. See our review.

CIDER HOUSE BED & BREAKFAST **(616) 947-2833**
BED & BREAKFAST

Enjoy cider and Scottish shortbread overlooking the apple blossoms. Pick your own apples in fall. Contemporary country inn is only minutes from downtown Traverse City. Beautiful oak floors, fireplace, canopy beds. Country style breakfast. 5 rooms w/private baths.

Daily $69-$79

The Grainery — **(616) 946-8325**
Ron & Julie Kucera — **Bed & Breakfast**

Relax in this 1892 Country Gentleman's farm on 10 lovely, quiet acres. Decorated in the country Victorian tradition. A/C, coffee pot, fridge, CATV and outdoor hot tub along with 2 golf greens and a pond. Full country breakfast. 5 rooms/private baths (2 rooms feature Jacuzzi and fireplace).

Daily $75-$130 (In-season); $65-$130 (Off-season)

Jim & Connie Legato — **(616) 946-3842**
Home

Well maintained older home, 3 bedrooms, (total 5 beds/sleeps 9). Features cable CATV, VCR, phone, and fully equipped kitchen. Linens provided. Quiet in-town location 2 blocks from swimming beach on Grand Traverse Bay and 4 blocks from town. Available year around. Pets welcome.

Weekly $650 (Summer); $400 (Winter)

Ranch Rudolf — **(616) 947-9529**
Lodge/Bunkhouse

Entertainment Friday and Saturday nights. Restaurant and lounge with fireplace. Enjoy the hay rides, sleigh rides, river fishing, backpacking, horseshoes, hiking, tennis, swimming pool, badminton, volleyball and a children's playground. Visa and MC accepted.

	Bunkhouse	Lodge
Weekly	$105 (per day-assumes 6 days)	N/A
Daily	$135 (per day)	$50-$60

Tall Ship Malabar — **(616) 941-2000**
Bed & Breakfast

Unique "floating" B&B! This large traditional sailing vessel offers overnight accommodations along with a 2-1/2 hour sunset sail w/picnic dinner and a hearty breakfast! Come join the crew for a special evening on this 105 ft., two-masted topsail schooner. Reservations 1 month in advance. May-Sept.

Daily $95-$175 (children 8-12 $45)

WEST BAY

La Petite Maison Sur L'eau — **(616) 386-5462**
Theda Connell — **Vacation Home**

Intimate, charming, attractively furnished, 1 bedroom property features a large window overlooking the lawn to Grand Traverse Bay, fireplace, fully equipped kitchen. Secluded, ideal for honeymooners or small family. Safe swimming, hiking, walking. No pets.

Weekly $525 (call for lower off-season rates)

Editor's Note: Small but very well maintained. Good value. See our review.

LEREW'S COTTAGE — **(216) 826-4069**
BECKY — **HOME**

3 bedroom home (sleeps 8) on 200 ft. of private sandy beach near Old Mission Light House. It can easily be shared by 2 families. Includes dishwasher, washer/dryer. Shallow water, safe swimming. Tennis and docking nearby. No pets.

Weekly $1,200

RONALD MALLEK — **(616) 386-5041 • (810) 952-1945**
COTTAGE

This charming, 1 bedroom (sleeps 3), English country cottage features a private patio, many gardens and sandy beach. Fully furnished with fireplace and equipped kitchen. Linens provided. No pets/smoking.

Weekly $500

PRIVATE COTTAGE — **(616) 947-5948**
KEN — **COTTAGE**

One bedroom rental, large living room, private sandy beach, Grand Traverse Bay. Three blocks from downtown, 1 block to City tennis courts. Completely furnished, includes TV, microwave, canoe, rowboat. Please provide own linens. $100 deposit.

Weekly $700 (Cherry Festival Week $800)

Editor's Note: Small, private cottage with all the conveniences. Quiet setting, large windows with spectacular sunsets make this one a gem. We understand it's difficult to get reservations during prime season - so book well in advance or enjoy off-season.

STRAWBERRY HILL HOUSE — **(314) 726-5266**
CINDY CURLEY — **WATERFRONT HOME • LOG CABIN**

<u>Waterfront Home</u>: Peaceful and charming. Secluded 4 bedroom log home, south of Suttons Bay. Rustic but refined — with great views over orchards and water. Screened porch, stone fireplace, antiques, fully carpeted, 1-1/2 baths. Stairs down bluff to scenic private beach. Furnished except for linens. No pets/smoking.

Weekly $850-$1,100

<u>Log Cabin</u>: Next to Strawberry Hill House in north woods estate setting. This hilltop log cabin features sundeck and panoramic bay view. Enclosed porch, twin beds - suitable for 2 and possibly 1 child. Great beach. Furnished except for linens. Not far to restaurants, theaters, boutiques in Sutton's Bay and Traverse City. No pets/smoking.

Weekly $525

THE VICTORIANA 1898 **(616) 929-1009**
BED & BREAKFAST

Visitors to this Victorian B&B are greeted with exquisitely crafted tiled fireplaces, oak staircase, gazebo and carriage house. Located in a quiet, historic district, the lodging is close to West Bay, downtown. "Very Special" breakfasts are served each morning. A/C. 3 rooms/private baths.

Daily $60-$80

WYNDENROK ON THE BAY **(616) 386-5462**
THEDA CONNELL **VACATION HOME**

3 bedroom/1 bath, 1920's nostalgia summer home, on quiet, private, and wooded lot w/166 ft. bay frontage. Beautiful view from its 3 screened porches. French doors lead to outside balcony which overlooks Grand Traverse Bay. Comfortably furnished w/piano. A massive stone fireplace adds to the ambiance of the home. No pets/smoking.

Weekly $975 (Call for Lower Rates May/June/Sept./Oct.)

Editor's Note: Well maintained, invitingly decorated with a true 1920's ambiance ... which is particularly appealing for those who enjoy nostalgia. See our review.

CADILLAC & ONEKAMA

The **Cadillac** area is an excellent stop for fishing and water sports enthusiasts with its two lakes (Cadillac and Mitchell) within its city limits, and many other lakes not far away. Wild and tame game are abundant at Johnny's Wild Game and Fish Park which also stocks its waters with plenty of trout. In February, come and enjoy the North American Snowmobile Festival.

On the shores of of Portage Lake, with access to Lake Michigan, **Onekama** is a summer resort community with a charter-boat fleet, marina, white sandy beaches and lovely parks.

CADILLAC

AMERICAN INN BED & BREAKFAST **(616) 779-9000**
BED & BREAKFAST

Built in 1896, this home features stained glass, oak carvings, antiques. Guest rooms include queen/king beds, CATV, A/C. Sauna and hot tub available. Master suite offers private spa, spiral staircase to walkout deck. Hearty, continental breakfast. Corporate rates. 5 rooms with private baths.

Daily $65-$150

ONEKAMA

LAKE MICHIGAN CHALET HIDEAWAY **(312) 943-7565**
DONNA **CHALET**

An elegant, spacious 3 bedroom/3 bath, fully furnished home on Lake Michigan. This 3,500 sq. ft. home features fireplaces, a fully equipped kitchen with dishwasher and microwave, living room/dining room, CATV, VCR, CD stereo and sauna. Lake and sunset viewing deck in addition to a large attached deck with BBQ pit. Private setting. Weekly maid service and linens included. Winterized. No pets. Weekly, weekend and monthly rentals.

Weekly $1,300-$1,600 Monthly $4,000

REGION 6

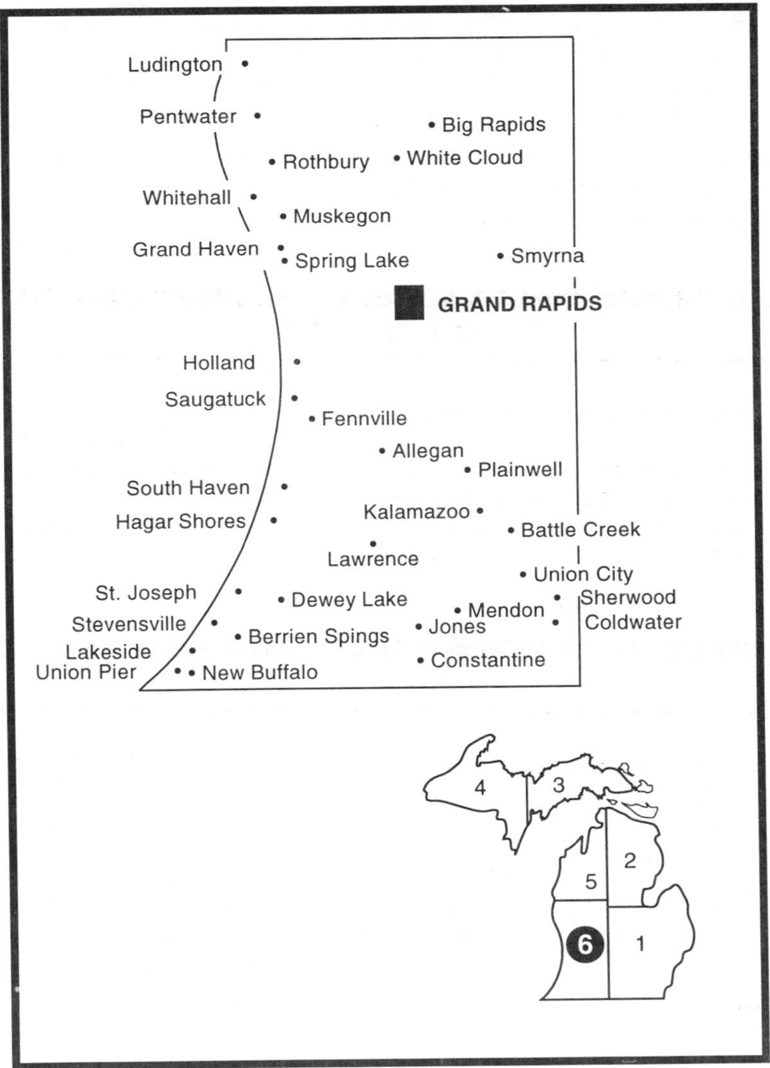

Ludington
Pentwater
Big Rapids
Rothbury
White Cloud
Whitehall
Muskegon
Grand Haven
Spring Lake
Smyrna
GRAND RAPIDS
Holland
Saugatuck
Fennville
Allegan
Plainwell
South Haven
Hagar Shores
Kalamazoo
Battle Creek
Lawrence
Union City
St. Joseph
Dewey Lake
Sherwood
Mendon
Stevensville
Jones
Coldwater
Berrien Spings
Lakeside
Constantine
Union Pier
New Buffalo
4
3
2
5
6
1

REGION 6

This unique region offers a variety of things to see and do. Where else would you find a city that can claim to have over 450 lakes. It also boasts over 100,000 acres of nature preserves, sand dunes, great fishing, golf, wonderful beaches, winter sports and one of the most scenic and elaborate bike trail systems in Michigan.

Sometimes referred to as the Riviera of the Midwest because of its land and climate, the area produces some of Michigan's finest premium wines. For something a little different in this orchard country, why not stop at the annual Cherry Pit Spitting Championship. You can relax watching the world's largest Music Fountain or add a new twist to fishing with Party Boat Fishing. If you feel daring, the area is also known for hang gliding.

You can spend the day with great shopping, theaters and double decker bus rides. There are plenty of festivals to enjoy, such as the famous Tulip Festival and Cereal Festival with the world's longest breakfast table.

Maybe you want to skip back in time. Try their museums or many historic districts which incorporate more than 1500 historic houses on 27 square blocks.

If you enjoy traditional vacation fun with a twist, this is the place.

LUDINGTON • GRAND RAPIDS • HOLLAND & SURROUNDING AREAS

COVERS: BIG RAPIDS • GRAND HAVEN • MUSKEGON • PENTWATER • ROTHBURY • SMYRNA • SPRING LAKE • WHITE CLOUD • WHITEHALL

Nestled between Lake Michigan and the Allegan State Forest is **Fennville.** This community is surrounded by vineyards, such as Fenn Valley Vineyards. Take a tour and sample the premium grape and natural fruit wines.

A boardwalk, stretching for 2-1/2 miles from downtown **Grand Haven** to its pier, is bordered by shops and eateries and many sandy beaches. Be sure to visit Moser's, a unique shop filled with dried-flower arrangements and country style decorations. For a grand tour, hop on board the Harbor Steamer. For a spectacular sight, see the World's Largest Musical Fountain and visit Michigan's second largest zoo which has 150 species of animals, an aquarium, herpetarium, and more.

Grand Rapids, a unique blend of old and new, the city has many activities to keep you busy! Heritage Hill contains almost 100 historical homes. You'll also want to visit the John Ball Zoological Gardens, Roger B. Chaffe Planetarium, and the Voigt House, a Victorian home built in 1895.

People from all over come to **Holland's** special May event, the Tulip Time Festival; but there is much to see here throughout the year. Dutch Village should not be missed — and don't leave without seeing the Wooden Shoe Factory or Windmill Island.

Ludington features one of the largest charter-fishing fleets on Lake Michigan and is well known for its coho and salmon population. A piece of history can be found at the White Pine Village, a 19th century pioneering town. Bike through 22 miles of nature in Michigan's first linear state park, the Hart-Montage Bicycle Trail State Park. Several notable restaurants in the area include *P.M. Steamers* for a good view of marina activities or *Gibbs Country House* to indulge in their truly sticky, sticky buns and well prepared American cuisine in a family atmosphere.

For a change of pace, enjoy the New England charm of **Pentwater**, with its cozy cafes and double-decker bus. Build a sand castle in the Silver Lake State Park which features a huge sandbox with 450 acres of dunes for off-road vehicles and 750 acres for pedestrians only.

LUDINGTON • GRAND RAPIDS • HOLLAND & SURROUNDING AREAS

(continued...)

Hungry? Try some of Pentwater's unique restaurants: *Historic Nickerson Inn* for a warm and charming atmosphere (reservations requested); the *Village Pub* for casual pizza and fish sandwiches and evening entertainment of comedy or jazz; the *Antler Bar* known for their special burrito; and *Gull Landing* serves up steak and seafood.

With plenty to do in this great lake playground, you will find the atmosphere relaxed, the people friendly, and the scenery beautiful.

BIG RAPIDS

Hillview Resort **(616) 796-5928**
Greg/Patti Beduhn **Cabins**
Seven knotty pine cabins located on Hillview Lake, have 1-3 bedrooms, space heater, shower, picnic table, firepit, and screened porches. Kitchens fully equipped, double beds have pillows and a blanket. Great fishing (blue gill, sunfish, bass, pike), 5 row boats, 2 canoes and 1 paddle boat, included with rental. Sandy beach and swimming area. Boat landing if you would like to bring your own boat.

Weekly $250-$300 Daily $30-$50

GRAND HAVEN

Boyden House Inn Bed & Breakfast **(616) 846-3538**
Corrie & Berend Snoeyer **Bed & Breakfast**
1874 Victorian Home. Its eclectic decor represents our varied interests and welcomes guests. Enjoy cozy rooms, delightful breakfasts, books, flowers, walks on beaches and boardwalks. Air conditioned rooms feature TV, some with fireplaces, balconies and whirlpool tubs. An exciting day may be concluded with whirlpool baths or a fireplace room, creating a memory worth recalling. 7 rooms/private baths.

Daily $85-$120

GRAND RAPIDS

CHICAGO POINT RESORT **(616) 795-7216 • (517) 321-4562**
MARGUERITE STRAYER **COTTAGES**
Located between Kalamazoo and Grand Rapids, on the southeast side of Gun Lake. Near Yankee Springs Recreation Area with 5,000 acres of country wilderness trails. Al Capone was said to have paid a visit here! The resort features 2-4 bedroom cottages, fully furnished and equipped (provide your own blankets, sheets and towels), private beach, fishing docks and picnic area. Rowboats, canoes, paddle boat and sailboat available. No pets.

Weekly $500-$800

BRUCE & LAUREL YOUNG **(616) 942-6568**
VACATION HOME
Lake Michigan cottage located on 100 feet of low bank sandy beach. Four bedrooms (sleeps 10), 2 baths, fireplace, fully equipped kitchen, heat, bed linens provided, deck, gas grill. Limit of 3 car parking, private association. No pets.

Weekly $800-$1,500

HOLLAND

DUTCH COLONIAL INN B&B **(616) 396-0461(FAX) • (616) 396-3664**
PAT & BOB ELENBAAS **BED & BREAKFAST**
1928 Dutch Colonial Inn features elegant decor with 1930 furnishings and heirloom antiques. All guest rooms have tiled private baths, some with whirlpool tub for 2. Honeymoon suites available for that "Special Getaway". Also close to shopping, Hope College, bike paths, x-country ski trails and beaches. Business people welcome/corporate rate available. A/C. 5 rooms.

Daily $75-$150

EDGEWOOD BEACH **(313) 692-3941**
GERALYN PLAKMEYER **COTTAGE**
Located just north of Holland, in Beach Front Association. Home has 2 bedrooms, 1 bath, fully furnished, equipped kitchen, fireplace, central heat and CATV. 150' back from Lake Michigan, stairway to long sandy beach complete with sunsets and fire pit. Provide your own linens. Available June to Sept. No pets!

Weekly $500

North Shore Inn **(616) 394-9050**
Beverly & Kurt Van Genderen **Bed & Breakfast**

An elegant historical estate overlooking Lake Macatawa. Three guest bedrooms, furnished with antiques and handmade quilts. A three course, home cooked breakfast is served on the porch or formal dining room. Guests may choose king, queen or double beds, private or shared bath.

Daily $90-$110

Editor's Note: Beautiful gardens and landscaped yard with a breathtaking view of the Lake make this elegant B&B an excellent choice. See our review.

The Old Holland Inn **(616) 396-6601**
Dave Plaggemars **Bed & Breakfast**

Nationally registered B&B features 10 ft. ceiling, brass fixtures, stained glass windows and a lovely brass-inlaid fireplace. Antiques, fresh flowers decorate each air conditioned room. Enjoy special house-blend coffee, fresh muffins, fruit and cheese plates each morning.

Daily $40-$75

The Parsonage 1908 **(616) 396-1316**
Bonnie Verwys, Hostess **Bed & Breakfast**

Near Hope College and the Convention Center. Elegant European styled lodging, AAA approved. Featured in Fodor's Guide and Detroit Free Press . 4 rooms with A/C (private or shared baths). Full breakfasts. Close to beaches, x-country skiing/bike trails, theater, fine dining, and more No pet/smoking.

Daily $90-$100 (dbl)

LUDINGTON

Bed & Breakfast at Ludington **(616) 843-9768**
Grace & Robert Schneider **Bed & Breakfast**

Hills, dales, woods, pond and trails, big breakfast, big hot tub, barn loft hideaway. Children invited. Toboggans, snowshoes provided. 3 miles out of Ludington. 3 rooms with private or shared baths.

Daily $40-$60

Doll House Historical Inn **(800) 275-4616 • (616) 843-2286**
Joe & Barbara Gerovac **Bed & Breakfast**

Gracious 1900 American Foursquare. 7 rooms including bridal suite with whirlpool tub for two. Smoke and pet free, full Heart Smart breakfast. A/C. Corporate rates, bicycles, x-country skiing. Walk to beach, town,

Doll House Historical Inn (continued...)
transportation to car ferry and airport. Surrounded by antiques, modern facilities. Murder mystery weekend packages. Closed Jan.-March.

Daily $70-$110

The Inn at Ludington **(616) 845-7055**
Diane Shields **Bed & Breakfast**
Elegant accommodations in this 106 year old Queen Anne Victorian. Lovingly decorated with family heirlooms and cherished collectibles. Also features a bridal suite, CATV, fireplaces, family suite. Breakfast here is an event — not an after thought. Walk to shops, restaurants, beach, marina. 6 rooms/private baths.

Daily $65-$85

The Lamplighter B & B **(616) 843-9792 • Res. (800) 301-9792**
Judy & Heinz Bertram **Bed & Breakfast**

Victorian Style, European Elegance and American Comfort are the hallmarks of "The Lamplighter Bed and Breakfast". Your stay in our individually decorated rooms with queen size beds, private baths, A/C, CATV and phones will be the most relaxing possible. 2 rooms feature a whirlpool for special occasions. All rooms as well as the common areas—parlor, living room and dining room—are decorated with original art and antiques. Full gourmet breakfasts are served either in our dining room or outdoors in the gazebo. Our premises are "protected" by our Cocker Spaniel "Freddie".

Daily $75-$135

Editor's Note: Charming accommodations and gracious owners. We also loved Freddie!!! See our review.

Parkview Cottages **(616) 843-4445**
Dennis & Jill **Cottages**
Nestled in a grove of shade trees only a block from the park on Lake Michigan, these cottages sleep from 2-6. Each features knotty pine interiors, private bath with ceramic tiled shower, fully equipped kitchen, gas heat, CATV (with HBO), fieldstone fireplace (firewood included). Large wood deck with grills and patio furniture. Across the street from public beach. Open year around.

Rates $68 daily (assumes 7 days or more); $78 daily (assumes 6 days or less)

SCHOENBERGER HOUSE **(616) 843-4435**
MARLENE SCHOENBERGER **COTTAGES**

This singularly beautiful neoclassical mansion, built by a lumber baron in 1903, has been home to the Schoenberger family for nearly half a century. Included in *Historic Homes of America* and *Grand Homes of the Midwest*, this elegantly furnished B&B features exquisite woodwork, magnificent chandeliers, 5 fireplaces, 2 grand pianos, a library, and 5 bedrooms each with private bath. Just minutes from the Lake Michigan beach, city marina, car ferry and the majestic dunes of Ludington State Park. Visa/MC accepted. Smoke-free.

Daily $120-$195

TWIN POINTS RESORT **(616) 843-9434**
JIM & BARB HUSTED **COTTAGES**
10 cottages (1-3 bedrooms) rest on 2 wooded bluffs overlooking lovely Hamlet Lake. Walk down to large and sandy swimming beach. Boaters can back their trailers down with ease. Moor your boat in covered docks. Motors and boats available for rent. Cottages are fully furnished and equipped. Most have knotty pine interiors. Close to Ludington State Park.

Call for Rates

WILLOW BY THE LAKE RESORT **(616) 843-2904 • RES. (800) 331-2904**
GORDON/DAVID BETCHER & MARTIN LUTZENKIRCHEN **COTTAGES**
Attractive, clean, 1-2 bedroom cottages with equipped kitchens. Guests provide linens/towels. Beautiful view of sand dunes and sunsets from east shore of Hamlin Lake. Sandy beach/play areas for children. Dockage/boat rentals available. Open May-October. No pets.

Weekly $325-$410

MUSKEGON

IDLEWILD RETREAT **(616) 842-5716**
CAROLYN MILLER **VACATION HOMES**
Beautifully decorated home on Lake Michigan with adjoining efficiency and loft (sleeps 5/efficiency 4). Both have supplied kitchens, baths, linens, TV, phone and heat. Main cottage has dishwasher, washer, dryer and fireplace. Rented together or separately. Private beach. Available May-Dec. No pets.

Call for Rates

PENTWATER

The Candlewyck House B&B **(616) 869-5967**
John & Mary Jo Neidow **Bed & Breakfast**

This 1868 home offers a unique and comfortable place for families. 5 rooms/ private baths, individually furnished with Americana and folk art from our gift shop, The Painted Pony Mercantile. Walk to shops, beaches and pier fishing. Bikes, skis and sports equipment on premise. Full country breakfast.

Daily $75-$95

Historic Nickerson Inn **(616) 869-6731**
Harry & Gretchen Shiparski **Bed & Breakfast**

Serving guests with "Special Hospitality" since 1914. On a bluff overlooking Lake Michigan. Completely renovated, all rooms have private baths and A/C. Two Jacuzzi suites with fireplaces and balconies overlooking Lake Michigan. Two blocks to beach and shopping district. Casual fine dining, cocktails. Consider romantic getaways, workshops retreats, marriage encounters. 12 rooms/private baths.

Daily $100-$185 (June-Oct.); $85-$160 (Off-season)

Pentwater Inn Bed & Breakfast **(616) 869-5909**
Bed & Breakfast

This beautiful 1869 Victorian home is located on a quiet village street just a short walk from Lake Michigan sandy beach, shops and restaurants. 5 antique-filled rooms with private baths. A large parlor with CATV. Full gourmet breakfast. Featured in The Bed & Breakfast Cookbook of Great American Inns.

Daily $75-$95

Perkins Place **(616) 869-8751**
M.A. Perkins **Cottage/Apartment**

On Lake Michigan, in a quiet residential area between Pentwater and Ludington. Clean sandy beaches are good for sunbathing and walking. Each rental unit has 2 bedrooms (limit 4), bathroom, living/dining area and fully equipped kitchen. Bring sheets and towels. Cleaning products are supplied. $100 deposit.

Weekly $450

ROTHBURY

DOUBLE JJ RESORT **(616) 894-4444**

HOTEL/CONDOS

Horseback riding, championship golf, archery, rifle range, swimming, boating and a whole lot more at this adult-exclusive ranch/resort. Rooms vary from basic sleeping rooms to luxury condos and hotel rooms. Activities too numerous to mention. Entertainment nightly. Price includes all activities, entertainment, and meals! Call for special package rates.

Weekend $209-$375 Weekly $549-$1.041

Editor's Note: Excellent horseback riding, top-rated golf course, beautiful grounds and friendly ranch hands too...Yee-haw!

SMYRNA

DOUBLE 'R' RANCH RESORT **(616) 794-0520**

CHALETS/BUNK HOUSE MOTEL

Lets go tubing on the Flat River! Great fishing too — pike & small mouth bass. Shuffleboard, volleyball, horseback riding, golf, canoeing, hay rides. Each chalet has electric stove, refrigerator and all dishes. Chalets rent by week. For overnight stays, try the rustic western atmosphere of the Bunk House Motel.

Call for Rates

SPRING LAKE

SEASCAPE BED & BREAKFAST **(616) 842-8409**

SUSAN MEYER **BED & BREAKFAST**

On a private Lake Michigan beach. Enjoy the hospitality and "country living" ambiance of this nautical lakeshore home. Full breakfast served in gathering room (with fieldstone fireplace) or on sun deck with panoramic view of Grand Haven Harbor. Stroll or x-country ski on dune land nature trails. 3 rooms.

Daily $75-$90 (Special rates Sun-Thur.)

WHITE CLOUD

THE CROW'S NEST **(616) 689-0088**

JOYCE & DICK BILLINGSLEY **BED & BREAKFAST**

Experience the warmth and charm at this renovated home on the banks of the White River. Stroll by the river's edge, pick blueberries. Enjoy a full breakfast served in the formal dining room or the glass/screen enclosed porch overlooking the river. 3 rooms with queen beds, 1 with private bath. Open year around.

Daily $45-$65

WHITEHALL

MICHILINDA BEACH RESORT (616) 893-1895
COTTAGES/LODGE ROOMS

Modified American Plan resort with weekly activities and plenty to do. Well groomed grounds on scenic location. In operation almost 60 years. Cottages and lodge rooms offer private baths and most with sitting areas (no kitchens). Many rooms with lake views. Prices include breakfast and lunch. 49 rooms available. Open May to early October. No pets.

Lodge Rooms	Daily	\$130-\$161	Weekly	\$680-\$,1025
Cottages	Daily	\$210 (and up)	Weekly	\$1,075-\$1,310

Editor's Note: Well groomed, picturesque resort with plenty to keep families and couples very busy. Rooms comfortable and clean.

WHITE SWAN INN (888) WHT SWAN (TOLL FREE) • (616) 894-5169
RON & CATHY RUSSELL BED & BREAKFAST

1880's Queen Anne home with screened porch. Spacious rooms, delightful mix of antiques, wicker and eclectic furnishings. 2 blocks from shops and restaurants. 1 block from White Lake; across from Fine Arts Summer Playhouse. Enjoy our bicycles on nearby 22-mile paved trail. Features interior design studio and gift shop. Open year around.

Daily \$67-\$77

SAUGATUCK • KALAMAZOO • UNION PIER & SURROUNDING

COVERS: ALLEGAN • BATTLE CREEK • BERRIEN SPRINGS • COLDWATER • CONSTANTINE • DEWEY LAKE • HAGAR SHORES • JONES • LAKESIDE • LAWRENCE • MENDON •PLAINWELL • ST. JOSEPH • SOUTH HAVEN • STEVENSVILLE • UNION CITY • UNION PIER/NEW BUFFALO

Battle Creek, home of the cereal pioneers W. K. Kellogg and C. W. Post, has given this city the name of "Cereal Capital of the World". It is also the site of Fort Custer National Cemetery and the International Hot-Air Balloon Championship which last for 8 days in June.

Kalamazoo — how very diverse. Whatever you wish to do, or see, is here. From Victorian homes and quaint inns, tours, classic cars and aircraft, museums, theaters, sports or historic districts. For galleries and antique shops stop at **Lakeside**.

Relax amid historic homes, bed and breakfast inns, fragrant orchards, boat cruises, dune rides, golf courses and antique shops in **Saugatuck**. Take a cruise on the Queen of Saugatuck, a 67 ft. stern wheel riverboat, or ride across the sand dunes. Take a tour of the Tabor Hill Wine Port, and taste Michigan premium wines.

SAUGATUCK • KALAMAZOO • BENTON HARBOR • UNION PIER & SURROUNDIN

(continued...)

South Haven not only prides itself as the "Blueberry Capital of the World" it is also one of our major yachting and sport fishing ports. Explore the many parks, hike over the sand dunes or, if you dare, go hang gliding in the Warren Dunes State Park just south of **St. Joseph**. In the fall, harvest festivals and color tours are popular. Ice fishing and skiing attract enthusiasts in the winter. May brings The Blossom Time Festival celebrated for over 80 years. In mid-July the Venetian Festival turns the lakefront park and boulevard into a giant midway. You don't want to miss this one!

Getting hungry yet? Try out *Jenny's* on Lakeshore Road (between New Buffalo and Union Pier). Creatively prepared food and homey atmosphere featuring Great Lakes Indian art and high-beamed ceiling with skylights make this a worthwhile stop! Also, *Schu's Grill & Bar* on Lake Boulevard (St. Joseph) prepares excellent meals — their Blackout Cake is a wonderful treat. We understand the *North Beach Inn* serve's up very memorable blueberry pancakes or waffles. For casual dining on the water, give *Three Pelican's* (South Haven) a try.

ALLEGAN

ALVA SPRIENSMA — **(616) 538-2575**

COTTAGE

Modern lakefront (110 ft. frontage) cottage on Miner Lake near Allegan (Southwestern MI). Miner Lake covers 350 acres, excellent for fishing, swimming, skiing. 2 baths, 2 bedrooms, queen sofa sleeper (sleeps 6). Paddle boat, raft included. Excellent beach. Cooking utensils, dishes provided. Bring linens. No pets. Available spring/summer.

Weekly $400 Weekend $175

BATTLE CREEK

GREENCREST MANOR — **(616) 962-8633**

TOM & KATHY VAN DAFF — **BED & BREAKFAST**

This grand French Normandy mansion situated on the highest elevation of St. Mary's Lake is constructed of sandstone, slate and copper. Formal gardens include fountains and cut stone urns. A/C. Private baths. 5 rooms. Featured in "Country Inns Magazine" as "Inn of the Month" and Top 12 Inns of North America of 1992.

Daily $75-$170

BERRIEN SPRINGS

PENNELLWOOD RESORT **(616) 473-2511**
JACK & PAT DAVIS **COTTAGES**
One price includes everything—meals, lodging, recreation and entertainment. 39 cottages have 2 and 3 bedrooms. Bring beach towels, life jackets & tennis racquets. Enjoy pontoon rides, volleyball, softball, shuffleboard, archery, tubing, wine tasting and Monte Carlo night. Reservations require deposit. No pets.

Weekly $330-$360 (per adult - children less)

COLDWATER

BATAVIA INN **(517) 278-5146**
FRED MARQUARDT **COUNTRY INN**
An 1872 Italianate country inn with original massive wood-work, high ceilings and restful charm. Near antique and outlet shopping, lakes, parks, museums and recreation. Seasonal decorations a specialty. In-ground pool. Guest pampering is the Innkeepers' goal. 5 rooms.

Daily $64-$104

CHICAGO PIKE INN **(517) 279-8744**
REBECCA SCHULTZ **BED & BREAKFAST**
Turn of the century reformed Colonial Mansion adorned with antiques from the Victorian era. Six guest rooms in main house, two with whirlpools in Carriage House, all with private baths. Formal dining room, library, and reception room feature sweeping cherry staircase and parquet floors. Full country breakfast and refreshments.

Daily $80-$165

CONSTANTINE

"OUR OLDE HOUSE" B&B INN **RES. (800) 435-5365 • (616) 435-3325**
JAN MARSHALL **BED & BREAKFAST**
Located in Historical Village near antique centers. Inn features antique fireplace mantels, European antiques, in-ground pool. Rooms offers private bath (2 with Jacuzzi) and fireplaces. Full breakfast. Near Amish Shipshewana, Indiana. Canoeing, carriage rides, fishing on St. Joseph River/lakes. 5 rooms/private bath.

Rates $80-$125

DEWEY LAKE

SHADY SHORES RESORT **(616) 424-5251**

COTTAGES

On Dewey Lake, 30 miles east of Benton Harbor. Furnished and equipped housekeeping cottages have electric ranges, refrigerators, heat, private bath, blankets and cooking/eating utensils. Includes boats, bicycles, playground, badminton, shuffleboard, croquet, and tennis. Safe swimming on sandy beach.

Weekly $325-$450

HAGAR SHORES

THE SAND CASTLES **(800) 972-0080**

COTTAGES

EDITOR'S ★ CHOICE!

10 housekeeping cottages sleep from 2 to 10. Each has a kitchenette or full kitchen w/ cooking utensils, coffee maker and toaster, ceiling fans, some separate living/dining/kitchen areas w/microwave, A/C. Bedding included (bring your own towels). Cable hook-up offering HBO. Lake Michigan beaches, restaurants nearby.

Weekly $250-$600

Editor's Note: These traditional cottages should be noted for their exceptionally well maintained interiors with some nice features including ceiling fans and air conditioning. Sizes range significantly. Beach access 1 mile. See our review.

JONES

SANCTUARY AT WILDWOOD **(616) 244-5910 • (800) 249-5910**

BED & BREAKFAST & COTTAGES

Lodge and cottages rest on more than 90 acres of woods and meadows. The Sanctuary provides security for 2 herds of whitetail deer as well as many waterfowl that visit the pond. Nature is emphasized throughout the lodge.Private decks/ balconies. Each room with private baths, fireplace, Jacuzzi and refrigerators. Ask about their special romantic, canoe or golf packages. Deluxe breakfasts served each morning. Conference room available.

Daily $139-$179 (rooms- 2 night min.); $159-$179 (cottage - 2 night min.)
Editor's Note: The rooms and location are beautiful.

KALAMAZOO

Hall House **(616) 343-2500**
Jerry & Joanne Hofferth **Bed & Breakfast**

"Experience the Difference". Premier lodging in National Historic District. Enjoy the exceptional craftsmanship, polished mahogany, gleaming marble and cozy fireplaces of this 1923 Georgian-styled city inn. Near college/university, theatre, shopping and dining. 5 rooms offer private bath, TV, telephone and A/C. Complementary afternoon refreshments. Smoke free.

Daily $89-$140

LAKESIDE

The Pebble House **(616) 469-1416**
Jean & Ed Lawrence **Bed & Breakfast**

1912 Craftsman style buildings connected by wooden walkways and pergolas. Furnished with arts and crafts style antiques. Fireplaces, rocker filled porches, wild flower gardens, tennis court. Lake Michigan beach access. Scandinavian style breakfast. Suites. Outdoor smoking only. 7 rooms/ private baths.

Daily $95-$150

LAWRENCE

Oak Cove Resort **(616) 674-8228 • (630) 983-8025**
Historic Lodge/Cottages/Homes

Nestled on 16 wooded acres overlooking beautiful Lake Cora. 7 cottages (no kitchens), 7 lodge rooms plus 4 spacious homes (includes full kitchens and living area). All linens provided. Heated pool, sandy beach, boats, fishing, hiking trails, bicycling, recreation room, FREE golf. Nearby antique shops, flea markets, wine tasting and tours. 3 hearty meals like mother used to make included in price. See our Web Site: http://www.oakcove.com

Call for Rates

Editor's Note: This traditional cottage resort offers a beautiful lake view, friendly owners, great food and plenty to do.

MENDON

MENDON COUNTRY INN **(616) 496-8132**
DICK & DOLLY BUERKLE **BED & BREAKFAST**

Overlooking the St. Joseph River, this romantic country inn has antique filled guest rooms with private baths. Free canoeing, bicycles built for two, fifteen acres of woods and water. Restaurant and Amish Tour guide. Featured in Country Living and Country Home magazines. 7 Jacuzzi suites w/fireplace. 18 rooms/private bath.

Daily $69-$159

Editor's Note: The Buerkle's will definitely make you feel at home. Charming historic inn. For those seeking contemporary styling, the Creekside Lodge rooms (in the back of the lot) make for one romantic stay.

PLAINWELL

THE 1882 JOHN CRISPE HOUSE **(616) 685-1293**
NANCY LEFEVER **BED & BREAKFAST**

Museum quality Victorian elegance, on the Kalamazoo River, featuring original gaslight fixtures, plaster medallions, and 1882 furnishings. Between Grand Rapids and Kalamazoo off U.S. 131. Close to fine dining, golf, skiing, and antique shops. Full breakfast. A/C. Visa/MC. Gift certificates. 5 rooms. No smoking/alcohol/pets. "A step back in time."

Daily $55-$110

SAUGATUCK

BAYSIDE INN **(800) 548-0077 • (616) 857-4321**
KATHY & FRANK WILSON **BED & BREAKFAST**

Once a charming boat house now a contemporary B&B. Watch the water activity during the summer or gather around the fireplace in the winter. Located on the water in downtown Saugatuck with 6 guest rooms and two efficiency apartments, all with private bath, private decks. 8 rooms.

Daily $95-$225 (May-Oct.); $60-$175 (Nov.-April)

BRIAR-CLIFFE **(616) 857-7041**
DAVID & SHIRLEY WITT **LUXURY GUEST SWITE**

Luxury suite on a scenic bluff overlooking the sandy shores of Lake Michigan. Comfortable sitting rooms with woodburning fireplace, TV/VCR. 5 acres of woods provide a relaxing view from the queen sized canopy bed. Ceramic bath with Jacuzzi for two. Small refrigerator, microwave and coffeemaker in room. Private stairway takes you to sandy beach.

Daily $125

Editor's Note: Classic stylings combined with antique-filled rooms and a very quiet setting make this a good spot for that special getaway. See our review.

GOSHORN LAKE RESORT **(800) 541-4210 • (616) 857-4808**
RIC GILLETTE **COTTAGES**

19 housekeeping cottages. Some with wood burning fireplaces, A/C. Fully equipped kitchens, picnic tables & BBQ grill. Beautiful sandy, private swimming beach, volleyball, horseshoes, basketball, fire pit area, and boat rentals. Near Saugatuck, Lake Michigan beaches and golf. Nearby hiking trails, x-country skiing. Pets allowed.

Weekly $490-$700 Daily $85-$125

HIDDEN POND BED & BREAKFAST **(616) 561-2491**
PRISCILLA & LARRY FUERST **BED & BREAKFAST**

Accommodations of quiet traditional elegance. Two bedrooms with private baths, plus five common rooms. 28 acres of private ravined grounds with wildlife and pond. Selected by Frommer B&B North America Guidebook as one of the "50 Best B&B Homes in America". 2 rooms.

Daily $64-$110

THE KINGSLEY HOUSE **(616) 561-6425**
GARY & KARI KING **BED & BREAKFAST**

Located in Fennville, only minutes from Saugatuck, this 1886 elegant Queen Anne Victorian B&B. Featured in Innsider Magazine, rated as a "Top Fifty Inn" in America by Inn Times. AAA approved, it is located near Holland and Saugatuck and has sandy beaches, x-country skiing, bicycles. Private baths, whirlpool/bath. Special getaway/honeymoon suite. Beautiful surroundings, family antiques. Homemade breakfast. A/C. 8 rooms/private baths.

Daily $80-$145

Editor's Note: Well appointed rooms and welcoming proprietors make this a good choice.

THE KIRBY HOUSE — **(616) 857-2904**
LOREN & MARSHA KONTIO — **BED & BREAKFAST**

The most popular bed and breakfast in the Saugatuck/Douglas area. Furnished with antiques of the 1890's. Most rooms with private baths, air conditioning and fireplace rooms available. Pool, hot tub and bicycles. Full breakfast buffet. Near shopping and Lake Michigan. Advanced Reservations imperative.

Daily $85-$125 Dbl.

THE PARK HOUSE — **(800) 321-4535 • (616) 857-4535**
LYNDA & JOE PETTY — **BED & BREAKFAST**

On National Historic Register. Saugatuck's oldest residence (1857) hosted Susan B. Anthony. Queen beds and private baths. Fireplace, A/C, close to town, beach and ski trails. Two luxury suites and Rose Garden Cottage offer jet tubs and fireplaces. More than a night's stay—a homecoming! 9 rooms.

Daily $65-$150

THE PARK HOUSE COTTAGE COLLECTION — **(800) 321-4535 • (616) 857-4535**
LYNDA & JOE PETTY — **COTTAGES**

6 beautifully decorated cottages located in and around Saugatuck. Lodgings range in style from historic to contemporary and feature fully equipped kitchens, A/C, telephones. Some with Surround Sound stereos systems, TV/VCR, hot tub, or fireplace. Linens included. No pets.

Weekly $575-$975 Daily $115-$225

WICKWOOD COUNTRY INN — **(616) 857-1465**
JULEE ROSSO-MILLER & BILL MILLER — **BED & BREAKFAST**

A charming European-style Inn located in the beautiful Victorian Village of Saugatuck on the Eastern Shores of Lake Michigan. Owner Julee Rosso-Miller, serves up breakfast and hors d'oeuvres daily using recipes from her four best selling cookbooks. "The Silver Palate", "The Silver Palate Good Times", "The New Basics" and "Great Good Foods". 11 rooms with private baths.

Daily $125-$195

ST. JOSEPH

SAND RABBIT BEACH HOUSE — **(616) 468-3835**
BEACH HOUSE

This 3 bedroom Lake Michigan beach house is fully furnished and features CATV, A/C, microwave, washer/dryer, enclosed yard and deck. Sleeps up to 6. Includes 1 king WB — loft has large floor pillows and sleeping bags. Only 5 min. from downtown St. Joseph. $200 deposit (per week). No pets. No smoking.

Call for Rates

THE SILVERBEACH FUNHOUSES **(616) 983-2959**
CONDOS/HOMES

NEAR THE POPULAR SILVER BEACH & CENTER OF TOWN WITH 100'S OF SPECIALTY SHOPS & SIGHTSEEING ATTRACTIONS

The Cup & The Saucer

If you enjoy crystal clear waters and broad sandy beaches, this is for you! These quaint, clean cottages are close to the ever popular silver beach on Lake Michigan. *The Cup* (upstairs) sleeps 4 and *The Saucer* (down-stairs) sleeps 10. *The Dollhouse* is a miniature *Funhouse*, right next door and sleeps 6-8 (3 bedrooms). It is fully furnished and includes cable, phone and deck. *The Lighthouse* is a large, 3 unit home with view of the pier and lighthouse featuring 1 room to 3 bedrooms. Linens and bath towels are included. Enjoy swimming, fishing, roller-blading, wind surfing, shopping, free concerts. Reserve early.

Weekly $425-$850

Editor's Note: Comfortable rooms, fun decor and great location.

SOUTH CLIFF INN BED & BREAKFAST **(616) 983-4881**
BILL SWISHER **BED & BREAKFAST**

Overlooking Lake Michigan, traditional brick home has luxurious accommodations but relaxed atmosphere. Tastefully decorated rooms with traditional and antique furnishings. The private beach is just steps away. Continental breakfast. Room with whirlpool tub /fireplace available. A/C. 7 rooms.

Daily (Seasonal) $75-$150

SOUTH HAVEN

ARUNDEL HOUSE—AN ENGLISH B&B **(616) 637-4790**
PAT & TOM ZAPAL **BED & BREAKFAST**

Turn-of-the-Century, fully restored resort home. Registered with the Michigan Historical Society. Rooms decorated with antiques and maintained in English tradition. Continental buffet breakfast and afternoon tea. Walking distance to beach, restaurants, shops, marinas.

Daily $60-$110

Editor's Note: Delightful B&B ... in the English tradition.

A COUNTRY PLACE BED & BREAKFAST & COTTAGES **(616) 637-5523**
ART & LEE NIFFENEGGER **COTTAGES PLUS BED & BREAKFAST**

A restored 1860's Greek Revival furnished with American antiques. 5 charming guest rooms with private baths feature English country themes. A "sin" sational full breakfast served. All 3 cozy cottages feature fresh pine interiors, full kitchens, 1 & 2 bedrooms. 2 have fireplaces, 2 have private beach. Remaining cottage and B&B access Lake Michigan 1/2 block. B&B open all year - Cottages open April-October.

Cottages $500-$750 (weekly) Bed & Breakfast $70-$95 (daily)

Editor's Note: Gracious owners, very inviting accommodations — all of the Niffenegger's lodging are outstanding, P.S. We liked their cat, Munchken, too!

COTTAGE AT GLEN HAVEN SHORES **(616) 455-5602**
ANDREA KULDANEK **COTTAGE**

Cottage on Lake Michigan Bluff between Saugatuck and South Haven. 1 bedroom and sleeping loft (sleeps 8), full bath. Equipped kitchen, wood burning stove, TV/VCR, screened porch. Access to tennis court. Bike trail nearby. Provide your own linens & paper products. May-Oct. No smoking. No pets.

Weekly $900 (Weekend rates available after Labor Day)

GREENE'S VACATION HOMES **(616) 637-6400**
MERYL GREENE **COTTAGES**

Vacation homes near town and marinas. Many lakefront or with beach access. Linens provided (bring towels). All lodgings have fully equipped kitchens, baths. Many with telephones, CATV and ceiling fans. Sleep 6 or more. Monthly and off-season rates available.

Weekly $600 (and up, July-Aug.)

LAST RESORT B&B INN **(616) 637-8943**
BED & BREAKFAST

Built in 1883 as South Haven's first resort inn. Watch Lake Michigan sunsets from the deck. Most rooms w/view of the Lake or the harbor. Penthouse suites provide best views and feature Jacuzzi's. A/C. Open April-Oct. 14 rooms /private baths.

Daily $45-$185

LOKNATH-CHANDERVARMA, HARBOR'S UNIT #32 **(616) 344-3012**
CONDO

2 bedroom/2 bath condo (sleeps 7). Elegantly furnished, large master bedroom. A/C, CATV, equipped kitchen, microwave, dishwasher. Panoramic view, private beach, pool, laundry, garage. Provide your own towel and linens. Minimum 7 day stay. Available all year. No pets.

Weekly $900 (May-Sept.)

MICHI-MONA-MAC **(616) 637-3003 • (847) 332-1443**
COTTAGES

Watch truly spectacular sunsets from the pure, spotless beach. Very clean and well maintained cottages with full kitchens, private baths, ceiling fans.

Michi-Mona-Mac (continued...)

beachside rooms with lovely bay windows and fireplace. Open all year. No pets.

Weekly $800 (and up)

Editor's Note: The beach is small but lovely with incline taking you to water's edge. Units are linked together apartment style. Small but well maintained interiors.

North Beach Inn & Pigozzi's **(616) 637-6738**

Inn

1890's Victorian styled B&B overlooks Lake Michigan Beach. All rooms offer private baths. Restaurant, Pigozzi, serves full breakfasts, lunch and dinners.

Daily $90-$135

Riverbend Retreat **(616) 637-3505**

Cottages

Cozy cedar cottages on beautiful Black River. Come and enjoy the peacefulness! Inground heated pool, boat dock, canoes, boat, private hot tub, stone fireplace, Kal-Haven pass. Fully equipped for 12 people, including towels and bedding, phone, TV, VCR, dishwasher, laundry. Open year around. Off-season priced for couples or groups. No pets.

Call for Rates

The Seymour House **(616) 227-3918**

Gwen & Tom Paton **Bed & Breakfast & Log Cabin**

Enjoy the unsurpassed beauty and magnificent grounds of this stately 1862 Victorian mansion on 11 wooded acres. Picturesque 1-acre pond for fishing, swimming or paddleboat ride and trails through the woods. Minutes to popular Saugatuck/South Haven, Lake Michigan beaches, restaurants, galleries, horseback riding, golf and orchards. 5 guest rooms w/ private bath, fireplaces and Jacuzzi. Guest log cabins. A/C, gourmet breakfast presented in style.

Daily $75-$129

SLEEPY HOLLOW RESORT **(616) 637-1127**

COTTAGES/APARTMENTS/DUPLEX

This 58 years old Art Deco style resort provides the "all in one" family vacation. Theater, restaurant and plenty of activities on the resort promises to keep you busy. Cottages and apartments include partial to full kitchens, private baths.

Weekly $450-$1,040

Editor's Note: Lots of activities at this American Plan resort have made it popular over the years.

SOUTH HAVEN VACATION HOME **(616) 637-5406**

AMANDA & CHARLEY SOUKUP **COTTAGE**

Vacation home features 3 bedrooms, large living room, kitchen, dining room and family room. Includes microwave, washing/dryer, CATV. Large yard for family recreation. Walk to Kids' Corner and Lake Michigan.

Weekly $850 (Off-season rates available)

TANBITHN **(616) 637-4304**

MARCIA ROBINSON **COTTAGE**

One bedroom (sleeps 5) cottage on North Shore Drive. Features CATV, telephone, ceiling fan and room air conditioning. Fully renovated in 1994 including bathroom fixtures, kitchen area. Linens provided (bring towels). Light and airy interior with wicker highlights. Only 1/2 block from beach, 1 block from marina. Fall/winter rates negotiable. No pets.

Weekends $125 (per night) Weekly $700 (May -Sept.)

THOMPSON HOUSE **(616) 637-6521**

JOYCE THOMPSON **HOME**

Charming home, sleeps six. 1 block to South Beach, Riverfront Park. Great garden, umbrella table, wraparound porch and deck. Enjoy all the modern conveniences including microwave, dishwasher, laundry, central air, electronic air cleaner, a water purifier and whirlpool bathtub. No pets.

Weekly $850 (June-Aug.); $700 (May, Sept., Oct.)

Editor's Note: Well maintained home on a quiet and relaxing side street. A nice place to be away from the maddening crowds. Good value.

VICTORIA RESORT B & B **(800) 473-7376 • (616) 637-6414**

BOB & JAN **COTTAGES/BED & BREAKFAST**

3 acre family resort with 17 cottages/rooms renovated in 1993. Located 1 block from Lake Michigan beach. Features 2-3 bedroom cottages plus B&B rooms. Includes A/C, CATV, VCR, full kitchen (in cottages), linens provided, playground area and evening bonfires. Full maid service. B&B rooms range from cozy to spacious, some with whirlpools. No pets.

Weekly Cottages from $800 Rooms from $49

Editor's Note: Comfortable and very clean accommodations for family fun.

YELTON MANOR BED & BREAKFAST **(616) 637-5220**
ELAINE HERBERT & ROB KRIPAITIS **BED & BREAKFAST**

On the sunset coast of beautiful Lake Michigan. 17 guest rooms with private baths. Some have Jacuzzi and fireplace. Extravagant honeymoon and anniversary suites. Evening hors d' oeuvres, fabulous breakfast and day-long goodies. A true make-yourself-at-home, luxurious getaway.

Daily $90-$220

Editor's Note: A premiere resort for executive retreats. A great way to FORGET ABOUT THE...STRESS.

STEVENSVILLE

CHALET ON THE LAKE **(616) 465-6365**
CHALETS/CONDOS

51 spacious, well equipped, 2-story duplex chalet-styled lodgings 7 miles south of St. Joseph. 27 acres by Lake Michigan Lodgings include 2 bed-room condominiums (sleep 8) with full kitchens, dining areas, living room, TV and patios. Resort features nature trails, volleyball, 5 tennis courts, 2 pools and large beach. Bring towels. Open year around. No pets.

Weekly $575-$930

UNION CITY

VICTORIAN VILLA INN **(800) 34-VILLA • (517) 741-7383**
RONALD J. GIBSON **BED & BREAKFAST**

Romantic, 19th Century Intalianate style B&B—perfect for anniversaries or any other special occasion. Tower suites with private parlor, offer an excellent birds-eye view of the town. Restaurant features menus which reflect the tastes and trends of the 19th century and are sure to please. Private baths. 6 rooms, 4 suites (2 with fireplaces). Major credit cards accepted.

Daily $85-$145

UNION PIER/NEW BUFFALO

GARDEN GROVE B&B **(616) 469-6346 • (800) 613-2872**
BED & BREAKFAST

Nestled in the countryside of Union Pier, a charming resort community along the shores of Lake Michigan. This quiet retreat is a reminder of times past when the world moved slower. Everything the discriminating inn guest has come to expect: charm, comfort, beauty and romance. 4 rooms with private baths.

Daily $69-$150

THE INN AT UNION PIER — **(616) 469-4700**
JOYCE ERICKSON PITTS & MARK PITTS — **BED & BREAKFAST**

An elegant Inn blending barefoot informality with the comforts of a well-appointed country home. Lake Michigan is across the street. Most rooms have porches and Swedish fireplaces. Relax in our sauna or outdoor hot tub. Linger over homemade breakfast. Hosting corporate retreats. Private baths. 16 rooms. Weekday specials. No smoking. No pets.

Daily $115-$185

PINE GARTH INN — **(616) 469-1642**
RUSS & PAULA BULIN — **BED & BREAKFAST/COTTAGES**

Restored summer estate and cottages, located in a quiet setting overlooking Lake Michigan. All guest rooms have spectacular lake views. Rooms have queen beds, private baths, VCR. Cottages have 2 bedrooms, kitchens, fireplace, hot tubs, gas grills and private decks with beach chairs. 7 rooms, 5 cottages.

	Rooms*	Cottages*
Daily	$115-$150	$210-$225
Weekends		$430-$485

* In season. Call for off-season rates.

SANS SOUCI BED & BREAKFAST — **(616) 756-3141**
ANGELIKA SIEWERT — **BED & BREAKFAST, COTTAGES, HOMES**

The sophisticated traveler may choose a secluded luxury suite, family home or modern lakeside cottage at San Souci, located in a pastoral countryside 70 miles from Chicago. We have 50 acres of spring-fed lakes, whispering pines and abundant wildlife near Lake Michigan beaches. Antique shops, galleries, fine restaurants nearby. Welcome all. Handicap access.

Rooms: Daily $98-$185 Cottages: Weekly $1,110; Daily $185
Homes: Weekly $1,176-$1,764; Daily $196-$294

Main Office:

MICHIGAN TRAVEL BUREAU
P.O. Box 3393, Livonia, MI 48151-3393
800-5432-YES (U.S. and Canada)
900-722-8191 (TDD for the hearing impaired)

Offices Listed Alphabetically by City

UPPER PENINSULA

Keweenaw Tourism Council
1197 Calumet Avenue
Calumet, MI 49913
906-337-4579
800-338-7982 (U.S. & Canada)

Delta County Tourism & Convention Bureau
230 Ludington Street
Escanaba, MI 49829
800-437-7496 (U.S. & Canada)

Keweenaw Tourism Council
326 Shelden Avenue, P.O. Box 336
Houghton, MI 49931
906-482-2388
800-338-7982 (U.S. & Canada)

Tourism Association of Dickinson County
P.O. Box 672
Iron Mountain, MI 49801
906-774-2002
800-236-2447 (U.S. only)

Iron County Tourism Council
50 E. Genesee Street
Iron River, MI 49935
906-265-3822
800-255-3620 (U.S. only)

Ironwood Tourism Council
100 E. Aurora Street
Ironwood, MI 49938
906-932-1000

Western Upper Peninsula CVB
137 E. Cloverland Drive
Ironwood, MI 49938
906-932-4850
800-272-7000 (out of MI)

Baraga County Tourist & Recreation Association
755 E. Broad Street
L'Anse, MI 49946
906-524-7444

Mackinac Island Chamber of Commerce
P.O. Box 451
Mackinac Island, MI 49757
1-800-4-LILACS

Manistique Area Tourist Council
P.O. Box 37
Manistique, MI 49854
906-341-5838
800-342-4282 (U.S. & Canada)

Marquette County CVB
2552 W. US-41, Suite 300,
Marquette, MI 49855
906-228-7749
800-544-4321 (U.S. & Canada)

Munising Visitors Bureau
422 E. Munising Avenue
Munising, MI 49862
906-387-2138

Newberry Area Tourism Association
P.O. Box 308
Newberry, MI 49868
906-293-5562
800-831-7292 (U.S. & Canada)

Ontonagon Tourism Council
600 River Road, P.O. Box 266
Ontonagon, MI 49953
906-884-4735

Paradise Area Tourism Council
P.O. Box 64
Paradise, MI 49768
906-492-3927

St. Ignace Area Tourist Association
11 S. State Street
St. Ignace, MI 49781
906-643-8717
800-338-6660 (U.S. & Canada)

Sault Ste. Marie Tourist Bureau
2581 I-75 Business Spur
Sault Ste. Marie, MI 49783
906-632-3301
800-MI-SAULT (U.S. & Canada)

LOWER PENINSULA

Lenawee County Conference & Visitors Bureau
1629 W. Maumee,
Adrian, MI 49221
800-536-2933 (U.S. only) or
800-682-6580 (U.S. & Canada)

CVB of Thunder Bay Region
133 Johnson Street, P.O. Box 65,
Alpena, MI 49707-0065
517-354-4181
800-4- ALPENA (U.S. & Canada)

Ann Arbor CVB
120 W. Huron Street
Ann Arbor, MI 48104
313-995-7281

Huron County Visitors Bureau
250 E. Huron Avenue
Bad Axe, MI 48413
517-269-6431
800-35-THUMB (U.S. & Canada)

Battle Creek Area Visitor & Convention Bureau
34 W. Jackson Street, Suite 4-B
Battle Creek, MI 49017
616-962-2240
800-397-2240 (U.S. only)

Bay Area CVB
901 Saginaw Street
Bay City, MI 48708
517-893-1222
800-424-5114 (U.S. & Canada)

Lake Michigan CVB
185 E. Main Street, P.O. Box 428
Benton Harbor, MI 49023
616-925-6100

Southwestern Michigan Tourist Council
2300 Pipestone Road
Benton Harbor, MI 49022
616-925-6301

Mecosta County CVB
246 N. State Street
Big Rapids, MI 49307
616-796-7640
800-833-6697

Cadillac Area Visitors Bureau
222 Lake Street
Cadillac, MI 49601
616-775-9776
800-22-LAKES (U.S. only)

Charlevoix Area CVB
408 Bridge Street
Charlevoix, MI 49720
800-367-8557 (MI only)
616-547-2101

Cheboygan Area Tourist Bureau
124 N. Main Street, P.O. Box 69,
Cheboygan, MI 49721
616-627-7183
800-968-3302 (U.S. & Canada)

Frankenmuth CVB
635 S. Main Street
Frankenmuth, MI 48734
517-652-6106
800-FUN-TOWN

Gaylord Area Convention & Tourism Bureau
101 W. Main Street, P.O. Box 3069
Gaylord, MI 49735
517-732-6333
800-345-8621 (U.S. & Canada)

Grand Haven-Spring Lake CVB
One S. Harbor Drive
Grand Haven, MI 49417
616-842-4499
800-303-4094 (U.S. & Canada)

Grand Rapids Area CVB
140 Monroe Center, NW, Ste. 300
Grand Rapids, MI 49503
616-459-8287
800-678-9859

Grayling Area Visitors Council
213 N. James Street, P.O. Box 217
Grayling, MI 49738
517-348-2921
800-937-8837

Oceana County Tourism Bureau
P.O. Box 168, Hart, MI 49420
616-873-7141

Elk County Visitors Bureau
P.O. Box 507
Hillman, MI 49746
517-742-3739

Holland Area CVB
100 E. Eighth Street, Suite 120
Holland, MI 49423
616-394-0000
800-506-1299 (U.S. & Canada)

Houghton Lake Area Tourist & Convention Bureau
370 Cloverleaf Lane
Houghton Lake, MI 48329
517-422-3931

Indian River Tourist Bureau
P.O. Box 414
Indian River, MI 49749
616-238-9325

Jackson Convention & Tourist Bureau
6007 Ann Arbor Road
Jackson, MI 49201
517-764-4440
800-245-5282

Kalamazoo County CVB
128 N. Kalamazoo Mall
Kalamazoo, MI 49007
616-381-4003

Greater Lansing CVB
119 Pere Marquette Drive
P.O. Box 1506
Lansing, MI 48901
517-487-6800
800-648-6630

Ludington Area CVB
5827 W. US-10, P.O. Box 160
Ludington, MI 49431
616-845-0324
800-542-4600 (U.S. only)

Mackinaw Area Tourist Bureau
708 S. Huron, P.O. Box 160
Mackinaw City, MI 49701
616-436-5664
800-666-0160 (U.S. & Canada)

Midland County CVB
300 Rodd Street
Midland, MI 48640
517-839-9901
800-678-1961

Mount Pleasant Area CVB
144 E. Broadway
Mount Pleasant, MI 48858
517-772-4433
800-77-CHIEF (MI only)

Muskegon County CVB
349 W. Webster, P.O. Box 1087
Muskegon, MI 49443
616-722-3751
800-235-FUNN

Four Flags Area Council on Tourism
321 E. Main Street, P.O. Box 1300
Niles, MI 49120
616-683-3720

Boyne County CVB
401 E. Mitchell St., P.O. Box 694
Petoskey, MI 49770
616-348-2755
800-845-2828

Blue Water Area Tourist Bureau
520 Thomas Edison Parkway
Port Huron, MI 48060
810-987-8687
800-852-4242 (MI only)

Rogers City Travelers & Visitors Bureau
540 W. Third Street
Rogers City, MI 49779
517-734-2535
800-622-4148 (MI only)

Saginaw County CVB
901 S. Washington
Saginaw, MI 48601
517-752-7164
800-444-9979 (U.S. & Canada)

Saugatuck-Douglas CVB
P.O. Box 28
Saugatuck, MI 49453
616-857-1701

Tawas Bay Tourist & Convention Bureau
402 E. Lake Street
P.O. Box 10
Tawas City, MI 48764
517-362-8643
800-55-TAWAS (U.S. & Canada)

Traverse City CVB
415 Munson Avenue, Suite 200
Traverse City, MI 49684
616-947-1120
800-872-8377

West Branch-Ogemaw County Travel
422 W. Houghton Avenue
West Branch, MI 48661
517-345-2821
800-755-9091 (MI only)

Ypsilanti CVB
301 W. Michigan Avenue
Suite 101
Ypsilanti, MI 48197
313-482-4920

The sun is setting. It's time to return to daily living. But you'll remember the excitement, the challenge, the peace and serenity ... of green forests, rolling hills, crystal waters and abundant wildlife. And you'll dream of the things yet to come.

For you are the dreamer,

and I am your dream maker ...

the vacation land for all seasons.

Michigan

Until We Meet Again...

Your Friends at the Michigan Vacation Guide

Send Us Your Comments!

We're always looking to improve this publication. So, let us know if our book was helpful — what improvements you'd like to see in our next edition — and your opinion of the place(s) you've stayed. ***We look forward to hearing from you!***

Do you have property you'd like to list in our next publication?

If you have a property in Michigan that you would be interested in listing, please send your name, address, phone number, along with a brief description of your property. We'll have you complete one of our Property Owner's Questionnaires and add you to our contact list. We'll be sure to notify you when we update the next edition!

Need Additional Copies of the Michigan Vacation Guide????

If you'd like to order additional copies of our Guide, please send $12.95 *plus* $2.75 tax and shipping to TR Desktop Publishing c/o The Michigan Vacation Guide at the below address:

TR Desktop Publishing
P.O. Box 180271
Utica, Michigan 48318-0271
(810) 228-8780

CHECK OUT OUR INTERNET AFFILIATE & WEB SITE AT THE MICHIGAN TRAVELER'S COMPANION
http://www.yesmichigan.com